Other titles in the series

Robert M. Gagné
Essentials of Learning for Instruction

Ellis D. Evans
Transition to Teaching

Donald M. Baer
Student Motivation and Behavior Modification

Irving E. Sigel/Rodney R. Cocking
**Cognitive Development from Childhood to Adolescence:
A Constructivist Perspective**

Hayne W. Reese
Basic Learning Processes in Childhood

Lauren B. Resnick
Psychology for Mathematics Instruction

Lucy R. Ferguson
Personality Development

D. Ross Green
Evaluating Instruction

Joel Levin
Learner Differences: Diagnosis and Prescription

Robert Glaser
Adaptive Instruction: Individual Diversity and Learning

Martin V. Covington/Richard G. Beery
Self-Worth and School Learning

Series Editors: William and Carol Rohwer
University of California, Berkeley

Cognitive Development from Childhood to Adolescence: A Constructivist Perspective

Cognitive Development from Childhood to Adolescence: A Constructivist Perspective

Irving E. Sigel
Rodney R. Cocking
Educational Testing Service

Holt, Rinehart and Winston
New York, Chicago, San Francisco, Atlanta, Dallas
Montreal, Toronto, London, Sydney

Library of Congress Cataloging in Publication Data

Sigel, Irving E.
  Cognitive development from childhood to adolescence.

  (Principles of educational psychology series)
  Bibliography: p. 235
  Includes index.
  1. Cognition (Child psychology) I. Cocking,
Rodney R., joint author. II. Title.
BF723.C5S56   155.4'13   76-55335
ISBN 0-03-015636-X

Foreword

The Principles of Educational Psychology Series

The materials used to present educational psychology to teachers should have two dominant characteristics—excellence and adaptability. The *Principles of Educational Psychology Series* aspires to both. It consists of several short books, each devoted to an essential topic in the field. The authors of the books are responsible for their excellence; each author is noted for a command of his or her topic and for a deep conviction of the importance of the topic for teachers. Taken as a whole, the series provides comprehensive coverage of the major topics in educational psychology, but it is by no means a survey, for every topic is illuminated in a distinctive way by the individual approach of each author.

Numerous considerations require that the materials used

for instruction in educational psychology be adaptable. One consideration is that the readership is heterogeneous, including students in pre-service teacher training programs, of whom some have and others have not taken prior work in psychology, as well as professional teachers in in-service programs who have already completed previous courses in educational psychology. The separate booklets in the *Principles of Educational Psychology Series* are intended to be responsive to these differences. The writing is clear and direct, providing easy access for the novice, and the authors' fresh and distinctive viewpoints offer new insights to the more experienced.

Another consideration is that the format of courses in educational psychology varies widely. A course may be designed for pre-service or for in-service programs, for early childhood, elementary, secondary, or comprehensive programs, or to offer special preparation for teaching in urban, suburban, or rural settings. The course may occupy a full academic year, a semester, trimester, quarter, or an even shorter period. A common set of topics may be offered to all students in the course, or the topical coverage may be individualized. The *Principles of Educational Psychology Series* can be adapted to any one of these formats. Since the series consists of separate books, each one treating a single topic, instructors and students can choose to adopt the entire set or selected volumes from it, depending on the length, topical emphasis, and structure of the course.

The need for effective means of training teachers is of increasing urgency. To assist in meeting that need, the intent of the series is to provide materials for presenting educational psychology that are distinctive in approach, excellent in execution, and adaptable in use.

William Rohwer
Carol Rohwer
Series Editors
Berkeley, California
February, 1974

Preface

Our purpose in writing this book is to review Piagetian theory and to provide our interpretation of how it is relevant to the educational enterprise, as well as to indicate some areas for further work. These issues are usually dealt with in courses in educational psychology, developmental psychology, cognitive development, and related courses in educational psychology.

Piagetian theory is of current interest to research, education, and many applied disciplines, even though it is not a fully evolved system. In his voluminous writings Piaget has touched on most issues germane to the understanding of cognitive growth, but he has not detailed the patterns of development in many of the relevant areas. We believe there is a need to come to terms with some of these issues, and to fill in some important gaps in the current Piagetian description of cognitive development.

For students to comprehend the cognitive growth of children requires an understanding of the theory. Piagetian theory is complex and expansive. We have made an effort to outline the significant concepts and describe in clear detail the growth patterns described by Piaget. Chapters 1 to 4 provide a summary of Piagetian theory for approaching the remaining four chapters. Chapters 5 and 6 focus on the interrelationship of language and cognitive growth, as well as the social and communication ingredients which stimulate cognitive development. These chapters provide conceptual and empirical substance to areas Piaget has but touched on or has not elaborated.

For those readers in education, however, a major task is the application of such a comprehensive theory to the practical world of the classroom. It is one thing to know a theory; it is another to be able to translate theory into everyday practice. To this end we have pulled together some of the major issues and research in a chapter on training studies, Chapter 7.

Piagetian theory is, as the reader will discover, a constructivist theory. Piaget contends that the individual constructs or builds a conception of the world through physical and/or mental involvement with objects, with people, and with events. Yet at another level, the interpretations, the attitudes, and the feelings aroused by that world may differ. However, we have each employed similar processes in building a sense of common reality. The important point is that reality is constructed by each of us. We extend Piagetian thinking, in Chapter 8, to show how constructivism is relevant to understanding individual differences.

If, in spite of the book's brevity, we have stimulated the reader to ponder and to reflect on issues relevant to cognitive growth, we will have fulfilled part of our goal. *But*, if in the process of such reflection the reader can relate to practical, real-life situations in either classroom or daily life, we will have met our objectives.

In this book, we have endeavored to provide illustrations and examples of applying the ideas. By using our suggestions, the reader will discover guidelines for pursuing practical aims. Practice without a conceptual base, however, is doomed to short-lived success and limited growth. It is to prevent this that we have embedded our practical issues and relevancies in a conceptual framework. Thus we hope this volume does provide stimulus for further thought.

It is customary for the authors to conclude a preface with acknowledgements to those responsible for the project. We shall follow this practice, but with one digression; namely, I (Irving Sigel) do wish to acknowledge the fact that the project could never have been completed had Rodney Cocking not joined me in a true partnership. Both of us, however, wish to acknowledge the patient and fine editorial assistance William and Carol Rohwer performed; to the former editor, Roger Williams, and to his successor, Richard Owen, thanks for the encouragement to bring this project to a completion; to George Forman, for sharing with us his thorough bibliography and thoughts on conservation studies in Chapter 7; and above all, to Linda Kozelski who patiently and thoughtfully endured the many revisions of this manuscript; and of course, above all else to Jean Piaget whose monumental contribution to developmental psychology has inspired so many of us to take a new look at old questions.

Irving E. Sigel
Rodney R. Cocking
Princeton, New Jersey
January 1977

Contents

1	Chapter 1	Introduction
13	Chapter 2	Overview of Piagetian Theory
37	Chapter 3	Cognitive Development during Preschool Years
64	Chapter 4	Periods of Concrete and Formal Operations
105	Chapter 5	Language Acquisition and the Early Stages of Cognitive Development
161	Chapter 6	The Development of Representational Thought: A Special Conceptualization—The Distancing Hypothesis
186	Chapter 7	The Modification of Cognitive Abilities and Implications for Education
217	Chapter 8	Modification of Piagetian Theory
235		References
247		Index

Cognitive Development from Childhood to Adolescence: A Constructivist Perspective

Chapter 1 Introduction

This is a book about how a person's thinking, reasoning, and judging processes develop. It is a book about how one gets to know the physical world, the social world, and the personal world. We can say that this is a book about *knowing*.

To *know* is to understand; to *know* enables one to act on that knowledge and to be aware of one's self in the complex world. Knowing is commonly referred to as "cognition," a continual change defined in the dictionary as "the process of knowing or perceiving, the act of acquiring an idea." This book describes how people adapt to their environment through knowing that environment and how the various levels of *knowing* are acquired.

The stated purpose of the book has many implications. It implies that there is a category of behavior we define as *knowing*; that knowing is developed—that it comes about over time and through experience; that knowing provides people with the schemes to cope daily with their environment.

Underlying these purposes are the assumptions that cognitive behaviors and processes can be systematically distinguished. Given the delineation of cognition as a behavioral system, we shall discuss how it develops, point out what kinds of individual and environmental conditions influence the direction and the quality of cognitive development, and finally, we shall thread throughout the discussion how the *knowing* process is central to adaptation to our world.

We are born with no knowledge of ourselves or of the environment. From the moment of birth onward, we are in the process of becoming knowledgeable human beings, developing a repertoire of information that makes it possible for us to master a wide variety of skills, from tying a shoe to sending a man into space. It may appear obvious, even trite, to point out that these events occur. In spite of the obviousness, psychologists, philosophers, biologists, and the public in general do not understand *how* this process works, *what* constitute the necessary and sufficient conditions for cognitive development, nor *what* comprise the limits of human competence in getting to know the world.

Interest in this problem is probably as old as civilization. From the time people began to reflect on themselves, they began to ask these questions. In every culture, humans have had to "know" how to behave, know what to know about their culture. Only in this way could they survive. The transmission of knowledge from one generation to another is one means of sustaining the culture. Thus not only did individuals have to acquire knowledge, they also had to transmit it. Procedures had to be developed to accomplish this objective. One way societies transmit knowledge is through language. Since language is a means of knowledge transmission, it required the development of a system of signs and symbols. The evolution of the symbol system illustrates how the language-communication system is inextricably bound to the "knowing" or cognition process. Language and cognition are closely intertwined, each fundamental to human survival. This fundamental problem will be discussed at some length in Chapter 5.

Knowledge is transmitted not only through language but

through other modes such as gestures, pictures, and various signs. The individual comes to understand the meaning of the messages in a mode as a prerequisite to understanding the symbol system of one's group. Cultures devise various ways of achieving this goal. In some societies, for example, oral traditions were developed where the elders would instruct the youth in the history of the group by oral presentation, expecting the youth to commit the information to memory. Oral traditions were limited, being subject to bias and distractions of memory. The breakthrough in this process of knowledge recording and transmission was the concept that ideas and events can be represented in other ways, such as through writing and drawing. Transforming oral language into arbitrary signs (written language) that could be precise descriptions of events was a major cognitive leap.

At issue now is how the individual acquires knowledge, not only when presented orally, but graphically. Some knowledge is acquired by direct practical experience—learning through action and by observing others. Other types of knowledge, however, cannot be gained through direct experience. The history of the group, for example, comes through some form of recording. Every society developed what it felt was a functional system by which to record and transmit its heritage and way of life. The way societies elect to preserve themselves is to create some form of "educational" institution. In preliterate societies this may have taken the form of initiation rites at predefined ages, when children learned the traditions, duties and obligations from their elders. For modern societies education is formalized into schools and universities employing a complex set of strategies to initiate the individual into the culture.

What does all this have to do with cognitive development? Education subsumes a system of knowledge of the physical and social world which is organized and transmitted through some institution. In other words, to a degree knowledge transmission is institutionalized. For example, curricula in elementary and secondary schools express society's way of revealing what the relevant knowledge base is and how it is organized. An examination of textbooks or teaching strategies shows how knowledge of the traditions, history, and customs of the society, and the physical world (science) are conceptualized. The contention is that all this material, by its very construction, orients the child to the world in a particular way. Western society tends to emphasize the rational scientific organization of knowledge. Note, for example, how college courses are defined—we separate physical science from social science and science from art and humanities. Ask yourself how these categories developed. What are the criteria for creating such organizations? You will discover that knowledge is organized in particular and arbitrary ways. For those interested in anthropology, it would be important to examine how preliterate and nonwestern societies cope with the problem of cultural continuity through educational and quasieducational institutions. Assimilation of this knowledge and development of ways of using it are covered by cognitive development.

Much knowledge is acquired outside the formal classroom. A child comes in contact with people, objects, and events. These experiences provide the individual with sets of knowledge, however informal and nonorganized. The influence of daily activities in the environment on the child's understanding of the world and the child's place in it must not be underestimated. But, experiences open to the child, types of objects, the styles of living arrangements, personal interactions, and the limitations placed on the child by adults, will all vary as a function of the particular culture into which the person is born. Opportunities that the child in a metropolis has differ from those a child in the countryside might have; the child in the jungle has a different world of natural phenomena than the child growing up in the desert. These environmental differences have diverse impact on how the child defines the world and copes with it. The contents of the problems faced by the child in the metropolis are far different from those faced by the child in the desert. Where the city child has to acquire a set of cognitive skills involving utilization of three-dimensional space filled with tall buildings and hence obstacles in long range distance perspective, the child in the desert has to learn how to deal with vast spaces, and with obstacles such as buildings. It is only within recent psychological thinking that we have come to appreciate the profound effects of these types of experiential variations (Cole and Scribner, 1974). The child engages the environment, not as a passive recipient of external forces, but rather as an active organism seeking and organizing experiences, thereby coping with the world.

One other critical aspect involved in the accumulation of information[1] is the medium in which the information is transmitted. The question is, does the mode of transmission place another cognitive demand on the developing system? In western societies information is transmitted through oral and written language, pictures, and other sign systems, all of which involve understanding the principle that experiences and thoughts can be represented in various forms. It is not only important because it provides a more efficient and reliable way of preserving the past and transmitting current knowledge, but it is also important in that it makes new demands on the individual to master the systems used in these representations. Although there are problems for some in mastering oral language, they do not compare in number to the difficulties children have in mastering reading, for example, which is a representation of oral language. Understanding that knowledge can be represented in various forms is a skill the child has to acquire. The society has to train the child to master this skill. Acquisition of the representational system then places demands on the child's developing cognitive system. For example, understanding that marks on the page have concrete and abstract referents is a highly complex and not very well understood process that requires considerable training.

The discussion so far can be summarized as follows. Irrespective of the culture, the developing individual assimilates the cultural definitions of social and physical reality; this process of assimilation is a universal cognitive process. In many cultures the body of knowledge is transmitted through a sign and/or

---

[1] While the point is not crucial to the present discussion, a word should be added about the distinction between information and knowledge so as to be consistent with the theoretical position which we will be developing throughout the text. In the Piagetian system, the process through which the person takes in information which is experienced is termed *assimilation*. If those experiences alter the individual's behavior so that we may say that the person adjusted his behavioral repertoire in some way, we say that the person has *accommodated* to his new experiences. It is our view that *knowledge* is information to which the individual has accommodated. The distinction between assimilation and accommodation processes will be elaborated in Chapter 2.

symbol system which the child has to master—another profound cognitive demand. Cultures have both formal and informal modes of achieving the transmission of its essential requirements. An educational system or its prototype are the formal modes, while every day movements and activities are the informal modes. In essence, adaptation to the personal, social, and physical world is essentially a cognitive demand, for only through understanding and knowledge can people make the necessary adjustments to insure their own and their society's survival.

How is this process of acquiring knowledge more than learning? Learning defines a more or less permanent alteration in an individual's behavior. Gagné confines the definition of learning to "that which occurs when the organism *interacts* with his environment" (Gagné, 1974, p. 6). If learning consists of interactions with the environment that result in changes which persist over time, how is learning different from cognition? How is learning different from development, a term also applied to change which persists over time as a result of interactions with the environment?

The answer to the above, in part, is what this book is all about. As we shall see, learning depends upon development. Learning is a statement which defines a process, but learning is *not* cognition. Cognition is knowing, understanding what is learned; and by implication, knowing is the organization of knowledge.

As the reader will soon discover, the conceptual framework of this volume is derived from the theory and research of Jean Piaget, the noted Swiss psychologist and epistemologist. A conceptual framework serves as a map, providing needed guidelines to define issues, establish priorities of problems to be studied, influence methods of such study, and orient the interpretations of the results of such investigations. All conceptual systems are arbitrary since they are based on assumptions whose validity is untestable. The particular system one elects as one's guide is based on a variety of rational and nonrational factors. It may be that after weighing various explanations from some phenomenon or investigative methods, one accepts the framework because it fits with one's experience or style of working. For example, in psychology some individuals are more prone to be introspective and feel the import of internal emotions as critical in coping with the world. Psychoanalytic writings may appeal to these individuals. Or incidentally, an individual may be exposed to a teacher or an educational program that fosters a particular point of view. The young, untrained student is quickly taught the system; some stay forever, others move about. It is very difficult to "prove" the virtue of one system over another on purely rational grounds. A good example in psychology will be exemplified in this book.

The selection of a Piagetian perspective is based on the assumption that Piaget's image of human development touches on a number of issues that are vital for education. Piaget is the only psychologist who presents a comprehensive theory of intellectual development involving three critical areas: (1) a developmental point of view—a conviction that intellectual growth proceeds in orderly stages, each of which defines what the individual is capable of learning; (2) a substantial body of knowledge describing the developmental course of how children acquire information about the physical world, for example, number, quantity, time, space; the *social world*, for example, morality, social conventions; and *logical-mathematical reasoning*, for example, classification, hypothetical-deductive reasoning; and (3) a description of a methodology, a clinical method of inquiry which reveals *how* the child thinks and reasons, rather than just what the child knows (see Chapter 4).

It is important to reiterate that its value rests in what the method contributes to the larger goal of scholarship and to the enhancement of our understanding of the subject in question.

Piagetian theory was initially derived from studies of his own three children, but has since been extended to include exhaustive studies with thousands of children all over the world. Piaget and his collaborators in Geneva have worked intensively with infants, preschoolers, and elementary and secondary school children. Each child is interviewed individually. From Piaget's point of view, a detailed inquiry is the only way to discover, not only what the child thinks, but how he or she reasons and reaches conclusions. Piaget discovered that children think and reason differently at different periods in their lives and that the *same* task is responded to differently at various periods. He learned this by presenting children with tasks to perform, such as number, classification, or cause-effect sequences, and then asking them to explain their answers. For example, when a four-year-old is asked, "Which weighs more, a pound of feathers or a pound of lead?" the child at this level does not understand the question. The six- to seven-year-old, however, will say that the pound of *lead* weighs more "because lead is heavier than feathers." This child focuses on the material to be weighed rather than the unit of measure and does not solve the problem. But a nine- to ten-year-old will say, "They both weigh the same, because a pound is a unit of measure, and a pound of anything weighs the same." This example demonstrates Piaget's profound contribution: the discovery that *how* the child reasons about such a problem reveals *how* he thinks, and how he thinks is the result of his developmental level, not merely a lack of information. Piaget uses the child's wrong answer, not as a mistake to be ignored, but rather as a diagnostic aid to unravel the child's reasoning.

The methodology employed by Piaget is far different from that traditionally used by educators and psychologists in the United States. Because of this difference, many investigators and educators regard the Piagetian system as inadequate according to their scientific standards. Yet Piaget argues that his standards for judging his work and that of others are rigid and scientific. The issue is one in which investigators differ in their conception of science. We, then, confront the controversy of what is science, what is a scientifically correct theoretical perspective and logical methodology. However, it is not our function to delve into the complexities of defining science and the scientific methods.

The use of Piagetian theory in education should not be interpreted as suggesting that Piaget and his colleagues have all the answers. Rather, it is a system that offers a framework in which to work, assuming that the problems studied are important, relevant, and, at this writing, offer new insights into the complexity of cognitive development. More and continued research and evaluation must go on to test the theory and make necessary modifications.

For us, then, the problem of interest is cognitive development. Time will tell which system has most furthered this study. The history of science is replete with theories that have proved useful and influential in the course of scientific growth. Some have been validated, some merely heuristic, but there are probably more that have been discarded. As in so many other human endeavors, time becomes the best test of the validity and value of a theory. For science there is the added advantage that the theory or the paradigm has to prove itself by showing results. These results may occur in the practical world as in technology or in the world of ideas. Thus as you read this volume, you may consider the degree to which the discussion agrees with some of your conceptions of cognitive functions.

Relevance of Cognitive Development to the Educational Process

The relation between a psychology of cognitive development and education rests in one's conceptualization of education. If education is viewed as a process involving an instructional model comprised of teacher-student-content interactions, then understanding the interaction among these components can be best understood by knowing something about the characteristics of each component. The student is the central character in our educational system. Our interest is the student's transformation from an untutored, unskilled individual to a *tutored*, competent person. The transformation takes place in part through the complex instructional process. Two processes are involved: (1) the learning process (described by Gagné, 1974, in another volume in this series) and (2) cognitive processes, mental activities such as thinking and reasoning, processes used with learning materials (for example, thinking in terms of arithmetic processes requires previous knowledge about numbers and reasoning requires material about which to reason). Learning, then, is the application of an already acquired pattern of knowledge. Learning and reasoning go hand in hand and are not, in reality, separated. We learn how to think and reason as well as what to think about. From a developmental perspective, children learn and think differently at different stages. Children cannot learn multiplication until they know addition; they cannot understand that rules can be changed until they learn who makes rules and how they are made. This point can serve as a guiding principle for education. The conception of development and its relation to learning should not be confused with the commonly used, vague term called *readiness*. Readiness is used to denote *when* the child is ready for school learning. As we shall see later, describing the child's "developmental state" helps us to understand *what* the necessary patterns or preconditions are that encourage learning.

Educators who understand the course of cognitive development use this knowledge to gauge what material can be introduced, how and when to introduce it, and how to interpret the child's responses. Thus teaching strategies and teaching materials can be guided by an understanding of cognition.

Plan of the Book

In the following chapter, we shall present an overview of cognitive development from a Piagetian perspective. We present the basic Piagetian concepts which give a framework within which the substantive aspects of the theory are understood.

We, then, move to a detailed discussion of the substantive matters in each of the major stages of development. Chapter 3 describes the steps in development from the beginning of life to kindergarten age. It might be mentioned here that the age gradations are only estimates and should not be taken literally. As we shall see, while the stages proceed in consistent order, the ages at which they appear may vary. Chapter 4 covers the cognitive developments during the elementary and secondary school periods, with particular attention to the patterns of thinking and reasoning used in working with physical and social tasks.

With the basic presentation of the Piagetian perspective—concepts, substance, and method—we proceed into critical issues in language development, a vehicle for expression and representational thinking. Piaget tends to treat language as a method of expressing thoughts, rather than as thinking itself. This fundamental issue is discussed in Chapter 5.

While Piaget acknowledges the significance of the social environment in cognitive growth, he does not specify the conditions for cognitive growth. In Chapter 6 we fill in this gap by describing a class of social behaviors which we argue influences the quality of children's thinking. Proceeding through these chapters, we will provide illustrations to indicate how our point of view applies to the educator.

Having described the concepts and substance of cognitive development, we come to a central issue. Is the course of cognitive development fixed or is it subject to modification? In other words, can rate and sequence of development be altered? This question and related ones are addressed in Chapter 7. Much research has been done to test the Piagetian contention that the stages of development are invariant, that rate of growth cannot truly be accelerated, and that the optimal environment involves minimal pressure. The human organism has regulatory processes which affect the course of adaptation to the physical and social environment. The lines of the argument are drawn between "acceleration" and "natural growth." As shall be shown, the evidence does not definitively support either position. These complex issues are discussed. Further, particular teaching strategies are shown to have different effects.

As indicated in our opening comments, not all educators and researchers accept Piagetian theory. In the last chapter (Chapter 8), we discuss some aspects of the Piagetian framework which need elaboration, revision, or further explication. Finally, we conclude the chapter with an epilogue that is a restatement of the constructivist perspective, consistent with the Piagetian epistemological approach.

With this we come to the end of our journey into the realm of Piagetian conception of intellectual growth, amplified and extended by us. The relevance of Piaget and of cognitive psychology to education is fraught with many problems, possibly a function of the complexity and the comprehensiveness of the theory and the differential acquaintance educators have with it. Also, many educational issues are not directly mentioned in the theory. It is difficult to assert, then, that a one-way approach is the most consistent. But what is consistent is the need for verification, a point of view Piaget would favor. For as a scientist philosopher, he is a strong advocate of verification and experimentation. The issue confronting educators is the translation of developmental theory into pedagogy. Educators must do the best they can with what is known and orient themselves to consistent and careful observation of processes and outcomes. Hopefully, sensitized to the complexity, the teacher can tune in to the classroom and reflect on what is happening. The teacher's task, according to Piagetian theory, is to learn to assess levels of cognitive functioning from child behaviors, and then provide some discrepant information which the child has not taken into account due to a limited view of the world. This should energize the child toward problem solving. The plea, in a sense, is for the teacher to be reflective in assessing classroom procedures and activities. Finally, the teacher in this case has to be willing to be innovative. By trying new methods, the teacher can discover ones which appear to be effective, and in this way define the conditions under which such effectiveness occurs.

Chapter 2 Overview of Piagetian Theory

The concepts central to a full discussion of Piaget's theory are the topic of this chapter. We present them separately because we wish to point out that the terms that Piaget uses to describe processes of development are economical ways of conveying a great deal of information and therefore need fuller elaborations than simple definitions transmit. These concepts will then be brought together in Piaget's theory in Chapters 3 and 4.

Piaget's theory, a developmental one, has as its central interest the investigation of how cognition evolves from infancy to later stages in adolescence. The theory is referred to as genetic because it is concerned with development of the individual (ontogenesis). Thus Piagetian psychology is called "genetic psychology," referring to individual development.[1] For Piaget, genetic psychology is not to be confused with child psychology.

Where child psychology deals with the child for his own sake and does not consider his eventual development into an adult, we tend to use the term "genetic psychology" to refer to the

[1] Piaget's system is also referred to as *genetic epistemology*. Epistemology is the science that studies the origins, growth, and nature of knowledge; "genetic" refers to the developmental point of view. Therefore genetic epistemology is the study of how the individual acquires knowledge. Since

study of developmental processes that underlie the mental functions studied in general psychology (intelligence) . . . interest
in psychological investigations of the child . . . explains the man
as well as and often better than the man explains the child
(Piaget and Inhelder, 1969, viii–ix).

For genetic psychology the following areas are of central
interest in understanding the development of intelligence: biological factors, factors in individual development, social factors
which influence the growth of knowledge, and cultural or environmental factors.

Core Concepts

The core concepts which guide genetic psychological research
and which are important for interpreting the Piagetian theory
and the research which has been done relevant to it are deline-
ated as follows:

1. biological-experiential
2. assimilation and accommodation
3. constructivism
4. stages
5. factors influencing development
     maturation
     experience
     action
     equilibration
6. structure
7. operations

Biological-Experiental Factors

Piaget's theory is a *biological-experiential* and *interactionist*
model, in which cognitive development is a mode of adaptation
to the world. Cognitive growth derives from the organism's biological nature, starting with the infant's reflexes and proceeding
by invariant stages to the eventual capability of abstract, log-

---

in his 1969 discussion of his system Piaget refers to the notion of genetic
psychology, we shall use that designation for this portion of our discussion.

ical reasoning. Cognition is a particular instance of biological adaptation. For Piaget, cognition or intelligence "is one kind of biological achievement which allows the individual to interact effectively with the environment at a psychological level" (Ginsburg and Opper, 1969, p. 14).

Assimilation and Accommodation

Cognitive growth proceeds via two fundamental processes, *assimilation* and *accommodation*. For Piaget, assimilation means "taking in"; just as the body assimilates food through the digestive process, so does the organism take in information. As the body can only accept appropriate nutrients and reject others, so too the human organism can only take in or assimilate that class of information which the cognitive system is capable of dealing with at that point in time. When assimilation of information alters the individual's understanding of events, this alteration is referred to as *accommodation*. The individual assimilates knowledge and virtually at the same time makes accommodations to this new knowledge. The knowledge that is learned from this process is organized into what Piaget calls a *schema* (pl. *schemata*), a coherent, organized set of "information" about objects, events, or whatever may be the content in question. The important conceptualization is that these processes of assimilation and accommodation refer to the means by which knowledge is mentally constructed. If information is "taken" into a system and the organism attempts to cope with these new "intrusions," the changes which result from this coping (the accommodations) leave the individual intellectually different. Let us take your reading this book as an example. You already have explicit or implicit ideas about how the mind works. You are coming upon a new theory, a body of new information, which you "take in" (assimilate), while at the same time your previous view is being altered. You are accommodating your previous view to account for new information.

Constructivism

The child, for Piaget, is an active organism who assimilates information, thereby creating a knowledge base. Piaget asserts that to know and construct knowledge of the world, the child must act on objects and it is this action which provides knowledge of those objects. This concept of action on objects is a critical feature of Piagetian thought. Action of the individual on the object is not a one-way activity, but is an *interaction* between child and object which yields new insights into a personal effect upon the environment and the environment's responsiveness to activities which have been initiated. A child bounces a ball and the ball reacts, perhaps in ways unexpected by the child. How the object reacts irrespective of the child's intention, adds to the child's knowledge. With each interaction between the child and the object, the child's knowledge of the object becomes altered. Piaget maintains that knowing comes not from the object alone nor from the child's actions alone, but from constructions of the interactions between the child and the object. The child increasingly becomes able to objectify his or her knowledge; that is, to know that the child's actions and the object's actions are separate. In other words, objectivity is learned.

Since objective knowledge of the world is not given and if the child's knowledge is not a copy of reality, how is sensory information transformed into knowledge? Knowledge is built from actions, experiences, and the interactions with the world. For example, if the child releases an object, it falls. The object might be returned and the same object is released again. The child begins to construct a notion that flexing the palm leads to the object's falling and that grasping leads to its retention. In this process, the child is an active participant in constructing a mental picture of the physical and social environment.

Arguing about human nature in this fashion clearly implies that one is not a passive organism moved about by forces beyond one's control. Rather, one is active, modifying the environment. Humans engage actively in the transformation of their reality. This perspective clarifies the role action plays as a universal human characteristic.

Constructivism refers to that process of constructing, in effect, creating a concept which serves as a guideline against which objects or people can be gauged. During the course of interacting with objects, people, or events, the individual constructs a reality of them. The object, for example, is defined mentally. This mental construction then guides subsequent actions with that object or event. For an example, knowledge of the object *orange* is built through actions and reactions of that object until a construction of an orange results and we *know* the orange. This knowledge of *orange* influences subsequent interactions. Construction of objects, their characteristics and their place in the scheme of things is an outcome of direct and indirect contact with these objects. Not only is the concept of constructivism appropriate for construction of knowledge of physical objects, but it can be used as a generic concept identifying a process by which reality in general is systematized and ultimately schematized.

Piaget argues that through actions with objects the child comes to experience the object. Eventually the actions become internalized, become part of the child's mental awareness of the object. As we know, however, action with objects involves various experiences. The child interacting with the ball comes to experience its bounce, its roll, its texture, and its temperature. Much of what is learned about an object occurs in the course of interacting with the object. The role of actions with objects is central to the Piagetian explanation of how we come to know the world about us. In the course of this interaction, however, the child begins to know the object on many levels and to develop different interpretations of the object. In effect, he establishes different levels of meaning. We will turn to this issue later when we extend Piagetian theory, by pointing up a critical issue which argues that we come to know an object through action on many levels.

Development Proceeds by Stages

The concept of stages describes the orderly appearance of behaviors. Certain clusters of behaviors are successively ordered and the appearance of each group is necessary for the emergence of the next array. Development follows a sequential order such "that each of its stages is necessary to the construction of the next" (Piaget, 1970b, p. 711). This is in contrast to the behaviorists who do not espouse stage-dependent theories. The distinction is very important. If the stage concept is accepted, it follows that development of knowledge, and learning specifically, is limited by the stage in which the child is at that time. Then, for example, the fact that a young child cannot learn to add or subtract is not necessarily a function of inadequate teaching strategies but rather the fact that the child's level of development precludes his being able to assimilate the necessary information with which to learn arithmetic. For Piaget, development means movement from stage to stage, resulting in changes both in what one *can* understand and *how* one understands.

Factors Influencing the Course of Development

Development occurs as an orderly process in a biosocial context, according to Piaget. He takes into account the biological nature of the individual interacting with the social world. Four factors account for the sequence of development: *maturation* (biological); *experience* of the physical environment; the *action* of the social environment; and *equilibration* or self-regulation by the organism.

Maturation refers to the growth of the biological structure in the individual. The evolving biological organism with increased specializations of functions of the brain also has increased capacities for learning. As children mature, they are able to be sociable, thereby extending environmental contacts. The human organism is programmed to grow in size, in degree of equalization of various body parts. Piaget, however, is very explicit in stating that intelligence is *not* programmed.

We cannot assume there exists a hereditary program indulging the development of human intelligence, there are no innate ideas. . . . Even logic is not innate. . . . The effects of maturation consist essentially of organizing new possibilities for development; that is, giving access to structures which could not be evolved before these possibilities were offered. But between possibility and actualization, there must intervene a set of other factors such as exercise, experience and social interaction. (Piaget, 1970b, pp. 719–720).

That is, while the capacities are part of the individual's biological inheritance, their realization is very much influenced by *experience* in a particular culture—another one of those crucial factors necessary for intelligence to develop. Among the biological factors which Piaget enumerates as a research problem area studied by genetic psychologists is epigenetic development, the development of factors which contribute to an entirely *new* organism. The epigenetic view holds that the development of the organism is not just of growth, but proceeds toward adult structures not seen in the embryo. This conceptualization is in sharp contrast to points of view which propose that development consists only of growth and/or elaboration of structures which are present in the embryo.

Experience, for Piaget, encompasses sensory and motor exercise, experience with the physical world, and experiences in reasoning. *Exercise* involves action and reaction of both the individuals and objects, and thereby leads to knowledge through direct experience. The infant in grasping an object, releasing it, and watching it fall acquires new information while at the same time consolidates the capability to repeat the action, resulting in competence.

A dramatic illustration of this phenomenon was observed in a study of children's classification behavior (Sigel, Secrist, and Forman, 1973). Children, aged two, were presented with a set of multicolored blocks of various shapes. Although they were asked to classify the objects, they were not expected to organize them on any principle, and the chances are that they did not understand the concept of grouping or classification. The primary interest was to observe the kinds of actions children employ in working with such materials. The children were able to extract information from their interactions with the objects as expressed in their ability to make decisions in their activities. Most children built towers and made serious and persistent attempts to pile blocks on one another until the towers fell. Gradually the children showed hesitation in placing a block, as if they were testing the appropriateness of each block for the tower. Holding the block in midair while examining the relationship between the surface of the block in one hand and the surface on which it was to be placed, the child demonstrated the testing of relationships between the two blocks. The child extracted this knowledge about relationships from the situation.

In addition to physical experience, there is another factor

that promotes reasoning about the validity of experiences. This type of experience plays an important part at all levels of cognitive development when fully logical deduction is still not possible. The child is not merely manipulating objects as in the case of sensorimotor experience, nor simply abstracting singular attributes about experienced objects. The child is now deducing interactive relationships because he is repeating actions on objects. In the example given above with the surfaces of the blocks, the child learns through action that stacking can only occur with proper relationships between surfaces of blocks. Thus if the child is asked to build a tall tower, having had this experience he will make certain that proper relationships between surfaces are established.

Piaget offers another example in the area of learning about the properties of number. A child playing with a row of stones lines them up, counts them from right to left or left to right, and finds the same number, in each case. She places them in a circle and counts them and discovers again that the number is the same. These are logico-mathematical experiences, not physical ones, because nothing in the objects yields information about their similarities but rather relationships emerge when the child orders the materials. Piaget purports that two kinds of knowledge come from interaction with objects: knowledge of the object, this includes the information contained in the object itself; and knowledge gained through constructive activities with objects. Knowledge gained through constructive activities with objects involves both discovery and invention. To paraphrase Piaget, each time one teaches a child something he could have discovered for himself, the child is kept from inventing it and consequently from understanding it completely.

Action of the social environment. In the cross-cultural research cited by Piaget, children from Iran were shown to lag behind European and American children by one to two years in mental development, *while demonstrating the same sequence of stages.* In addition, these results have been replicated to demonstrate that the same stages are exhibited by urban and rural children and that rural children usually fall behind their city peers in attaining these stages. Piaget, therefore, concludes that the experiential features of the environment exert tremendous impact upon the developing organism. The impact appears to be demonstrated most dramatically at ages 4 and 5 (Piaget, 1973, p. 152).

We may say, therefore, that knowledge of objects does not occur in a vacuum but rather in a social milieu. The stages enumerated

are accelerated or retarded for the average chronological ages according to the cultural and educational environment. But the fact that the stages follow in any environment is enough to show that the social environment cannot account for everything. This constant order of succession cannot be ascribed to the environment (Piaget, 1970b, p. 721).

Equilibration is the fourth factor that Piaget contends is the critical organizing factor. Again, this concept, as we shall see, is important theoretically, as well as in its practical educational application. Simply, equilibration means that there is a requirement for maturation, experience, and the social environment to be in balance. The organism comes to each situation with its own cognitive structures, which may be as diverse as the infant's reflex action patterns or the adult's accommodated structures. The discrepancy between the new objects or experiences and established structures sets up an imbalance, termed disequilibrium. Piaget maintains that growth of knowledge is due to the conflict between structures and events, the imbalance between what the individual knows and new experiences. If the new experiences are neither too novel nor too familiar (internalized concepts), they may be assimilated and may influence or change those existent structures. In this case we may say that the structures have accommodated to the new information. This conflict creates the transition from one stage to another.

Transitions from Stage to Stage

Since transition from stage to stage is an integral concern in the Piagetian system, we shall direct our attention now to some of the key concepts that will help provide perspective at this point and in subsequent discussions. Piaget offers additional concepts which help us to understand stage transitions, *logical necessity* and *cognitive conflict*.

Logical necessity may appear pretentious for a two- or three-year-old child, but for the paradigm or model that we are referring to it is appropriate. Certain environmental demands and events require actions that have an inherent or built-in logic. The child does not have to be taught that if he wants to put on his shoes and his socks, there is a fixed order defined by the necessity of that situation. In this circumstance the child has usually heard an order which is the reverse of logic ("put on your shoes and socks," rather than "socks and shoes"), and yet the child, out of logical necessity, responds appropriately. There are other such situations which are built out of reality. "You can't close your mouth and eat." "You can't sleep and watch television." There is a built-in logic to these situations, and this inherent logic of events helps the child learn certain kinds of logical sequences out of necessity.

These situations of logical necessity often create what we could also call a *cognitive conflict*. One cannot engage in one act and the other at the same time. Two objects cannot be in the same space at the same time unless one is on top of the other and then it is not in the exact space; it is in an approximate space and time. A child begins to learn the *principle of displacement*. That is, if you put something in one place, it takes up that space which does not allow for something else unless the former object is moved. Two people can't sit on the same chair if it is an ordinary chair. We notice arguments in children's play over territory where children are struggling with this concept of displacement when two children want to be at the same spot. The conflicts that the children have in their own activities as well as in interactions with other people, create a *disequilibrium*, a tension, and it is the solutions of these problems that help propel the child from one competence level to another.

The logical necessity and conflict explanations are appropriate ways to explain transitions between stages. These, however, are essentially social experiences and Piaget contends that more than social experience accounts for transition. Although he does not detail the nature of the transitions between later stages, he does provide an additional factor accounting for the transition from sensorimotor to empirical thinking; this is the advent of language. Language becomes the intermediary providing the means by which later concepts and conceptual thinking are furthered (see Chapter 5 on language).

Thus, the transition between stages can be attributed in part to social demands and in the early years to the advent of language (Piaget, 1951).

The Concept of Structure

As we have indicated, Piaget's theory can be called developmental constructivism. Its basic postulate is "that no human knowledge, with the obvious exception of the very elementary hereditary forms, is preformed in the structures of either the subject or the object" (Inhelder, Sinclair, and Bovet, 1974, p. 8). Piaget contends that the "knower" or learner is constantly active in elaborating knowledge and changing perspective. The individual builds, literally, a knowledge base through acting with objects.

The knowledge acquired and the processes by which the constructions are achieved form an organization, or in Piagetian terms, a *structure*. A structure is a metaphor to describe the relationships among mental actions or transformations involved in thinking. Piaget employs mathematical analogies, that is, models by which to specify the organization (structure) of reasoning. Thus the child develops a system of reasoning; she shows *how* she can solve certain problems. For example, Piaget and his colleague Szeminiska asked four-year-old children to show, in a small construction game, how they went from home to school. The children knew how to make the trip, but they could not represent the trip. Their cognitive structure, that is, their system of reasoning, precluded their solving this problem. The system was in a state of equilibrium (in balance) and the children were unaware of their inability to accomplish this task. For reasons yet to be clearly identified, older children, about age seven or eight, become able to deal with the problem; they develop a different type of logic. The cognitive structure changes, and the child's logic includes the ability to reconstruct and represent experiences by thinking and reasoning different from younger children. No single mental act such as simple reconstruction can solve the problem; many different mental acts are necessary, forming a whole. Another illustration from Piaget, which demonstrates the same structure concept, is the understanding of elementary arithmetic problems. To understand that $8+6=14$, and that $14-8=6$ is its reverse, requires three operations: combining (adding), separating (subtraction), and reversibility. The organization of these parts (combination, separation, and reversibility) forms a system needed to understand and reason about the arithmetic problem.

Cognitive structures are used to adapt to the environment. The particular structures are not inherited but depend on the individual's history. Recall the significance of the social and physical environment as it influences the individual's construction of reality. What is biologically based, according to Piaget, is the tendency to organize one's intellectual processes. The tendency to organize and adapt results in a number of psychological structures takes different forms at different times in an individual's life (see Chapters 4 and 7). These are the stages of development.

Concept of Operations

In Piaget's theoretical system, *actions* are eventually internalized by the performer into *operations*. The scheme of the permanent object is part of knowing that an object can be taken away from view and reintroduced again, which is the notion of *reversibility* of actions. These are all part of the operations for conservation. For Piaget, the operation is the unit of logical thinking. We may say, then, that *process* describes a general state of mental activities that are necessary in order to derive a product. *Operations* specifies what particular mental activity is involved. Operations will be described in Chapter 4 since they emerge and function during the elementary school period, near the ages of six or seven.

The significance of this concept resides in the identification of mental activities involved in logical reasoning. Defining these mental activities enables specification of the relevant units of logical thinking for particular problems. Finally, operations form the crux of thought for Piaget because they are expressions of certain forms of "coordination which are general to all actions" (Inhelder and Piaget, 1964, p. 29). That is, operations are general in application. In sum, then, understanding the processes and operations leads to the understanding of how thought functions.

Although the constant order of stages cannot be attributed to environmental conditions, and although some evidence supports the idea that the sequence of stages is universal, valid evidence suggests that the rate of emergence of stages will vary with the culture.

Cultural Perspective

That cultural forces influence human development is not a new idea. From the earliest years of recorded history, differences between groups have been reported. This information is readily available in any anthropology text. For our purposes, of importance is the current integration of anthropological thinking and cognitive development. At one time it was assumed that cultures could be characterized by their degree of primitivization in terms of levels of mental ability. Thus, characterization of cultures as primitive was often based on the assumption that inherent biological differences exist between cultural groups. Some still hold this position. What is relevant for us is the intimate relationship between culture and cognitive functioning.

Culture exerts influence through the language one learns, the patterns of relating to the world, the available objects, how these objects are used, and so on. In fact, virtually no aspect of life is not touched by the culture within which one lives.

It can be said that the culture binds people, setting limits that define ways of thinking, reasoning, relating, and hence developing. For example, expectations of thinking and reasoning skills of children may be defined differently depending on whether a culture is age graded or not and what the age grades are. In some cultures children are not thought of as being able to think and reason for themselves until about age three. This means that the children below three years old are treated as not being responsible for their actions. They can make errors and adults will take the responsibility. After age three, however, these children are considered independent and able to understand. They are expected to comply and carry out certain requirements. This is not different from the concept of puberty rites in other societies where there is the expectation that certain responsibilities can now be carried out which heretofore were not possible because the individual had not yet reached a certain stage in development.

Culture plays a more subtle role through language. The way individuals express themselves and their ideas and the way they communicate feelings, attitudes, and knowledge, depend not only on the form of the language but also on a culturally defined style. Some cultures may heavily use metaphors; some may speak indirectly, while others do not; some languages are undifferentiated in their terms for particular events or objects, while others may be highly differentiated. The well-known example of the latter phenomenon is from the language of the Eskimos. While most standard English-speaking people use the nondifferentiated word "snow," Eskimos distinguish among the different kinds of snow with a specific term for each. Though we can distinguish among the varieties of snow, Eskimos can communicate that distinction more easily because their language has specific terms which enable them to do so.

At issue, however, is the degree to which the expression of the language is indicative of what the person may or may not say. This is an important distinction. If the language is restrictive by its very organization, then we do not know what range of expressive ability the person has. All we know is what is determined by that linguistic structure. On the other hand, if we have other sources of information, we can discover that the individual had more ability than is being exhibited in conversation. A good example of this is the work of Gladwin (1970) on the sailing skills of a Melanesian group. These people are able to sail in their outriggers for long distances without compass or sextant, with no land cues and usually arrive safely at their destination. There is no oral or written tradition which explicitly describes the rules of navigation. Youngsters observe and participate with their elders in navigational activities. Yet, Gladwin asks, "How do the Melanesians do it? How do they transmit this information from one generation to another?"

The culture, in its broadest sense, includes the total environment in which the individual lives. It permeates all of one's life, through one's way of thinking, relating, believing, expressing oneself, and so on. That it usually also includes a location, a country, does not mean that this is always the case. Cultures frequently exist in particular locations, but locations do not necessarily define a culture. Jews have lived in every part of the world and share cultural patterns, such as their religious beliefs, but they are not bound by location. Currently, when populations often migrate over long distances, individuals carry their cultures with them. Cultures transcend location. Thus a Puerto Rican culture can function in New York City and in San Juan and in Los Angeles and in Buffalo, New York. Even though there are limitations defined by the locale (for example, rural and urban patterns cannot coexist in New York City), there can be significant overlap such as language, religious practices, family relationships that transcend the locational differences. Thus, cultural patterns as potent and cogent influences on cognitive functioning, must be reckoned with irrespective of time and place.

Here again psychologists tend to treat this issue naively. Some have believed, for example, that comprehension of the language of another culture is sufficient for communication. This point of view overlooks the issues and problems in learning a second language and thinking in that language. There is no reason to believe that learning a second language, which is part of another culture, results in thinking and reasoning patterns which are similar to those of people who live in that culture.

The significance of culture is that it characterizes how people define their environment, their places in it, and relationships to each other. It is necessary to take an anthropological perspective here. Otherwise we overlook the significance of this critical, permeating, differentiating, and constraining force in human life, the cultural milieu. As Cole and Scribner put it:

as it is fanciful to conceive of man existing outside of social life, we cannot imagine any intellectual function that does not have sociocultural character. Perception, memory, and thinking all develop as part of the general socialization of a child and are inseparably bound up with patterns of activity, communication and social relations into which he enters. The very physical environment that he encounters has been transformed by human effort. His every experience has been shaped by culture of which he is a member and is infused with socially defined meanings and emotions. Consider language for example; it is at one and the same time a vital social force and an individual tool of communication and thought; it is so to speak, on both sides of the culture-cognition relationship (Cole and Scribner, 1974).

It might be argued that the individual is not part of the culture, but an expression of the culture. The person and the culture in a sense are one. Experiences within a cultural context are not actions on the person; they contribute to defining the person. Can you think like a Chinese, or a Japanese? Are you aware that you think differently? Rather, we contend that one is so enmeshed in a culture that one believes it is reality. That which we find general among ourselves, for example, scientific thinking or the object-person distinction, we hold to be a universal thought. However, when encountering other cultures, Oriental or American Indian, for example, we discover that what we consider to be a universal way of defining reality is not universally shared, but is an outcome of our own embeddedness in a belief system, a culture. In fact it is so internalized that it is difficult to realize that it and we are the same. The person then evolves in and with an environment. Humans are self-monitoring organisms, aware of their own awareness. In this context we can turn to a seemingly contradictory aspect. Namely, that in a given culture, each person is not a carbon copy of a cultural other. If that were true, there would be no individual differences among people. Yet we know that individual differences do exist within our own culture. Then, we must consider *individual–culture intertwining*. When we previously spoke abstractly about the characteristics of people, the ethological and the cultural ones, we implied that people residing in a common culture are alike. Being of the same species, they are all alike. Thus, if you know one you know them all. This, unfortunately, is an attitude that leads to prejudice. We realize that each of us as a resident of the United States is still vastly different from others living here. Even if we look within similar ethnic family groups, we are aware of the individual variations among people. If that is true of us why should it not be true of others? Frequently we make the mistake of assuming that because a culture looks simple or homogeneous, everyone in that culture is the same.

Variations among individuals within cultures as well as between cultures are bound to exist if for no other reason than humans are mongrels. We all are different, irrespective of cultural or species similarities. As Luria said,

It is remarkable that all individuals of a species, except identical twins, should be so different that their cells are recognized as foreign. Evidently each man is unique because his set of genes is unique. Slightly different versions of a gene will produce slightly different proteins which are often equal or nearly equal in effectiveness of function. Yet the small variation will cause a protein to be considered foreign by antibodies which recognize the fine details of its chemical surface (Luria, 1973, p. 112).

Thus he concludes that the chance that two individuals are identical is infinitesimal, so that "not only in his thoughts and feelings and his will but in the chemical markings of his body each individual is unlike any other that has ever existed" (Luria, 1973, p. 112). The biological makeup of humans then is toward individuality.

The impact of one's environment is considerable since it permeates virtually every aspect of one's life. Awareness of this issue sensitizes one to a major source of individual differences equally in a multi-cultural society such as ours.

Some Critical Issues of Stage Theory

Since the stage issue is so central to Piagetian theory, it is necessary to discuss it in some detail. Further, to create balance in our presentation and provide a basis for healthy skepticism of the stage descriptions, we shall present some of the major issues prior to describing the three major stages defined by Piaget: sensorimotor, concrete operations (and its preliminary stage of preoperations), and formal operations. These stages are the topics of the following chapters.

Recall that development refers to change that occurs through time. One basic question is whether development always follows the same general pattern; or, stated more formally, whether it proceeds in the sequential, invariant order proposed by Piaget. There are those who hold that it does (Goldstein and Scheerer, 1941; Inhelder and Piaget, 1958; Kohlberg, 1963; Laurendeau and Pinard, 1962, 1970; Piaget, 1952a, 1954, 1960, 1961; Tanner and Inhelder, 1960; Werner, 1948). These stage-dependent theories maintain that for the child to arrive at stage B in his development, he must first have reached and passed through Stage A. The order is fixed; stage B cannot be arrived at until stage A has been mastered (see Chapter 8).

For some investigators, this invariant order is accepted as being hereditarily based (Gesell and Amatruda, 1941). But for others "the order is assumed to be a fixed feature of the organism-environment interaction, to be both organismic and experiential" (J. McV. Hunt, 1961, p. 256; Piaget, 1970b; Tanner and Inhelder, 1960). Those assuming a fixed order also accept the position that the age at which stages appear and their length will vary as a function of hereditary potential and experience (Tanner and Inhelder, 1960). Studies with mental defectives indicate that the order of the stages is present but appears at different chronological periods, and that the rate of change varies from that of normal children (Inhelder, 1968; Woodward, 1961). Thus ages and stages are not necessarily linked, although in normal situations some correspondence is generally found.

There are others who believe that stages as invariant sequences do not hold but, rather, that the child is a product of learning experiences, showing different levels of ability, knowledge, and skills as a function of each experience. Order of development is not invariant; instead, the rate and quality of change depend on the particular kinds of experiences (Ausubel, 1957; Bijou, 1975; J. McV. Hunt, 1961).

Laurendeau and Pinard (1962, 1970) provide discussions of the issues involved in this controversy. They give three reasons for the criticisms of the stage-dependent theory. The first is that there is considerable overlapping among chronological age groups in all kinds of responses and concepts children employ. Not all children at chronological age four, for example, are in the same stage but show a variety of stages. Second, there is apparent continuity in the development of the child so that gaps are not directly observable. Finally, the tremendous instability found among many young children results in their giving inconsistent answers, so that it is difficult at times to determine whether a child is or is not at a particular stage. Some studies tend to refute the stage concept because they find no evidence supporting it (Brainerd, 1974; Ezer, 1962; Mogar, 1960).

Another critique raises the question that if stages have this invariant sequence, then "of what do the individual differences in intelligence of children from seven to nine (for example) consist?" (Hunt, 1961, p. 257). Individual differences in performance still have to be accounted for in stage-dependent theories.

Those upholding a stage-dependent theory assert that stages are not found frequently because of the methods employed in working with children. The experimental studies must be set up so as to ensure the child an opportunity to express herself completely and clearly. In refuting the argument of instability or inconsistency, Laurendeau and Pinard (1962) maintain that it is illogical to insist that children always reason the same way when attacking different problems. The stages are not to be described as universal but, rather, as particular to particular classes of situations. For example, one of the concepts widely described in stage terms is *animism*, attributing life to inanimate objects. Laurendeau and Pinard report that the child goes through a variety of steps before she shifts from an animistic point of view to an objective one. When and how she does so depends upon the objects with which she is dealing. Where rocks and tools are concerned, she loses the sense of animism earlier than would be the case if she were dealing with such objects as automobiles and airplanes. Children tend to lose the concept of animism in relation to the amount of knowledge they gain about particular objects.

Another critical question facing proponents of the stage theory is how to explain the transition from one stage to another. A pertinent discussion is presented by Laurendeau and Pinard. What is presumed to happen is that the child goes through a set of steps, which are then transformed into a new level. During this period, as he proceeds from one stage to the next, continuous integrations and reintegrations are made (Flavell, 1971; Laurendeau and Pinard, 1962, 1970; Piaget, 1970b; Werner, 1948).

Development from one stage to another can also occur through the substitution of one kind of activity for another. In this case, an inferior performance disappears and a superior one emerges. Development explained this way does not imply integration of one stage with another but, rather, that some approaches, habits, and ideas drop out and others appear. The implication is that continuity does not necessarily exist in development, but that a new process may appear with no apparent previous manifestation. For example, the child's walking is not continuous with his crawling; rather, crawling drops out and walking emerges (Flavell, 1971).

The best test of the validity of the invariant order of concept development would require longitudinal studies, with the same children being consistently studied over long periods of time. Only in this way could investigators trace the invariant order of stages for each child. To date, no published studies of this type are available (Wohlwill, 1973).

A second test is to ask whether external influences, such as teaching, affect the stage development. Laurendeau and Pinard, again, maintain that home or school experiences are not of sufficient moment to alter the natural processes of adaptation which take place in the children's adjustment to their objective world. Even though the child's verbalizations suggest a more advanced stage, the child will "quickly abandon the explanations received and revert to his primitive schemata or else he distorts the adult interpretation to adjust it to his own current beliefs" (Laurendeau and Pinard, 1962, p. 260). This fixed evolution is presumed to be natural and cannot be altered by external forces. Other writers do not take such a firm position, considering the question to be still open (Flavell, 1963, 1971). The evidence on the teaching of concepts, like that on the invariant order of their emergence, is as of yet inconclusive (Brainerd, 1974; Strauss, 1972). (See Chapter 8.)

Although the invariant order of stages awaits clarification, its acceptance by some writers is based on inferences from cross-sectional studies (Elkind, 1961a, 1961b; Kooistra, 1963; Laurendeau and Pinard, 1962; Piaget, 1950; Wohlwill, 1960a, 1960b).

In these studies children of different ages are compared as to their ability to perform various tasks. The younger children usually perform at a stage inferior to that of the other children. It is assumed that if the same child were followed from one chronological age to another, he or she would show the same developmental pattern as do the cross-sectional groups. Some of the empirical studies employing cross-sectional procedures will be discussed later.

In spite of these critical issues in evaluating the stage concept, practical value is derived from identifying the characteristics of the broad stages described by Piaget. There seems to be agreement that the way children think and reason fits into the broader stage characterizations. In a sense, this information can be used as criteria for categorizing children's competencies.

Summary

We have presented some of the basic concepts of Piaget with occasional elaboration on the implication of the ideas, especially on environment and stages. Presenting these constructs in isolation does not reflect the holistic nature of Piagetian theory. Holistic refers to the interdependence of the parts of the system. Thus, as Ginsburg and Opper state "Piaget believes that the functional invariants—organization and adaptation (assimilation and accommodation)—and the psychological structures are inexplicably intertwined" (1969, p. 22). As a result of the tendency toward adaptation and organization, new experiences occur which result in new structures—all functioning as a whole coherent system.

Piaget's system is organized to show how the individual builds upon biological origins while *adapting* to the world. The emphasis is upon *adaptive* behavior, which is distinguished from repetitive behavior by the slight changes occurring with each new performance. Piaget points out that these changes, however slight they might appear to be, are *systematic*.

In order to adapt, the individual must be able to utilize the experiences of the past as directional cues. . . . The child's early adaptive responses are directed toward the outside world and initiated almost entirely through stimulation to the exteroceptors rather than the interoceptors (Goodenough and Tyler, 1959, p. 152).

Piaget formulated the constructs discussed in this chapter to account for the human's systematic adaptation to the world and the individual constructions of the world resulting from organism-environment interactions. The basic units of organized behaviors which are first evident are the reflex structures, like the sucking reflex and the tendency to turn the head toward auditory sources. The concept introduced in this chapter which describes organized patterns of action or perception (or both) was the *schema*. Schemata (plural) are not limited to reflex patterns, but also describe new organizations of behaviors which emerge as the child continues in its interactive adaptations to the world. The reflex schemata, however, are built upon through *assimilation*, the concept Piaget uses to describe the taking-in of new information from its surroundings, and *accommodation*, the concept used to indicate that the organism is always changed by its encounters with the world.

We have tried to point out briefly how each of these concepts conveys a complexity of theoretical ideas. In fact, we will devote the next several chapters to discussing the implications of these concepts as the core of Piaget's developmental theory. To acquaint the reader with a "glossary" of terms in order to understand the theory we are about to discuss we have had to rely upon comprehensive definitions of the concepts. This approach works sufficiently well for concepts such as schema, accommodation, and assimilation. We acknowledge that the complexity of ideas embodied by *structure*, *stage*, and so forth is too great to be covered thus far. The following chapters provide fuller discussions. As a continuation of the summary, let us state briefly that the adaptive organization of the individual's behavior does not cease with schema, assimilation, and accommodation. "The adaptation and organization are complementary aspects of a single cyclical mechanism" (J. McV. Hunt, 1961, p. 111) which continues throughout the life of the organism.

Schemata are organizations of actions. When these actions are internalized, Piaget refers to them as *operations*. Operations are given various names depending upon the specific *mental* activity involved. Further organization of operations into related patterns comprises mental *structures*. Remember that these concepts are Piaget's notation for showing the organization of human adaptation.

We have pointed out that adaptation is an interplay between biological and environmental factors, and that cultural variations contribute heavily to the environmental side of this interaction. The result of these person-environment interactions are the individual's interpretations (constructions) of the world. We do not all have the same world view because we have different experiences. However, since learning depends upon development, we all have the same delimiting factors to cognitive growth which make us similar. Piaget uses the term "stage" to indicate that our learning from experience is limited by the biological growth factors of maturation. For example, no amount of exposure to ambient adults will help the child to walk earlier than his development will allow. This analogy is applied to cognitive growth to illustrate the correspondence between learning and maturation.

A gap in the holistic nature of Piagetian theory is that two critical functions have not been discussed: *language*, a uniquely human characteristic, and *affect* (emotions and feelings). A discussion of the role of language has been presented in terms of the significance of social factors. The special role of language and representational thought in Piagetian theory are discussed in Chapter 5.

Finally, Piaget has been criticized for ignoring, or at least underemphasizing, the role of affect (emotions and feelings) in the development of intellect. Such assertions are far from the truth. For Piaget, affect and cognition are interwoven and hence indissociable, even though distinct systems (Piaget, 1973). The affective system is the energizer, and by its positive or negative connections, it may cause the acceleration or the delay of cognitive development. To quote Piaget, "this does not mean that affectivity produces or even modifies the cognitive structure (reasoning or thinking system) whose necessity remains intrinsic . . . it goes without saying that if the affective stems from an energetic then the cognitive stems from structures" (Piaget, 1973, p. 47). This means then that there are two systems, the affective (the energizer, the mover), and the cognitive (the organized system of thinking and reasoning). Piaget's research effort tends to emphasize the cognitive system through which the child constructs knowledge. Theoretical and empirical work still needs to be extended into the affective domain (see Chapter 4).

These concepts form the overall set of factors essential to the development of the stages of intelligence. Now, we shall move from consideration of these developmental concepts to the processes involved in development of cognition.

Chapter 3 Cognitive Development during Preschool Years

The previous chapter identified a number of key concepts integral to Piagetian theory—constructivism, assimilation and accommodation, stages, equilibration, structure, and operations. The theory describes the stages of development by analysis of changing cognitive structure.

Piaget has identified four major stages: sensorimotor, preoperational, concrete operations, and formal operations. For this chapter we shall describe the first two periods, sensorimotor (covering approximately birth through eighteen to twenty-four months), and the intuitive and preoperational periods (covering from eighteen to twenty-four months to about four or five years).

In reviewing these stages, however, it is important to realize that they are abstractions and do not necessarily characterize the total individual. The child may show characteristics which fit across stages. The critical criteria for defining the child's

stage are those characteristics which typify the child's behavior.

Periods of Intellectual Development

Sensorimotor Period (Birth to Two Years)

The first two years of life have been described by Piaget (1954)
as the *sensorimotor period*. The infant moves from a primarily
reflexive organism, responding in an undifferentiated way to the
environment, to "a relatively coherent organization of sensorimotor actions vis-à-vis his immediate environment" (Flavell,
1963, p. 86). The evolution of cognitive operations begins at
birth with the initial use of inherent reflexes, part of the child's
biological endowment, interacting with external environmental
excitation.

The infant's movements, physical and intellectual, lack pre-
cision and her activities and attention are dominated by external stimulation. The infant has been described as approaching the environment in an undifferentiated, unreflective, and
unspecified manner (Koffka, 1928; Werner, 1948).

Piaget has extensively studied infant development during
the sensorimotor period (1954). In general, he reports that the
child accomplishes the following tasks: attaining rudimentary
knowledge of objects, people, and events, which become the
basis for later concepts; differentiating the self from objects;
localizing the self in physical space; establishing the beginning
awareness of cause and effect and of time and space—in part
this happens because the child has acquired the ability to identify the permanence and substantiality of objects during this
period.

In the course of this development the child goes through six
stages. In the first stage, which lasts about a month, the child
shows little besides reflexive behavior. In the second stage, from
about one to four months, various reflex activities become modified with experience and coordinated with one another. In
stage three, between four and eight months, infants begin to
act toward objects and events outside their own bodies as
though they have some permanence and stability. In effect, each
child is beginning to demonstrate intentional or goal-directed

activity, becoming purposeful in the search. Intentionality of purpose is observed in children between eight and twelve months, during the fourth stage, with the beginnings of what are called means-end relationships. The child tends to use what has already been learned in searching for objects, as well as repeating patterns of behavior. Children reach stage five between twelve and eighteen months of age. They now begin to experiment, to search for new ways to solve problems, and to become excited about novelty for its own sake. Finally, at stage six, between eighteen months to approximately two years, children show the capacity for primitive symbolic representation. They may invent solutions mentally, that is, symbolically, rather than by trial and error. With the beginning of symbolic thought, they approach the next phase of development. Much of the accomplishment of intellectual development occurs as the child is developing and learning motor coordination, for example, reaching precisely for an object and bringing it to his mouth or seeing an object and walking toward it.

CIRCULAR REACTIONS. The achievements throughout this period can be characterized as *circular reactions*, actions and reactions, that is, the interaction between the child and the environment. The child, by acting on an object, makes the object "perform." Initially, this happens reflexively with no deliberation or purposeful basis for the action. Piaget offers this example.

As soon as the hands reach the lips, the sucking reflex is relearned. The child sucks his fingers for a moment but, of course, does not know either how to keep them in his mouth or nurse them with his lips. . . . For some children contact of the lips and probably the tongue with the nipple suffices to produce sucking (1952a, p. 25).

During the course of this sucking, the child incorporates (assimilates) many other experiences and sensations occurring during the sucking process. There is a tendency toward repetition. This tendency and the concomitant experiences set up the basis for the circular reactions which are a synthesis of assimilation and accommodation. The assimilation is evident in the child's reflexive sucking. Circular reactions, however, are also accommodative in that the child has now learned when to suck, building a new set of coordinations. These circular reactions are essentially feedback mechanisms. The concept here is that, given the effects of the action, the child seeks to carry out an action to produce or reproduce the previous result. Incidentally, this is an instance where the idea that pleasure or reproducing a pleasurable outcome indicates an implicit motivational basis for action. This primary circular reaction contributes to the production of voluntary behavior. As the child begins to repeat the activity, and to do so voluntarily, she is developing new schemata enabling her to carry out single actions at will.

Sucking, grasping, and looking are but some of the reflexes which become organized and enable the child to carry out single actions on objects. Subsequent to the primary circular reactions, are those which Piaget calls secondary and tertiary. Each is in principle analogous to the primary circular reactions, and increasingly complex, involving coordination of various actions (for example, visual coordination, coordinating looking and grasping).

During the sensorimotor period, the child begins to show preliminary activities which lead to one of the most significant achievements, *object permanence*, the awareness of the stabile existence of objects. During the first two stages of the period, the child spends time looking for an object where it disappears. By the third stage the object is completely gone as far as the child is concerned and attention is turned elsewhere. The child has some memory of the object, exhibiting some recognition when the item reappears. But what is critical now is that the infant does not have the conception that objects exist even though they cannot be seen.

In the third stage, with the appearance of *secondary circular reactions*, the child is now not only discovering new interests, but also discovering the power to make objects reappear. The child is moving toward the understanding of the meaning of the object, not just a recognition of familiarity. In summary, this achievement is coupled with an increased awareness of the permanence of objects and the idea that the child can make things disappear and reappear. The sense of some mastery of and competence in controlling the environment begins to emerge.

These actions and learning occur in a context characterized

by certainty and regularity. The presence of the familiar mother, father, and other family members, the constant presence of objects, and the child's home are all supportive of the regularity of the environment. Consistencies give rise to the predictability of the child's world. As the child in this stage is aware of the appearance and disappearance of objects and people, she also becomes aware that she can search for verification of her hypothesis that the object is, in fact, there.

By stage four, the child is able to coordinate the previous learning into secondary organizations. Now, the infants are combining aspects of their learning and organizing them more coherently, purposefully, and consequently intelligently. For example, the child learns about his relations to objects, if he pulls something, it will come toward him; if he pushes something, it will go away. If he pushes something and it goes away behind another object, he can retrieve it by his own actions. The child is learning not only about the functioning of objects, but also about people. The child can be expected to know that father will do something with her which is perhaps different from mother. When she is hungry and cries, she expects mother or a caregiver to come to feed her. There are many false starts at this period in imitating and solving primitive problems.

From stage four, at about ten-to-twelve-months-old, the child moves to what Piaget refers to as stage five, when *tertiary circular reactions* characterize child environment interactions. This stage covers the ages of twelve- to eighteen-months-old approximately. While prior to this period the child is *conservative*, repeating familiar actions to provide some sense of mastery and control, the child is now more exploratory and curious. At this stage Piaget calls the child inventive, especially at solving problems such as achieving a goal or removing obstacles that are in the way. The child works at solving conflicting situations more directly. Behaviors are more organized, purposeful, and reflect an increased understanding of the spatial role of objects. The child had previously searched in a relatively random way for objects that had disappeared; the behavior is now more systematic and directed toward the proper place. As he searches for hidden objects, already believing in the permanence of place, he eventually learns that an object, hidden from sight, still exists. This remarkable intellectual achievement for an organism so young leads us to realize that infants are more competent than had been believed (Bower, 1974; Moore and Clark, 1975; Moore and Dawson-Myers, 1975). The child now attempts to utter sounds that become associated with particular situations. This fosters the ability to imitate actions of others as well as anticipate their movements and actions.

During this and the previous period, dramatic changes are occurring in the biology and the environment of the child. She has begun to sit up in stage three, and now her visual perspective of the world is changing. The ability to sit unattended gives the child a new perspective of the environment approximating how it will look when she learns to walk. The child begins to crawl and so is able to voluntarily make contact with objects and individuals directly rather than primarily visually. The child is not only eating liquid or soft foods, but is having a different set of oral experiences. In addition to these changes, major changes are taking place in the child's use of vocalizations. In effect, contact with the world changes, in part, due to the individual's body growth. These interactive possibilities provide new and different experiences.

By the time children reach stage five, at twelve to eighteen months-old, some are already standing. By the end of this period, most children are walking. This upright movement and the opportunity to locomote farther than before give the child a chance for considerable exploratory adventures. The child now gets into situations which result in parental controls and limitations. These new capabilities bring the role of the parent into sharp relief. Strategies to control children serve three objectives: (1) to keep them from harming themselves; (2) to keep them from harming property; and (3) to promote understanding that they are living in a world of and with others. In essence, socialization becomes increasingly important in daily experiences.

As children move from stage five to stage six, they enter a major transitional period of preoperational thought. The child begins to enter the onset of representational thought. In addition to using previous experiences, the child begins to articulate his earlier experience with language and symbolic understanding. The child is now engaged in what Piaget refers to as the *semiotic function*, the ability to employ language, signs, and symbols as a means of expressing thought. A number of new

competencies emerge at this time. The child is able to anticipate mentally, that is, have an idea which he wishes to execute.
The child can imitate models which are no longer present,
deferred imitation in Piagetian terms. The child can reconstruct
ideas on the basis of language and represent a previous experience for others as well as for himself.

Activities are now more complex. The child becomes involved
in play behavior which for Piaget is assumed to be assimilation.
There is some question about this, however, since as the child
engages in play, he may also accommodate, that is, adapt old
schemata as a result of playing.

To summarize, the individual through complex learning processes acquires data from the environment. Stimulation is reciprocal; environmental sensations stimulate the person and the
various sensations eventually become identified, named, and
organized. Through increased ability to discriminate and generalize, the child develops schemata. In doing so, the individual
becomes increasingly emancipated from the perceptual and
sensory aspect of the environment, and is able to approach it
conceptually.

The long-term significance of intellectual development from
birth to two years still needs examination. Early significance of
these periods relative to the eventual attainment of concepts
and intellectual functioning needs to be studied longitudinally.
To illustrate, it may be that one reason children from economically impoverished backgrounds have difficulty in kindergarten
and first grade is that they did not have appropriate stimulation during these early years. The assumption is that adequate
or inadequate experience in the first two years of life influences
the rate of development. Therefore, if intellectual stimulation
begins earlier, we can prepare children for necessary knowledge
acquisition.

In the first two years, the infant generally begins with undifferentiated views of the self and the environment, then gradually begins to differentiate the self from the environment. In
the process the child also learns that the environment functions
on a basis of certain physical properties, such as space, object
permanence, and causality. The child at this period also has
been called preabstract, or not able to grasp what is called in
biology a "genus-species" relationship, that is, a higher class

concept. For example, he cannot yet understand that a dog is in the broad general class, *animal*, although he can understand that a particular dog, Rover, is a member of a smaller class, DOG (Welch, 1940). At the end of the second year, the child has acquired intellectual skills that enable him to function on a more symbolic level. The child now prepares for and begins to organize concrete operations (White, 1971). But what, we may ask, propels the child to move from a sensorimotor stage to the concrete operational stage through the preoperational transition?

TRANSITIONS FROM SENSORIMOTOR PERIOD TO PREOPERATIONAL PERIOD. The question can be posed succinctly: "What promotes change from sensorimotor to preoperational thought—a shift toward conceptual intelligence?" This transition can be characterized as a move from a period

which does not aim at explanation or classification or taking note of facts for their own sake: it links causally and classifies and takes note of facts only in relation to subjective goals which are foreign to the pursuit of truth. Sensorimotor intelligence is thus an intelligence in action and in no way reflective. (Piaget, 1950, p. 121).

The shift from sensorimotor intelligence to conceptual intelligence can be best understood by identifying four fundamental differences between the two periods: (1) Piaget claims that the child in the sensorimotor does not have a general overview of events. He uses the metaphor of a movie film to describe this state. "Sensory-motor intelligence thus functions like a slow motion film, representing one static image after another instead of showing a fusion of the images." (Piaget, 1952a, p. 239). (2) The infant is searching for sources of personal action, in a sense for the achievement of a practical aim. For example, finding the missing object is rather a search for understanding, or, as Piaget says, the infant searches for proof. (3) The child acts only on the apparent characteristics of objects, not on the symbols, signs, or schemata related to them. The child relates to objects in the immediate sense as individual objects, not as members of a class. (4) Finally, the child is essentially a self-centered individual whose social interactions reflect only her perspective. She is not able to employ abstractions to represent objects and events and is very literal.

If these four characteristics differentiate the sensorimotor stage from the preoperational (conceptual), four conditions would then explain the transition to the conceptual intelligence stage. Recall in our previous use of the film metaphor, we described the static film moving a frame at a time. In the beginning of the preoperational period the film metaphor is still appropriate, but now it changes from a static set of images to a continuous integration, a systematic integration of behavior. As Piaget says:

A speeded-up film of the behavior thus becomes an interior (mental) representation. With this newly acquired development, the child becomes able to unwind the film in both directions so [that] . . . the pursuit of a practical aim . . . [is] replaced by recognition and explanation . . . based on the classifying of objects and being aware of the fact that events and objects are ordered by grades (seriation). (Piaget, 1952a, p. 231)

The child is able to extend the processes of assimilation and accommodation, as perceptual and motor experiences are assimilated and applied to subsequent experiences. This latter process involves using acquired knowledge in order to anticipate outcomes and reconstitute previous experiences. Thus, the child is beginning to use representation as in film images while moving toward logical thought.

For Piaget, what is critical then are the constructions of representation. Language serves as the critical facilitator of this transition (see Chapter 5). Detailed discussion of the transformations occurring during this period are found in Piaget, *Play, Dreams, and Imitation in Childhood* (1951) and *The Construction of Reality in the Child* (1954).

Language emerges as a result of the maturity of the organism. The kind of language, its richness and the degree to which it allows for complex thought patterns depends on the culture and social experience. Thus, we come full circle back to the significant role of the three factors Piaget identifies, motivation, experience, and culture (see Chapter 2).

Finally, during interaction in the world of objects and events, logically necessitated conflicts occur. Conflict refers here to the discrepancy between events and experiences. For example, the child tries to fit a square piece of puzzle into a round inset.

After trying hard, he fails. A discrepancy exists between what he wants to do and what is possible. This is not random trial and error, but a case of miscuing spatial relationships. Thus, we can answer our question, Why does the child make the transition from sensorimotor to conceptual schemata? with three reasons: (1) The child develops a capability to represent experiences, anticipate outcomes, and reconstitute previous experiences; (2) acquires language and is able to evoke previous experience; and (3) has learned the coordination of representational ability which combines with language acquisition to enable the child to engage in socialized and conceptual thinking.

Preoperational Period (Two to Seven Years)

In the previous discussions we detailed the child's behavior during the first two years of life. The infant moved from a prone, nonverbal organism to an upright, verbal, and mobile child. Previously dependent on adults, now the child is increasingly independent. At first the child's wants and needs had been communicated indirectly, now language is employed. Not only qualitatively but emotionally the child is beginning to define a self and person separate from others.

As we proceed into the next stage it is important to think of this as a reorganization of the child's physical, mental, and social situation. In this complex context we can better understand the dynamics of cognitive development. This period is characterized by two subphases, preoperational and intuitive.

PREOPERATIONAL PHASE (TWO- TO FOUR-YEARS-OLD). In this phase instead of thinking and reasoning through action, that is, experimenting and operating externally and concretely, the child is approaching the ability to function symbolically. He is able to distinguish between the signifier—that which stands for something—and the actual object. With the beginning of symbolic thought, language plays an increasing role. The distinction is presented very clearly by Flavell.

First, the sensorimotor intelligence is capable of only linking, one by one, the successive actions of perceptual stages with which it gets involved. Piaget likens it to a slow motion film which represents one static frame after another, but can give no simultaneous and all-encompassing purview of all the frames. Representational thought, on the other hand, through symbolic capacity has the potential for simultaneously grasping, in a single internal epitome, a whole sweep of separate events. It is a much faster and more mobile device which can recall the past, represent the present, and anticipate the future in one temporally brief, organized act (1963, pp. 151–152).

Characteristics of preoperational thought during the early phase. However, this preoperational thought is not mature. During the preoperational phase (ages 2 to 4), the child is egocentric, using herself as the standard of judgment and unable to take the viewpoints of other people. She is egocentric with respect to representations and symbolic activities. She still judges by face value and not reflectively. Categorizing on the basis of single characteristics of objects, she is unable to classify the multi-faceted aspects of stimuli simultaneously. For example, she cannot take into account an object having width and height simultaneously. The child is conceptualizing on single, salient features of the environment. Egocentrism as defined by Piaget is not to be viewed as a personality trait, rather it denotes the child's frame of reference. At this time, it is the self.

This inability to handle multiple characteristics of objects is one reason that Piaget refers to this time as one in which the child is operating on preconcepts. Although the child has already acquired the concept of the object and has some idea of classes of objects, he is not able to incorporate the variety of characteristics of an object into a single classification. He can grasp ideas such as men and women being classified as people, or that potatoes and apples are food. These are called first-level concepts. But he cannot employ two attributes of the same object, that is, break up a group of apples along the multiple dimensions of big, red apples and small, green apples.

The child's conceptualization is perceptual-dominant, since organization, classification, and primitive conceptions are determined to a large measure by the potency of the apparent physical attributes. However, what makes this different from the sensorimotor stage is that the child approaches objects symbolically rather than through direct motor actions. Werner cites an example of the child's using the word *papa* not only for father, but for all objects belonging to father. These ways of relating different kinds of objects, by applying to them either the same name or the same behavior, reflect the child's selecting a particular characteristic deemed relevant as the basis of organizing diverse materials. In effect, the child sees objects as belonging together because from the child's experience and perspective they are, in fact, together. The reasons given for their grouping, however, are not logical. For example, a cat and a dog are classified together not because they are animals, but "because I like my cat and I like my dog." At this point the child's thinking is what Piaget calls *transductive*; that is, the child tends to relate the particular to the particular. If *A* is like *B* in one respect, then *A* must be like *B* in other respects.

For some writers children's conceptualizations are described as *syncretic*, since diverse items are grouped together in an egocentric fashion, often in disregard of their intrinsic relationships. For children at this period, all events may be related to each other—even assumed to be causally related—not on the basis of objectivity nor on an accurate cause-effect basis, but rather because they are juxtaposed in time and space. In the most literal sense, then, children are realistic; whatever they see is taken at face value and accepted (Piaget, 1954; Werner, 1948).

INTUITIVE PHASE (FOUR- TO SEVEN-YEARS-OLD). The next phase of intuitive thought (ages four to seven), is still somewhat part of the same epoch but with a transition to increased symbolic functioning (Flavell, 1963; Piaget & Inhelder, 1969). The child is still egocentric, dominated by her perceptions, and subjective judgments. Three fundamental operations now appear: the ability to think in terms of classes, to see relationships, and to deal with number concepts. The child can classify material on the basis of objective similarity. When presented with a group of squares and triangles, she can classify objects on the basis of triangularity or color, but still only on the basis of one of these characteristics. At the same time she is increasingly able to comprehend the meaning of similarity and classification. It is now possible to see relationships such as "Mrs. Smith is the mother of John," as a result of the ability to perceive relations as well as to compare and order items. The child is now said to be intuitive because she does not necessarily verbalize or indicate awareness of classification. She is also beginning to utilize numbers and to order things in terms of quantity. Because she is becoming able to disregard certain properties of items and see that a relationship can exist on a numerical basis even though the objects differ structurally, she can now count different objects, thereby producing a sum, which is an abstraction.

Summary—Characteristics of Preoperational Thought

This period is one of widening horizons of the child's cognitive structure as it is embedded in an increasingly complex social and emotional framework. The major acquisition for the child here is what Piaget calls the *semiotic function*. Piaget uses terms such as the signifier which means one thing that stands for another, and the significate which is that which is being signified. This process of the semiotic function can also be termed *representational thinking*, when the child is able to represent experiences of an object, a person, or an event in another form. The semiotic function is expressed in language, a system of acquired signs. Language provides a means of referring to existent and nonexistent objects, events, and persons. Further, language provides a mode of thought.

The major cognitive development then in this preoperational stage is moving from the sensorimotor plane to the plane of representation. Instead of engaging in activity on a motor level, the child becomes able to engage in the same activity transformed into a mental state. In the sensorimotor period a hidden object is found by the child's search behavior; now, he may have an image of that object and coordinates his actions to achieve it. In other words, the child's thinking is more internalized, that is, mental, instead of being tied solely to actions.

Transitional Processes

Piaget contends that the steady advance toward logical thought involves shifts from imitational behaviors in the immediate context to deferred imitation, from egocentrism as a frame of reference to the ability to take another's perspective, and from figurative to operative knowledge (p. 59). These changes become apparent in the intuitive phase of operational thought. Since, however, these developmental shifts are not isolated occurrences, but emerge from the context of a previous developmental context, we shall discuss each of them as general trends.

Imitation in Preoperational Thought

Internalization is further evidenced in the child's imitative behavior. In the sensorimotor period, imitation was observed very early but the child had to have the model present in order to imitate it. At the very beginning of the preoperational stage the child is capable of what Piaget refers to as *deferred imitation*, that is, after observing an event, the child repeats what she has seen when the model is not present. Remember that imitation for Piaget is not an exact copy of what was seen, but rather the child's interpretation and construction of what was seen which is then re-presented in the child's activities. Deferred imitation is related conceptually and pragmatically to much of the discussion of modeling and observational learning. In those instances, the child observes a model doing something and reiterates that action either in the presence of the model or at some later time. There seems to be little question that much learning occurs through what Bandura and others have referred to as "observational learning" (Bandura, 1974).

Imitation is a very critical problem in need of more study. There is no definitive answer to why a child imitates, what he imitates, and what he elects to retain and imitate at a later time. No doubt, deferred imitations serve an adaptive function. The child may see how someone uses a knife and fork and use them appropriately when faced with that requirement. The child may observe how someone plays with an object and engage in that play at a later time. These observations and their retention of the experiences provide the child with the necessary options for solving subsequent problems. Deferred imitation is a necessary prelude to representational thought. To imitate in the absence of the model necessitates an internal representation of that event. The child pretending to repeat a recently heard word or throwing a ball after watching a model are cases in point. As adults, we engage in deferred imitation quite frequently, for example, in learning how to hit a tennis ball. Thus there is an adaptive function for deferred imitation. It becomes particularly relevant when we relate it to the whole problem of observational learning. It is impossible for us as human beings to learn everything from textbooks, or to learn everything the first time. Just think how many times children see their parents drive a car. It may be that the continual exposure of children to driving significantly decreases the amount of time it takes an individual to learn to drive. As Piaget has indicated, the individual's increased experience with particular objects or events enhances the rate at which he assimilates new learning and evolves new accommodations to these objects or events. Observational learning is an important mode by which much information is accumulated.

In this context, representation and symbolic activity become critical. Although at this time we do not know the form in which this information is stored, Piaget has suggested that what happens is that the individual forms schemata, organizations of knowledge related in varying ways. These schemata are, in fact, representations of concepts of reality, physical and social. Thus, the child is beginning to construct an internal map, or conception of reality, during the preoperational period.

Children's Frame of Reference—Egocentric

Egocentrism at this period is a very important consideration in our understanding of the child's cognitive behavior. The considerable amount of research studying problems of egocentrism with preoperational children focuses on two areas: spatial perspectives and communication. The argument has been offered that spatial perspectives provide a basic insight into the child's use of self as a frame of reference in making decisions. Piaget's basic experiment is asking a child to judge how she sees a mountain scene. She is asked how that mountain scene would look if someone were on the other side of the mountain. In order to look at the scene from another perspective the child must project herself in space—in a sense, turn around and make judgments opposite to what she sees from her own vantage point.

Intuitively, one is inclined to see young children as essentially self-centered and believing that they are making judgments about events which are *the judgments* of events. For example, the child gets impatient when he uses words in sentences and finds that adults cannot understand him. Sometimes this impatience is due to the child's mystification that the adult cannot understand what seems so apparent. Part of the child's difficulty in taking the point of view of the other is that he has not learned how to make the appropriate inferences nor has he learned that other people's points of view are, in fact, different from his own.

Egocentrism among children is exemplified in preschool children's communications. The young child tells stories in a way that assumes the hearer knows the sequence or antecedents of events. An array of studies have been reported showing how difficult it is for young children to take the perspective of others, either in a physical situation, or in a social one. Recall our earlier example, where the child is in front of a mountain scene and is asked to describe it.

Next she is given a doll which is placed on the other side of the mountain. The child is asked to describe what the doll sees. At this age, the child does not discriminate between what she sees and what the doll sees. In other words, the preoperational child does not distinguish between her view and that of the doll. Later, she can make these distinctions.

Studies have been done using this paradigm with social situations, for example, asking children to take the point of view of another, asking how another child might feel if something happened to him, or asking a child to communicate instructions to a person sitting opposite him, that is, reversal in position. There is general agreement that children tend to use themselves as points of reference (Shantz, 1975).

Remember that egocentrism is an intellectual frame of reference that the child uses rather than being aware of the different positions from which other people view similar events. In other words, if adults are looking at a picture which is assumed to be obviously beautiful, they could say it is beautiful. To say a picture is beautiful implies that beauty is inherent in that picture. Yet another person viewing the same picture may say, "I believe that picture is ugly." The second person places ugliness not in the picture, but as his own invention or construction or

Figure 3.1
The three mountains

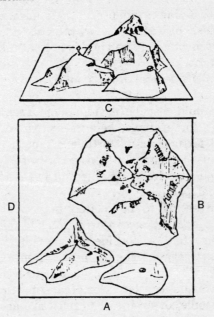

From J. Piaget and B. Inhelder, *The Child's Conception of Space*. New York: Norton, 1967, p. 211.

evaluation of that picture, not that the ugliness is an *objective* reality. The first viewer in our example would be the one who provides an egocentric response, thinking that beauty is inherent in the object. In effect, the way he sees the picture is the way the picture is, overlooking the fact that to others the picture is not viewed the same way.

Decentration—A Development toward Use of Alternatives

The gradual move away from egocentrism is referred to as *decentration*. That is, the child now begins gradually to move away from a single aspect of the environment and to take into account other factors that are there. The child gradually becomes aware of alternative points of view and/or choices. For example, in classifying a group of blocks, instead of classifying them on the basis of a single color, the child may now classify them on the basis of size. The child is able to take into account alternative criteria.

Decentration is a general process not limited to physical tasks. Becoming aware of alternative ways of looking at people or social events would also be examples of *decentration*. In the personal realm, for example, being sensitive to or empathetic with the good fortune or misfortune of another are instances where decentration occurs. In sum, decentration is the shifting from a single perspective of an object or event to an awareness of alternative perspectives.

Decentration seems to be related to two other important processes of Piaget's: *physical abstraction* and *reflective abstraction*. When the child is considering the physical criteria by which to organize events, she is, in effect, engaged in physical abstraction. That is, she is separating a perceived element from an array of elements as a basis for organizing those elements—be it blocks, people, or events. The reflective abstraction refers not to the discrimination of a perceived attribute, but to the child's mental representation of the item and using that information. It is, in effect, a representational process rather than a sensorimotor activity. We would expect, therefore, in the process of decentration that children engage in more reflective abstraction, when they are beginning to relate and combine elements.

Ontogenesis of Conservation

Related to the development of reflective abstraction is the problem of conservation. Conservation is a fundamental Piagetian concept which simply defined means that any attribute or quality retains its essential characteristics in spite of transformation in its physical appearance. The characteristics of the mountain remain constant irrespective of the position of the person observing it; the weight of an object does not change because the object is cut in half; the quantity of liquid does not change because it is poured into a different sized container; the chemical composition of an object may not change because its shape is altered. In effect, what Piaget argues is that there is a constancy of characteristics of an object and learning this is a critical base for subsequent logical thought.

Conservation is related to *object permanence* (see p. 40). The object is retained in memory; in effect, it is conserved in spite of its absence. The object has not lost any of its characteristics in spite of its absence.

We can begin to see places where the conservation principle is important and we will begin to talk about that as we proceed. When children are in the preoperational period, they are not conservers in the sense of truly understanding that when an object is transformed, disappears, or looks different, its essential characteristics are unchanged. The child now is tied to appearances; what he sees, is. If the child is given a whole apple which is then cut up into pieces, he thinks he may have more than he had before. It is not a question of his comprehension of the terms more or less; it is actually that what he sees is more pieces of apple and therefore more apple.

The problem of conservation permeates the discussions of the development of space, time, number, and relations, because the use of objects, establishing relations among objects, and determining classes of objects, requires the principle of conservation. It may well be for this reason that North American psychologists have found conservation of quantity, number, and space to be one of the most intriguing problems. We shall discuss the conservation issue again in a separate section describing older children (Chapter 4) and modifiability or change of children's capabilities on the cognitive level (Chapter 7).

Significance of Play in Cognitive Growth

One area of particular significance in the preoperational period is play, which has been receiving renewed attention in the psychological literature. There are some studies supporting the notion that play is a characteristic of cultures where there is a childhood. This may sound surprising to the reader but in some societies children are taught to engage in productive activity at a very early age. Thus the playful society and the play period as we know it are not part of their normal life style.

In western culture, Piaget's primary concern, play is an important developmental task, though play behavior is difficult to define. Adults distinguish between work and play. Work is considered purposeful, for economic gain, not necessarily pleasurable and so forth. The play of the child in the preoperational period should be viewed as analogous to adult work, if we think of work as a process of solving problems and engaging in activities which serve some purpose other than simple pleasure. For Piaget, play is essentially assimilative in nature; the child is acquiring, assimilating, and reiterating experiences. Sutton-Smith (1966) argues that play does involve accommodation since the child rethinks experience and also gains new knowledge. During play, the child not only deals with experiences on a physical level, but also learns about the functions and properties of objects and their relations to one another. The child also engages in fantasies, in role playing, and begins to work out some of her own reality notions and understandings.

Play, as distinguished from games, is assimilative and, in a sense, is initially symbolic. That is, the child's play contains elements that are identical to the reality (symbolic). For example, the child folds his hands and lies on them pretending to go to sleep, or the child sits on a chair and makes motions and noises very similar to a car or a bus or an airplane. These are deliberate and conscious activities in which the child engages, reproducing realistic elements. The function of this activity has not been studied too intensively in the past and we have only fragmented notions of their significance and understanding.

The psychoanalytic point of view describes play as serving the child's emotional life, enabling him to work through various emotional conflicts. The child works out his feelings toward siblings or parents. Thus the little girl playing mother, or the little boy playing father, or the little boy playing mother and the little girl playing father become instances where children attempt to resolve emotional conflicts, according to psychoanalytic theorists. However, this notion of conflict is different from the cognitive conflict referred to earlier which is a logical conflict between discrepant events in the environment.

Although Piaget does not deny the significance of fantasy and conflict resolution on the emotional plane, he tends to emphasize the cognitive elements of play in which the child assimilates new information while engaging in actions on objects. Nevertheless, there is reason to believe, as Sutton-Smith has argued, that play is more than assimilation. Play also involves new learning and understanding. This is compatible with the work of George Herbert Mead who maintained that children learn roles of others through games and this helps them define who they are and who others are. In other words, play becomes an important mechanism for the child's acquisition of roles and eventually for identification of the self (Mead, 1972).

Mead's work, however, has never been empirically tested. One study that seems relatively close to that test deserves detailed discussion because it serves to point out the significance of play and tends to illuminate some of the issues. The study referred to is by Robert Fink (1974) who worked with kindergarten children. Fink set up play situations for these children in small groups away from the school classroom. He then presented them with a play scene. For example, he announced that they were going to play restaurant. He assigned roles to each child, but some children elected to be waiters and other children asked to be the cooks or hostesses and so forth. After this introduction, Fink encouraged the children to play out a restaurant scene. He also did this for other themes. The control children as a group came into a room where Fink gave them toys and asked them to play as they wished, providing no structure to their activity. A third group had no contact at all of this kind. Observations were made of the children's play for both the experimental and control groups. The children were also assessed on a variety of intellectual measures, mostly dealing with conservation material. One of Fink's conservation interests was what he called conservation of social role, that is, when the child conserves the role of the individual in spite of transformation. For example, the father is still a father even though he goes to work to be a carpenter; the teacher is still the teacher even when she goes home to her family to be a mother; the mother is still a mother even though she is functioning as a teacher. It might be mentioned parenthetically that very young children frequently have difficulty in coordinating these bits of information and either one is a teacher or a mother, but to be a teacher and a mother is incongruous to a preoperational child. Fink evolved tests for conservations of social roles along with observations of some physical attributes, such as number and quantity. He found that the experimental children became more sensitive to and more competent in the conservation of social role than children in the control groups. In other words, Fink found that a structured play experience as he defined it, influences the acquisition of conservation of social role. This finding demonstrates that play serves an accommodative rather than a purely assimilative function. The child now has a new schema, a new organization, of persons and person conservation. Therefore, under those terms, we can see that Piaget is not entirely correct when he holds that play is purely assimilative.

What does play involve? First, the child must take the role of another. Involved with the present activity, the child must, second, imagine or fantasize what to be. Further, the child has to reconstruct or retrieve past information and use it in the present. Ordering the play theme and the sequence of events is not fixed in the physical world but rather fixed in the heads of the participants. Thus to engage in play, especially when it involves others, requires the child to engage in an array of interactions which can produce conflict, logical necessity, and consequently the need for resolution of these difficulties.

The above discussion, however, focuses on cooperative or corrective play, play in a group. But play is not restricted to group engagements; play can be individual or isolated. Thus when the child is playing alone, whether building a house or dancing to music or painting a picture or engaging in a variety of motor acts, these can all be classified as play. And what of this learning? Within the Piagetian framework, engagement in this form means that the child is learning the nature and functions of objects.

Meaning of Preoperational Thought

We should consider why certain phases are called preoperational. In preoperational phases the child is still engaged in mental activities which, although representational, are concrete and not abstract. The activities are very much tied to action, but mental, in contrast to sensorimotor thought which is external and nonreflective. The relationships between events are *figurative*. Knowledge is organized in pictorial mental images. For Piaget, acts such as labeling, classification, cause-effect, or activities such as play, are all inherently tied to the object-actions and reactions. Thus the operations are not serving as rules or principles which are in the child's conscious awareness. The child at this period does not monitor thought. This occurs later, when the operations become, in a sense, rules. The preoperational child, then, is not functioning on the basis of articulated conscious rules. Keep in mind we do not refer to these rules as only social norms, but also in other dimensions of knowledge, for example, mathematical rules for addition (one plus one equals two) or subtraction (when you have five objects and take away four you have one left). The rules of mathematics, the rules of relationships, and the rules of quantity do not govern the child's behavior in a deliberate, conscious way. The child can take four marbles from five and tell you that only one marble remains. He can also do this mentally, so long as the mental image of "marbles" can be employed. What the child cannot do is consider the abstraction of number independent of *number of objects*. He cannot tell you $(5-4=1)$. This example serves to illustrate another point and that is, while the child's behaviors are not "abstract," they are symbolic, as witnessed in this imitative behavior and language, all symbols for previous experiences. But the symbols, at this point, are very much bound to perceptual experiences.

Related to figurative knowledge is the fact that the child is tied to the present. There is the tendency for children to be time-bound when their time perspective is restricted. Early, between the ages of approximately two and three, time fuses from one day to the next. Concepts like today, tomorrow, and yesterday are not articulated and comprehended meaningfully. But the reader might argue that children at three might say: "Tomorrow I am going to the store," or "Tomorrow I am going to the zoo." Let us digress here for the moment to point out that mentioning the word is not a necessary indicator that the child has a true understanding of the concept. To test this, ask a preschool child to tell you "what is tomorrow?" or "when is tomorrow?" or "how you know it's tomorrow?" or "when is yesterday?" She will most likely answer vaguely that "yesterday is when I went to sleep" or "yesterday is when we had breakfast" or "tomorrow is when my Daddy takes me to the zoo." These are *action-based definitions* which are, in fact, not the concept; children are merely using actions to denote or indicate time differences. Thus to assume that because the children use the word they understand that word, would be erroneous.

Entering the *intuitive phase* of the preoperational period, the child is still inclined to be action oriented and tied to the present. What is misleading to the adult is that often children at this level appear to think logically, communicate in ways which suggest they take the perspective of others, and in general, appear as though they are thinking and reasoning at an operational level. This is why the term intuitive phase is used. It suggests that the child engages in logical thought without the consistency and the understanding found at later ages. Preschool children around age 4 or 5 will solve conservation problems, rudimentary number tasks and simple classifications. The solutions are not necessarily consistent from one time to the other and the reasons for the solutions for problems are not always clear. For example, in interviews with preschool children regarding friendships, a child was asked, "Do you have friends in school?" The child answered "yes." When asked to define *friend*, the child answered, "Someone I play with." Then the child was asked, "When you grow up, will your friend still be your friend?" The child answered, "No, because he will be too big for me to play with." Note, in this example, the child did engage in an appropriate discussion of "friend," but note that his definition of a friend is in terms of an egocentric relationship. Finally, he is unaware of the fact that he and his friend grow older together. His response, "He will be too old to play with" is another instance of egocentrism. In sum, we can conclude that during the intuitive phase, while moving toward an operational level, the child's thought is still preoperational. The important consideration here is that the evaluation of the child's level of thought must be judged by his explanations and reasons, not just by the words used or the actions engaged in.

Summary—Cognitive Growth from Birth to the Concrete Operational Period

From birth until about seven-years-old, the child goes through a series of changes which Piaget has defined in two broad stages, *sensorimotor* and *preoperational*. In the course of this period of growth the child becomes increasingly aware that objects exist independent of the self, that ideas can be represented mentally, and be presented in language. In these early years the child displays the prototypes that are manifested later.

Children change within this period in relation to objects as they become capable of representing these actions mentally. The children are able to become more economical in dealing with problems, but at the same time not as efficient as they will be when they are able to engage in *operational thought*. Part of this inefficiency is due not only to their limited ability to conserve and inability to disengage from what they see but also because they still have problems coordinating various experiences. This inability is a lack of *combinatorial thinking*. The adult can talk about big, red objects which particularizes some object in contrast to a small, blue one. The activity of combining two elements into one is a complex intellectual achievement which enables one to combine events and therefore be more precise. At the same time, one is also able to disengage the redness from the bigness and treat the attributes as separates. The child in the preoperational period is not able to do this combinative thinking. She can talk about a big object; she can talk about a blue object. But she cannot cope with the reasoning process of combining a big and blue object into words. Consequently, we can characterize this young child as an individual who is able to deal with one attribute at a time and is able to believe what she sees from her own point of view.

Gradually the child is more capable of appearing as if she understands—especially around four-through six-years-old. This understanding can be misleading, because the child may intuitively solve problems but cannot consciously and deliberately explain how. For Piaget the test for understanding a problem occurs when the child is able to articulate the reasoning. This, by the way, poses a problem for some because the argument is that Piaget really is studying verbal contents to justify logical or other cognitive activities. This is a moot point but an important one because for Piaget the self-consciousness, the awareness of one's own operations, is a test of whether or not one really understands something. If one cannot explain it and can only do it intuitively then there is really no way of knowing how the child solves the problem.

Relevance of Piaget for Preschool Ages

In recent years, Piaget's theory has been considerably important in preschool education. The renewed interest in cognitive development with the expansion of preschool programming for underprivileged children stimulated an interest in Piagetian theory, since it was one of the very few theoretical models that emphasized cognitive growth. During the 1960s and to the present, some preschool programs lean heavily on Piagetian theory (Kamii, 1972; Lavatelli, 1970; Sigel, 1972; Weikart, 1970), while others are influenced but not so labeled. A review of these programs is available in Evans (1973). For our purposes, we shall present a distillation of some of the key issues relevant to preschool education.

The nursery school must be viewed as a group experience in a particularly constructed space—containing a particular collection of materials. How this space, the group, and the adult-child interaction are used is a reflection of the conceptual basis of the nursery school. The significance of this environment in most general terms is that it provides the socialization experiences considered by Piaget as crucial to the development of intelligence.

The human being is immersed right from birth in a social environment which affects him just as much as his physical environment. Society, even more, in a sense, than the physical environment, changes the very structure of the individual, because it not only compels him to recognize facts, but also provides him with a readymade system of signs which modify his thoughts; it presents him with new values and it imposes on him an infinite series of obligations. It is therefore quite evident that social life affects intelligence through the three media of language (signs), the contents of interaction (intellectual values) and rules imposed on thought (collective logical or prelogical norms) (Piaget, 1963, p. 156).

With interaction from social agents (peers, teachers, parents) as well as the inanimate environment, the child acquires an objectified view of self and the world around him, for as Piaget maintains:

without interchange of thought and co-operation with others, the individual would never come to group his operations into a coherent whole: in this sense, therefore, operational grouping presupposes social life (Piaget, 1950, p. 163).

The significance of the social setting for cognitive growth becomes clear. How, then, should the social setting of the nursery school be organized? Piaget does not deal with this issue. Therefore we must extrapolate from his system. To do this requires greater specification of some of the characteristics of preschool children which would guide how the setting would be organized.

Since change occurs through a series of transformations, qualitative and quantitative, in perspective and in knowledge of the social and physical reality, the following guiding principles for program development are proposed.

(1) providing the child with activities and attendant verbal experiences to denote actions which will enable creation of schemata, for example, seriation and classification

(2) providing situations which involve conflict and confrontation with reality (involving direct teacher actions as well as peers)

(3) providing materials which allow for learning to be generalized

Within the context of the nursery school, then, the program should deal with those experiences that contribute to the transition from egocentricity to objectivity; facilitate decentration; and allow for articulating experiences involving the mental operations.

Chapter 4　Periods of Concrete and Formal Operations

Introduction

The previous chapter presented Piaget's description of cognitive development during the preschool period (birth to five-years-old). The change was dramatic—from a reflexive, noncoordinated infant to a verbally communicative, physically competent individual on the threshold of another major development transition, the move into the concrete operational stage.

In this chapter we shall describe the tortuous and complex paths the child follows through the *concrete operational* stage to *formal operations* stage—the most advanced stage in Piaget's description of cognitive growth.

As we indicated in Chapter 2, there is some disagreement as to the sharp demarcation between the stages, especially between concrete and formal operations. We shall discuss what distin-

guishes concrete operations from formal operations. Although
these distinctions may not be as precise as one would like, they
are sufficiently clear so that workers with children in the elementary and secondary levels can identify them in the context
of problem solving. We shall present examples of how children
at different developmental levels solve the same problem. Finally,
we shall conclude this chapter by identifying the relevance of
this period of cognitive development for education.

Period of Concrete Operations

A Schematic Description of the Concrete Operational Period

During the period from approximately seven to eleven years of
age, reasoning processes begin to appear logical. Even logicians
would be satisfied that a child is thinking in logical terms, using
mental operations. In the concrete operational period, the child
thinks in operations *but* is tied to the observable and needs
props to work with. The child, however, is able to think in terms
of classes, relations, and number. To be able to do that, he has
to be able to understand reversibility and conservation. These
are the topics we shall discuss in this section.

Piaget describes logical operations such as the ability to
return to the original point in thought (reversibility), organize
objects into hierarchies of classes (classification), or arrange
items along continua of increasing values (seriation). The consequence of the child's acquisition of these concrete operations
is an increasing ability to deal with *concepts*. For example,
number concepts require the child: (1) to perform reversible
operations; that is, for every action or operation there is an
operation that cancels it, such as eight times six is 48 and 48
divided by six equals eight; (2) to develop the *logic of classes*;
that is, grouping diverse items into a single classification (dogs,
cats, and horses are all grouped as animals); (3) to comprehend
and develop an understanding of asymmetrical relations; that is,
the ability to arrange items in order (seriation). A concrete
operation that enables seriation to appear is *reversibility*. For
example, if *A* is heavier than *B*, and *B* is heavier than *C*, then a

child knows the relationships among *A*, *B*, and *C*. The child is able to arrange items in a series along particular continua, such as weight in the example, going from light to heavy or heavy to light.

The child's ability to perform these various operations is critical to the establishment of a conceptual approach (J. McV. Hunt, 1961). She must be able to understand how attributes can belong to more than one class and that classes can be subordinated to others. A black cat can be a member of the class *cats* or class *black thing* or *four-legged animals*. The class *cat* is a subset of class mammals which is a subset of the class vertebrates and so on. Mental operations are employed to re-form classes. The child is increasingly able to deal symbolically with various materials, for example, words, numbers, and so on. In effect, the mental operations are integrated into a cognitive system (Piaget, 1950). The entire system evolves during this period to provide a mental structure increasingly capable of developing concepts for representational thought.

Genesis of Concrete Operations

After this overview of the concrete operational period, let us now consider the genesis of concrete operations in greater detail. The transition from the preoperational to the operational stage is exactly what the name implies, a move toward the competence to think and reason in operational terms. The child becomes capable of classifying, ordering, and relating classes of objects mentally rather than having to act out these processes as in the sensorimotor period. Concrete operational thought is an approximation of how adults think and reason. The major differences are twofold: (1) the child has had only limited experience and as a result has only limited knowledge; and (2) the child employs the operations in the presence of concrete objects, rather than in hypothetical reasoning.

Basic to logical thought is *conservation*, a principle we discussed in Chapter 2.

Prior to a discussion of the mental operations characteristic of the concrete operational period, let us first describe the child's solution to the conservation problem.

CONSERVATION PROBLEM. As we discussed in Chapter 2, one of

the major achievements that becomes possible at this period is the child's ability to *conserve*, previously not evident as a reasoned process. Conservation, it will be recalled, refers to the child's ability to understand that an attribute (for example, number, quantity, space) remains constant in spite of changes in its appearance. For example, the child may be presented with two rows of nine poker chips each, as in this diagram.

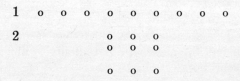

The child is asked if the two rows are equal: "Does row 1 have the same number as row 2?" If the child says yes, you ask him to show or tell you why it is so. He may say they are lined up one on the other, or for every chip in row 1 there is a chip in row 2. After the examiner is certain the child knows that the number in each row is the same, the examiner proceeds to alter the array.

Now the child is asked, "Do I have the same number of chips in row 1 as in row 2, or do I have more or less in row 1 than row 2?" The examiner points to the rows each time to be certain the child is attending to the proper row. If the child says that the rows are unequal, that one has either more or less than the other, then he is not *conserving* since he is not aware that the only change in the second row is its spatial rearrangement. The examiner did not add or subtract any chips. If, on the other hand, the child says, "They are the same," he is indicating an awareness that nothing was added or taken away. If the child attests to equality even after one row has been rearranged and he can justify his answer, he is *conserving*.

It is important that the examiner interviews the child to arrive at the basis for the answer, since it is only with the combination of a correct answer and a verbalized justification that the examiner comes to learn how the child reasons. Thus, it is necessary to employ the *method clinique*. This is the basic Piagetian interview strategy wherein the child is questioned to explain the basis for the answer. In the above illustration, for example, some children will say, "You just pushed these together." Others might say, "You did not add or subtract anything." Still another response could be, "They are the same, but these are spread out and these are bunched together." These answers, while providing an explanation, differ as to the underlying processing operations. The child, for example, who says, "You just pushed them together" is using an action criterion, not a logical one; whereas, the child who says "You did not add or subtract anything therefore they are the same," is using an addition-subtraction scheme, revealing an understanding of number or quantity. By using the *method clinique*, which is essentially an inquiry procedure, the examiner learns not only if the child has the correct idea (conservation) but how he thinks about the problem.

ANALYSIS OF CONSERVATION RESPONSES. Let us analyze this illustration so as to understand what appears to be going on in the child's mind as she faces this particular task. This classic problem contains all the necessary ingredients to illustrate some basic Piagetian concepts.

First, the child is presented an array too large for her to count. Thus, she is dependent on logic rather than another tool, enumeration, although enumerations may be mechanical or based on understanding of the principle of equality. That is, nine chips in row 1 equals nine chips in row 2. This answer may also be rote, "nine here, nine here, both have nine." If, however, counting is not possible the child has to create or construct some other system with which to solve the problem. What are some of the operations she can use? If the child focuses on the process of transforming one row from a line to a bunch, she will note that nothing but a spatial rearrangement occurred. She can stop here and say to herself, "The chips just changed places, nothing else changed." Here the child realizes that changes in spatial arrangement have to be discounted in order to solve the problem. Had she said that there are more in the bunched group, she would be functioning preoperationally, by basing her judgment on the spatial appearance. In the case where the spatial arrangement is emphasized, Piaget would characterize the child as prelogical.

Once the child sees that the arrays are indeed equal, we wish to know how she comes to this conclusion. Already we noted that it could be by ignoring spatial factors. A second trial is usually used here and instead of bunching one array, it is spread farther apart so that after a transformation, the arrangement looks as follows:

1   o o o o o o o o o

2 o   o   o   o   o   o   o   o   o

A similar inquiry is used by the examiner. Again, the child can justify the equality of the two arrays as she did in the bunching example.

For the child to understand what is going on in this task, two kinds of knowledge are necessary; first, to understand the principle of equality; that is, as in the case of numbers, for every chip in row 1 there is a corresponding chip in row 2. Unless she understands this, there is no point in going further. Understanding equivalence is the first and crucial step to becoming a conserver, whether it is quantity, space, number, or whatever.

Given that, the second kind of knowledge is understanding the instructions. Do the children know what "same," "more," or "less" mean? Children's knowledge of the terms should be routinely checked prior to assessing their ability to conserve. Understanding the terms does not, in fact, mean that the children can solve conservation problems. What it means is that they know quantitative terms and may be able to use them appropriately, but it does not necessarily follow that this knowledge enables the children to use it in a logical problem.

What is needed beyond the comprehension of the principle of correspondence and the language of the estimation to solve the number conservation problem? The solution to the conservation of number requires the child to attend to the relevant transformation of the array and not to be distracted by irrelevant changes in anything other than the rearrangement of chips. A related consideration is that the children have to be convinced that the issue is the number of chips, not how crowded or how far apart they are. This means that appearances of more or less have to be overlooked. It is true that there are differences between the rows (one row being farther apart than the others). They have to realize that this "move" is not the relevant "move," that *number* is the issue.

Conservation, irrespective of the subject involved, is not an all or none proposition. Every conservation proceeds in three developmental stages. Stage I, no conservation present; Stage II, transitional, where there is logical awareness and justification but inconsistently employed; Stage III, conservation, with a statement of logical justification. Children are not true conservers until they demonstrate an ability to solve conservation problems logically whenever they arise. This does not generally happen until the child is ten- or twelve-years-old. Thus conservation is a developing competence achieving its fulfillment through a gradual maturing process of experience.

Concepts of Number and Quantity

Conservation, as indicated above, is not an all or none achievement, but rather variations depend on the dimensions of the content involved. Number conservation is one of the conservations that emerges early. The operations that are functional now are *reversibility*, *classification*, *seriation*, and *decentration*. Let us discuss each of these operations and then show how they relate to the concepts of number and quantity.

REVERSIBILITY. Reversibility refers to the ability of the individual to rearrange thoughts mentally to return to the starting point. It is evident in all conservation problems and necessary in logical thought. For Piaget, reversibility is a "vital mechanism" for integration of cognitive structures in every stage (Inhelder and Piaget, 1958). For example, to solve the number conservation problem described earlier, the child must realize that if the changed *row* were returned to its original arrangement, it would be equal in number to the original array. This type of reversibility is a simple undoing. Reversibility also incorporates two other operations, *reciprocity* and *negation*. Reciprocity involves compensation. For example, if a piece of clay in the form of a sausage ⌒⌒ is rolled into a ball ◯ , the diameter increases as the length decreases, with no change in amount. Thus, the effect of the increase in diameter is compensated by a reduction in length. Negation refers to the cancelling operations. For every operation there is another operation which cancels it, as subtraction negates addition. Negation and reciprocity are two types of reversibility that are involved in operational thought.

CLASSIFICATION. Classification is the second operation involving organizing items into categories. Preoperational children can classify objects on the basis of perceptual attributes such as color or form. Grouping items by a single attribute, whether color, form, or use, indicates the child is overlooking other characteristics. During the period of concrete operations, children are beginning to demonstrate an ability to classify objects on the basis of more than one attribute simultaneously such as color and form. The child is evolving the ability to classify objects in a hierarchical order by creating more extensive classes. Let us illustrate this with a *class inclusion* problem, that is, the ability to realize that a superordinate class, such as animal, contains subclasses, such as horses.

Class-inclusion. Imagine the child has 10 white wooden beads and 10 brown wooden beads, a total of 20 beads. The child, when asked to create classes, may do so according to color as the only distinctive attribute. His ability to do that indicates the principle of grouping on one criterion. Let us now imagine pouring all the beads into a container and asking, "Which do I have more of, wooden beads or white beads?" White beads comprised a subset of wooden beads and if the child recognizes this he reflects an understanding of this *class* inclusion problem. He recognizes the hierarchical nature of the classes, and is able to combine the white and brown wooden beads into the class wooden beads, while recognizing that the white wooden beads are a subset of the total. This experiment can be made more complex by having fewer white beads, thereby creating a confusion, namely that there are more brown beads. In this case, the child has to disregard the greater number of brown beads, realize that the class under consideration is *wood* (material), and that every bead is wood.

To solve the problem the child has to *decenter*, a vital process in the development of thought. *Decentering* or *decentration* refers to the ability to shift the focus from one attribute to another, while *centering* or *centration* refers to the fixed, rigid and inflexible approach to the object (see the section on egocentrism in Chapter 3). For example, tumblers are for drinking and hammers for banging; tumblers are not vases nor are hammers useful in other ways. The move toward decentration enables the individual to engage in concrete operations. The preoperational child centers on one attribute and is not able to shift perspective. However, the concrete operational child decenters, altering perspective by combining two classes and simultaneously separating them based on other criteria. This process indicates the mental flexibility necessary to solve the class inclusion problem. For example, the hammer can be in the class, wooden-handled tools, in the class, metal tools, or in a combination class, metal and wooden tools. To combine these attributes requires decentration and, as we shall see, enables more complex categorization.

Thoughtful analysis of this problem shows how the operations of combining and reversibility are involved. The former is the awareness that classes can be combined on one attribute (white beads and brown beads = wooden beads and also that white beads are not the same as brown beads). Therefore, the negation of the class membership of brown beads into the class, beads, occurs by *altering* the criteria. As Piaget comments, "The child does not yet have at his disposal an integrated system that would enable him to pass deductively from one set of groupings to another and to compose thereby the inverse and reciprocal transformations" (Piaget and Inhelder, 1969, p. 138).

Class inclusion problems are structured to define the issue in terms of hierarchical relationships. Do children freely organize materials in this logical way?

A large body of research has examined how children organize familiar materials in *free sorting* situations. An array of materials is presented and the children are asked to organize the materials in any manner they wish, using whatever criteria they wish.

These studies tend to confirm the general trends described by Piaget. They have, moreover, described the kinds of classificatory behavior children show as well as pertinent bases for categorizing materials. Children at seven- and eight-years-old tend to categorize on the basis of the perceptual or concrete aspects of stimuli. Many of these studies employ sorting tasks containing familiar objects such as cars, furniture, animals, flowers, and so on. The child is asked to sort these on any basis she wishes and usually is asked to give the reason for the groupings. The results tend to agree that the younger children (about six- or seven-years-old) tend to perceive similarity on the basis of observable characteristics such as *structural similarities* (items all have *legs*, or a speck of brown), or on the basis of similarity of *use* (a hammer and a saw are used to build). With increasing age, the basis of categorization shifts to conceptual or categorical labels such as animals or tools, at least with lower- and middle-class boys between eight- and nine-years-old (Bolles, 1937; Sigel, 1953). For the younger children, seven- to nine-years-old, the concepts are still limited in inclusiveness, that is, not all instances of a category are included. The chosen categorical labels still have elements of concrete aspects as evidenced by the child applying the name *animal* only to animals that are structurally similar, for example, to four-legged animals while eliminating animals such as birds which are treated as a class by themselves. Gradually this increases to extensive categorization (Thompson, 1941), especially between nine and eleven years of age. The child's employment of conceptual labels does not necessarily mean that the underlying intellectual process is conceptual. The popular usage of the term *animals* accounts for the child's use of the label, rather than an understanding of the animal category for classification.

Nature of the materials. The nature of the items influences how children categorize. When meaningful materials are used (for example, animals) children between seven- and eleven-years-old tend to ignore structural properties such as color, texture, or materials the objects are made from, and focus on the meaning of the item (Sigel, 1954). Items depicting human figures are categorized on different bases from those depicting objects or animals (Sigel, 1961, 1963). Children at seven and eight years of age were presented with pictures depicting human figures such as fireman, cowboy, nurse, and so on. They were asked to classify these stimuli on the basis of similarity. They tended to use labels which were descriptive of parts of the stimuli; for instance, selecting the fireman and the soldier "because both have uniforms," or the boy and the girl "because they both have shoes." Given pictures of familiar objects and animals—furniture, tools, livestock—they tended to sort them by applying functional or class labels. Typical were the responses for a hammer and saw, "these are to build with," or for the cow, sheep, and chicken, "these live on a farm" (Sigel, 1961).

The results of these classification studies demonstrate that children elect different criteria as bases of ordering material depending on the child's age and the nature of the materials. Of interest is that the children are not inclined to use hierarchical classification unless requested to do so.

These free sort studies are significant because they demonstrate the degree to which children shift from spontaneous attention to single attributes to an ability to transcend physical properties of objects and treat them as members of a class. This ability is consistent with Piaget's assertion that understanding of the principles of classification emerges gradually during the period of concrete operations.

SERIATION. Another of the operations, *seriation*, consists of ordering elements according to an increasing or decreasing dimension (such as size or length). The children have to establish relations according to a descending or ascending order. Initially, children do not order things into a single series. If young children are given a series of different sized sticks, they may order the smallest and the longest, but will have difficulty in ordering the intermediary sticks. Operatory intelligence is evident when a systematic method of finding the smallest, then the smallest of the remainder, appears as the child's strategy in performing this task. The child now expresses a knowledge of ordering as a general principle.

After children have acquired seriation, they can solve problems involving one-to-one serial correspondence. This is a key prerequisite for understanding numbers and carrying out arithmetic functions (addition, subtraction, multiplication, and division). For example, give the child an array of boy dolls of various sizes and a series of beds also of various sizes. Ask the child to arrange the dolls in a row and for each one provide the correct sized bed and order the beds according to sizes, from long to short. With appropriate ordering the child reveals an understanding of seriation and one-to-one correspondence. He should, on request, be able to state the principle of one-to-one correspondence and serial ordering.

Transitivity. When the child finally achieves this operation, a mode of deductive composition previously unknown is achieved, *transitivity*; that is, $A < B$; $B < C$; therefore, $A < C$. *Transitive* literally means passing over to an object. In this instance it means that all elements need not be included in order to draw a conclusion. That is, the B term is not necessary in the final expression in order to know that $A < C$. Transitivity is an important logical reasoning operation which also involves identification of particular relevant attributes of a probe. A common example is this relation. Mary is taller than her sister Jane. Jane is taller than her cousin, Joan. Then Mary is taller than Joan. The question is who is the tallest. The solution to the problem is dependent on the child deciding that the critical variable is height and not kinship. The child has to separate the variables and attend to the significant ones. Preoperational solutions to this problem are unlikely since at that period children have difficulty identifying the relevant variable. The child at the concrete operational period has acquired the ability to discriminate the relevant variable.

COMBINATORIAL THINKING. The child in the concrete operational period shows the beginning of combinatorial thought, a fundamental formal operation which builds upon the classification system just discussed. The child can work with two independent attributes provided they are in our perceptual field. The problem used is illustrated below. The child has to fill in the missing cell of the matrix, a problem frequently used to study combinatorial thinking.

big and dark	big and darker	big and darkest
middle sized dark	middle sized darker	middle sized darkest
small dark	small darker	?

The solution to the problem requires the coordination of the horizontal change in color and the vertical decrease in size.

Thus the empty cell is a product of the two variables yielding a size (small) and color (darkest) combination. This example illustrates classifying on the basis of asymmetrical relations, in effect, a seriation problem. The child is also able to solve combinatorial problems that do not involve seriation. For example, imagine that a child has six large circles: three blue and three red; and six small circles: three blue and three red. The possible combinations are: (1) all circles combining color and size; (2) blue circles, combining just size; or (3) big circles, ignoring one size (small) and combining colors (blue and red). The child may also combine size and color, blue small circles, or large blue circles, thereby creating a subset. The concrete operational child is beginning to be able to create and understand some of these simple combinations. Here we are demonstrating combinatorial thought in symmetrical relationships as compared to the matrix on p. 75 which is asymmetrical (seriation). However, true logical combining of classes does not emerge until formal operations—about eleven-years-old and older.

Combining two or more attributes is another cognitive function children perform during this period. They are limited, however, in how many combinations they can make. Further, during the concrete operational period, the child is not able to create combinations if qualities of objects are not apparent. For this reason the child is limited to the number of combinations she can create, in contrast to the child during the formal operational period who can generate 16 combinations (see p. 90).

SUMMARY. We have emphasized achievements in the areas of reversibility, classification, and seriation because of their centrality in the cognitive operational behavior of children at all ages. Classification is central to the child's adaptation to the world for it allows for organization of reality in a way that is manageable and economical. It is manageable because it reduces the array of stimuli to fewer classes or instances, and thereby enables the child to treat instances as members of a class rather than as individuals. For example, if one believes that animals that are wild are dangerous, all that is necessary in making judgments about how to relate to the animals is to define their class membership. One does not have to make an independent judgment each time. In effect, a concept is defined in which each member of the class shares some commonality. There are individual differences among the class members, but this evokes the question of the defining characteristics of a class. Our example points to an instance in which the class is an overextension of the concept "wild," since not all wild animals are dangerous. Experience provides the challenge for the child to modify the concept. The place of reversibility in this discussion should not be forgotten. The problem we presented can be solved by a one-way operation, such as classifying animals into black and white or animals into wild and domestic. The reconstruction of the classes, so that black and white or wild and domestic equal the whole class, animal, requires the ability to return to the starting point of the operation in question. Unless children are able to do this they cannot solve logical problems. Understanding concepts, being able to decenter, and being able to engage in the operations of classification, seriation, and transitivity, require competence in reversibility. As we shall see this is critical in formal operational thought.

NUMBER. Closely allied to the child's understanding of seriation and class inclusion is the construction of whole numbers. Comprehension of number as a concept is more than simple counting. In fact, the ability to count is not necessarily evidence of an understanding of the concept of number. During the concrete operational period children begin to conserve number, which means that they can understand the principle of numerical *equivalence*; that is, one apple and one car are equivalent as far as number is concerned. The number is an independent issue, independent of the content which is enumerated. For Piaget, number is a synthesis of seriation and class inclusion. In the seriation problem, ordering items in terms of numbers (1, 2, 3, 4, 5, and so on) indicates that each number in the ascending order is one more than the previous number and one less than the subsequent one. To understand this principle requires the child to deal with the abstraction that in the world of numbers, it is the number that is equivalent and that on that basis a comparison is made. Thus one can compare five automobiles and three cows. If the child is asked, "Do I have more automobiles than cows, the answer must be in the world of numbers, not in the world of automobiles or cows. Yet, the class inclusion issue is also present. The child must treat the class cows as a subclass and distinguish it from another class, cars.

QUANTITY. Related to the number concept is the concept of quantity or amount. Number involves correspondence between frequency of objects and subsequent enumeration, while the concept of quantity relates to the mass that is involved. In the example, amount of clay or amount of water, the former is termed *continuous quantity* while the latter is called *discontinuous quantity*. Amount can be in terms of mass, weight, volume, or individualized items, as in grains of rice. Many conservation studies with children during the operational period have to do with the conservation of quantity. For example, the child is asked whether the same amount of clay exists when changed in shape from a pancake to a sausage. The child learns that the amount does not change in spite of the transformation in form. Similar investigations are made in terms of displacement of water; for example, does the water in a jar rise more if the piece of clay put into it is a sausage shape as opposed to a pancake shape? Another quantity dimension that is involved is weight: "Which weighs more, the sausage shaped piece of clay or the pancake?" This problem may remind the reader of the children's riddle, "Which weighs more, a pound of feathers or a pound of lead?" At issue in these examples is the child's awareness that the amount does not change in the face of physical transformation, just as the number does not change when different objects are enumerated. In each case the understanding of the concept is extant when the child demonstrates that he is not confused by the appearance. In the case of quantity, Piaget contends that the competence needed to solve these problems follows an invariant sequence.

The conservation studies have shown that conservation of mass (substance), precedes the conservation of weight and other volume. The order is invariant. They are not able to conserve generally, but rather the ability depends on the material. For example, in the experiment dealing with clay, the child is given two balls of clay identical in shape, size, and color. After the child agrees that the two balls are equal in all respects, one of the balls is rolled into a sausage and the child is now asked if the two pieces of clay still have the same amount. If the child can attest to the equality of amount in spite of shape, she is said to conserve quantity. Conserving quantity, however, does not mean that she can conserve weight, that is, being asked if the two pieces weigh the same. Although the child may conserve mass, this does not necessarily mean she is generally a conserver. Piaget refers to this development phenomenon as *décalage*, that is, a gap within the child's knowledge, for example, conservation, and ability to generalize it to other relevant problems (Sigel and Hooper, 1968).

Piaget has addressed himself to many other areas of physical knowledge (for example, number and space) that we do not need to consider here. However, for any area of knowledge in which we are interested, the format for Piagetian study is similar: defining the stages of knowledge acquisition from a nonexistent knowledge base to complete understanding. The operations are the same as discussed before; the content to which they are applied differs. For the interested reader, detailed discussions of the child's development of concepts of time, speed, and distance are described in Piaget (1970b).

Representation of the Universe: Transformations and Causality

One of the major attractions of Piagetian theory is the significance of the areas he studies. He has oriented us to what on the one hand appears obvious, and on the other hand what is esoteric and almost exotic. For example, few if any, writers in psychology have concerned themselves with the child's developing concept of reality, of the physical world, and of why children ask the kinds of questions they do. Yet all observant parents live with their children during those exciting and interesting periods when children ask "why" every 10 seconds, when they confuse what is alive with what moves, when they seem curious about their origins and where they belong. The adoption fantasy is a case in point. Many children ask the question of where they come from, who were their parents before, and the like. Children also become interested not only in the "why," but also in the certainty question. This is the question of consistency, change, and chance. In the Piagetian theory, causality, as with other intellectual achievements, has its roots in the sensorimotor period. Recall that we discussed the types of causal reasoning found among children in the sensorimotor and the preoperational periods. Let us now use causality as an illustration of the child's intellectual growth during the seven to eleven years of age range of concrete operations.

PHYSICAL CAUSALITY. The reader can probably figure out Piaget's reasoning in relation to causal reasoning by this time. Since the child is now at the level of concrete operations, his approach to causality problems begins to be operatory. This means that the child attempts to deal with causal problems from a rational approach, no longer totally egocentric, but rather assimilating new information and solutions to problems on the operatory level. At the concrete level, the child begins to make rational judgments, but they are not complete until the period of formal operations. Let us illustrate this by the experiment Piaget reports in what has been called understanding of _atomism_. The child is presented with a glass of water and into it some ice cubes are placed. The question is "What happens after the ice melts in the glass of water?" For the preoperational child, the ice vanishes; children aged 7 or 8 think ice is retained without its weight or its volume, in part because the children at this time are not able to conserve weight or volume. By the time the children are able to conserve weight and volume, they recognize that the level of water is raised when the ice is added, and that the level of water does not return to its original level after the ice has melted. They begin to understand that the ice has not been lost, but has been transformed. If the weight and mass of the ice are retained in a different form, then it should also displace some of the space and hence alter the water level.

In considering the above example, it is important to note the interlocking between the causal understanding of what happens to the ice and the operations involved in solving a conservation problem. It should also be kept in mind that the solution to this problem requires the child to be aware that disappearance of the ice does not mean that the matter no longer exists. This is the idea of object permanence. If the ice still exists and does so in a transformed state, why? The answer rests, according to Piaget, in the child's comprehension of the _principle of atomism_; that is, an item is composed of particles, and that by the act of melting the particles of ice they become small and invisible.

The explanation of the situation presupposes knowledge of certain physical principles or at least knowledge of physical facts, although not necessarily the principles. For example, in this case, the child is aware of the fact that some substances change in water; the process is called melting. Only through an understanding of conservation of mass does one realize that melting is disappearance but not nonexistence. Thus, in the solution to this problem the child must integrate previous knowledge and experience which lead to concepts of conservation, object permanence, and transformation.

We are still faced with two questions in our understanding of the theory. What prevents the child from understanding all this earlier? And why does the child eventually come to this understanding? Piaget argues that what prevents the child from understanding causality is "that reality resists deductions and involves a greater or lesser element of uncertainty" (Piaget and Inhelder, 1969, p. 112). Piaget explains this shift to logical operations in solutions of problems:

Three complementary processes are involved: (1) progressive relativity of ideas arising from the fact that the self gradually becomes conscious of the personal character of its own point of view and of the reciprocity between this point of view and other possible ones; (2) a progressive transformation of primitive mental experiments into constructions carried out by means of logic of relations; and (3) a progressive generalization, resulting from the fact that classes become rigid and well-defined (Piaget, 1973).

SOCIOCENTRISM. The transition from a precausal understanding of the objective world to a rational approach requires that the child reduce his egocentric view in favor of the progressive socialization of thought. That is, she must objectify her own viewpoint and understand that others may have different perspectives (reciprocity in viewpoints). In the earlier state, "the self is confused with the external world and with other people; the vision of the world is falsified by subjective adherences and the vision of other people is falsified by the fact that the personal point of view predominates almost to the exclusion of all others" (Piaget, 1930, pp. 301–302). This confusion is reduced and the child becomes increasingly aware of the other's point of view. This is referred to as sociocentrism.

What causes the shift from egocentric thought to sociocentric thought in the area of causality as in other domains is *the discovery that others do think as oneself*: "He makes the effort to adapt himself to them, he bows to the exigencies of control and verification which are implied by discussion and argument, and this comes to replace egocentric logic with true logic created by social life" (Piaget, 1930, p. 302). Thus, the comprehension of reality as with other dimensions of knowledge is an intimate relationship between development of socialized thought and intelligence. The child in the concrete operational stage begins to manifest logical explanations for his statement. During the egocentric period, the child, being very concrete, questions the need to justify a conclusion if he believes it is self-evident, that appearances are reality and what one sees is what one can believe. And as long as one feels that the point of view one holds is also everyone else's viewpoint, there is no motivation to seek further explanation or justification. The precausal child confuses motivation with cause, and in reasoning confuses subjective justification with verification.

A second and related factor that prevents the child from truly understanding causality is his inability to cope with uncertainty. Uncertainty, in effect, requires one to handle problems on a probability basis. The child has to learn that even though she cannot see an outcome, she can mentally anticipate outcomes on a probability basis. Children during this stage, seven- to eleven-years-old, evolve a conceptual organization that begins to be coherent and stable, possessing characteristics of logic and the ability to think in categorical terms. They are increasingly objective and manifest increasing emancipation from the perceptual dominance of the environment. They become able to use a conceptual framework as a way of organizing their surroundings. It is during these particular four or five years that the child makes great strides toward formal and adult conceptual functioning. What has preceded and what follows, however, should be considered interdependent.

Social and Affective Interactions

The foregoing discussion emphasized the development of logical reasoning processes with particular attention to questions relating to classes (classification), relations (seriation), and number. Yet, in our opening remarks we argued that Piagetian theory holds that "cognitive and affective or social development are inseparable and parallel . . ." (Piaget and Inhelder, 1969, p. 117). Thus, our previous discussion represents an emphasis on the cognitive, an emphasis which is certainly reflected in Piaget's own publications.

The preceding discussion emphasized that social interaction accounts, in part, for the transitions toward logical thought which occur during the concrete operations stage. In this section we shall direct our attention to what Piaget refers to as social and affective interaction. The term *social* corresponds to two very distinct realities in the affective sense. First, there is the relationship between the child and the adult which is the source of cultural transmission of specific sentiments, in particular the moral sentiments in the affective sense, through education and verbal interaction. Second, there are also the social relations among the children themselves (Piaget and Inhelder, 1969, p. 116). During the period of concrete operations when the children are beginning to think and reason operationally, new interpersonal interactions emerge. The child uses a newly developed cognitive apparatus to think and reason, and consequently to communicate with adults and peers. Thus, the child, during this period, is capable of understanding and expressing interest and concern toward others (empathy) and can understand the true reciprocal nature of cooperation.

These accomplishments evolve in stages commensurate with achievements in cognitive understanding. Piaget identifies three areas where the types of social development of interest have been observed; games with rules, group actions, and verbal exchanges.

GAMES. Games are social institutions—even children's games such as marbles. Some games are taught by adults (like baseball) and others, like hopscotch and marbles, are transmitted

among children. Part of what is transmitted are the *rules* of
the games. During the concrete operational period children are
beginning to engage in the common observance of rules. The
arguments among school-aged children engaged in a game are
a familiar sight. At issue is the interpretation or perception of
rules. Rules are viewed as immutable and fixed rather than
derived through social convention and through mutual consent.
Rules are usually complex so that initially the younger children
(preoperational) cannot grasp them in their totality or complexity. Also during this developmental period, the children
may not have the same body of information about the rules;
some may know more than others. The young child plays the
game as he understands it (egocentric) without either checking
on the others or knowing how to verify a rule, only reiterating
the rule verbatim. Not having a clear concept of the logic of
the game or the rules, the young child does not have a clear
concept of the fact that in games there are winners and losers.

GROUP ACTION. With the advent of concrete operations, group
actions alter because children are able to learn not only the
rules, but that rules are applicable to all participants and that
rules, while initially fixed, can be modified by cooperative agreement—the requirement being that children understand the
reciprocal nature of cooperation, the principle of give and take.

Cooperation requires decentration, the ability we discussed
earlier with regard to conservation of quantity problems. The
cognitive process is the same, a shift from one's own perspective to an awareness that the other person has a point of view
that must also be taken into consideration.

LANGUAGE. This awareness is expressed in verbal interchange
(language). The way children use language, for example; the
ability to explain something to one another, requires understanding that the other person does not necessarily understand
something because the speaker does. There is a new awareness
that *explanations* are sometimes necessary. Competency to engage in socially cooperative verbal activity occurs during the
middle childhood period and evolves consistently into the period
of formal speech.

Moral Feelings and Judgments

The role of games and rules and cooperation refers to social development, while morality is an outgrowth of affective relationships. "The affective relationship between the child and his parents or the adults who play the parental role, engenders the specific moral feelings forced upon one by one's conscience" (Piaget and Inhelder, 1969, p. 122). Piaget has studied moral development in children from the point of view of affect, whereas much recent work in the United States has emphasized the cognitive aspects of moral judgment. Let us now briefly present Piaget's perspective from the affective perspective and then present the stage concepts of moral judgment as developed by Kohlberg who based his work on Piaget's initial formulation of moral development.

AFFECTIVE BASIS OF MORAL FEELINGS. *Heteronomy*. Piaget's concepts in this area reflect the view that the origins of a sense of duty or obligation depend on orders given by others (for example, parents tell the child not to lie), and the child's acceptance of these orders. The child does not accept orders from anyone, however, but only from those whom he respects. For Piaget, respect is a combination of affection and fear. Where affection alone is insufficient and fear alone provokes submission, "respect involves both affection and fear associated with the position of the inferior in relation to the superior and therefore suffices to determine to acceptance of orders and consequently the sense of obligation" (Piaget and Inhelder, 1969, p. 123). Respect is initially one way—the child for the parent. Further, this respect initially gives rise to *heteronomy*, where the child believes that rules and obligations cannot be changed, but are fixed by some outside authority. Heteronomy holds not only for moral feelings but for social rules as well. The child becomes aware of rules and of the moral bases of behavior during the early stages of concrete operations. The intent of the rule, however, is irrelevant at this time. Piaget refers to this as *moral realism*. The child is told not to lie or steal before he understands the social value or intentions of the directive. To steal is initially absolutely wrong irrespective of motive.

Autonomy. With increasing awareness of social cooperation and corresponding progress in operational thinking, the child arrives at a stage of *autonomy.* Now rules, whether in games or in moral situations, are no longer sacred or unchangeable but are based on agreements or conventions and can be changed by mutual consent of the participants. The child begins to understand the notion of a contract.

Autonomy is based on the child developing a sense of mutual respect among persons. The sense of fairness and respect for others begins to emerge along with an understanding of operational thought (including negation and reversibility). The child can now reason that if she lies to someone, someone can also lie to her; if she steals from someone, someone can also steal from her, and so forth. The understanding of cooperation, mutual respect, and reciprocity result in justice and fair play even at the expense of obedience.

Thus, the child moves from heteronomy to autonomy in moral judgment and rule enforcement paralleling increases in operational thought. The interdependence among thought, social experience, and affect is well expressed in this domain. The child, now, is increasingly socialized and no longer believes in the fixed nature of rules, being aware that rules are made and can be altered. The child is increasingly autonomous.

DEVELOPMENT OF MORAL JUDGMENT. The broad description of moral judgment from heteronomy to autonomy discussed above has been studied over the past decade by Lawrence Kohlberg (1969). The Kohlberg system of stages of moral judgment is one of the developmental steps involved in the child's *cognitive ability* to solve moral problems.

Kohlberg used stories which presented moral dilemmas—for example, "a man's wife is dying but can be helped by an expensive drug. The druggist will not give the man the drug unless he pays for it. The husband, not having the money, breaks into the drugstore and steals the drug." Using similar stories, Kohlberg identified six stages of moral reasoning. The stages are described briefly by Selman (1971).

Preconventional Level
Stage 1: Obedience and punishment orientation. Egocentric

deference to superior power or prestige, or a trouble-avoiding set. Objective responsibility. Child's response is simply that it's wrong to steal.

Stage 2: Naively egocentric orientation. Right action is that instrumentally satisfying the self's needs and occasionally another's. Awareness of relativism of value to each actor's needs and perspective. Naive egalitarianism and orientation to exchange and reciprocity. "It's wrong to steal but the lady might get well; but it's still wrong to steal" are the responses which might be given here.

Conventional Level

Stage 3: Good-boy orientation. Orientation to approval and to pleasing and helping others. Conformity to stereotypical images of majority or natural role behavior, and judgement by intentions. "I would steal it for her" responses.

Stage 4: Authority and social-order-maintaining orientation. Orientation to "doing duty" and to showing respect for authority and maintaining the given social order for its own sake. Regard for the earned expectations of others. "I would steal it for her and then go to the police and turn myself in" reflects expectation and responsibility expectation.

Postconventional Level

Stage 5: Contract legalistic orientation. Recognition of an arbitrary element or starting point in rules or expectations for the sake of agreement. Duty defined in terms of contract, general avoidance of violation of the will or rights of others, and majority will and welfare. For example, "It's not wrong to steal to help someone; besides, I could probably find supporters to repay the druggist later."

Stage 6: Conscience or principle orientation. Orientation not only to actually ordained social rules but the principles of choice involving appeal to logical universality and consistency. Orientation to conscience as a directing agent and to mutual respect and trust. For example, "The higher order code is the personal conscience and sometimes personal conscience must take priority over social convention."

As we can see, not all of these stages occur during the period of concrete operations. Stages 5 and 6 occur during the period of formal operations, characteristically.

Moral judgment requires the use of cognitive operational thought. Unless the children can employ operations such as reciprocity, they reason on the concrete basis of rules and laws. Cognitive competencies such as understanding cause-effect, inferring outcomes, reconstructing past events, and so on are all cognitive activities involved in making a moral judgment. Thus, in the example of the drug, the husband can weigh the consequences of his act and decide if breaking a moral rule is more or less important than saving a life. These mental activities and cognitive activities are involved in responding to the dilemmas. Their resolution reflects the quality of moral judgment.

Considerable work has been done investigating moral judgment. Generally, there is agreement that the judgments show a stage-like evolution parallel to cognitive development (Hoffman, 1970). This is another example of the interdependence of operational thought and content (morality). As in each of the substantive areas (such as number and space), the knowledge acquired and its use are intrinsically dependent upon the child's level of cognitive development.

In summary, Piaget invokes a concept of "subjective centering" as a process which moves the child along in the concrete operational stage of development. The child is characterized as functioning intellectually on the basis of *figurative* knowledge, that is, in terms of concrete, descriptive aspects of his world. He is generally subjective in his judgments about people and events. But because of increased social contact after age 2, the child encounters points of view which conflict with his own. The centering begins to shift to decentering in cognitive, social, and moral domains. Piaget states that the changing perspective accounts, in great measure, for the child's move toward formal operational thinking.

Period of Formal Operations (Eleven to Fifteen Years)

The period of formal, truly logical operations, appears between eleven to fifteen years of age. It is at this point that children are able to take the final steps toward abstract thinking and conceptualization. They now may be guided by the form and logic of an argument while ignoring the specific content. Both

as preadolescents and adolescents they are able to make inferences and evaluate hypotheses. They can now operate in what
is called the hypothetical-deductive procedure of logical thought,
since they can create hypotheses and deduce logical conclusions.

A variety of intellectual skills become available at this time
of life. Considerable development occurs in mathematics; the
children are now able to handle calculus of proportions and logical reasoning both inductively and deductively in which they
employ propositions. During this period children can plan truly
scientific investigations because they are now ready to handle
combinations of variables in a systematic order whereas previously they could only handle one variable at a time.

We shall illustrate these abilities by describing an experiment
reported by Bärbel Inhelder, a close associate of Piaget's, in
this field of adolescent thought.

In experiments on proportionality the adolescent is given a
candle, a projection screen, and a series of rings of different
diameters; each ring is on a stick which can be stuck into a
board with evenly spaced holes. The instructions are to place
all the rings between the candle and the screen in such a way
that they will produce only a single "unbroken" shadow on the
screen—the shadow of "a ring." Gradually, the adolescent discovers that "there must be some relationship," and he tries to
find out what relationship it is by systematic attempts until he
becomes aware that it is a matter of proportionality. As one
bright 15-year-old said, "The thing is to keep the same propor-
tion between the size of the ring and the distance from the candle; the absolute doesn't matter" (Piaget and Inhelder, 1967).

The solution to this problem requires the child to establish a
hypothesis to guide his reasoning. The solution does not reside
in his manipulating objects, but rather depends on the individual's ability to go beyond the apparent, organizing all his perceptions and thoughts relevant to the solution of the problem.
One must be aware of the relationships among the parts: the
screen, the ring, and the light. Young children are distracted by
irrelevant cues. The formal operational individual segregates
the variables, eliminates contradictions, and combines variables
in a logical way. The child is capable of creating logical combinations, and verifying the hypotheses. In other words, solu-

tions to these problems involve utilizing formal operations which
are available to the child during the concrete operational stage,
but now are organized in such a way as to be allowed a range
of logical combinations. Recall that Piaget refers to this as
combinatorial thinking. To illustrate, let us describe an experiment reported in J. McV. Hunt (1961). The proposition involves
classes of animals. They are divided into two types, vertebrates
(*V*) and invertebrates (*I*). They are also classified as aquatic
(*A*) and terrestrial (*T*). The child is asked to describe the population of animals on a newly discovered planet. The child, who
is using concrete operations, gives four possible combinations,
vertebrates-aquatic (*VA*), invertebrates-aquatic (*IA*), verte-
brates-terrestrial (*VT*), invertebrates-terrestrial (*IT*). The combinations which are used by the concrete operational child are
only the obvious ones. The adolescent employing formal operations, however, can classify these into 16 categories, and he
might set up a table in the following way:

   (1) No animals at all
   (2) Only (*VT*)
   (3) Only (*VA*)
   (4) Only (*IT*)
   (5) Only (*IA*)
   (6) (*VT*) and (*VA*), but no (*IT*) or (*IA*)
   (7) (*VT*) and (*IT*), but no (*VA*) or (*IA*)
   (8) (*VT*) and (*IA*), but no (*VA*) or (*IT*)
   (9) (*VA*) and (*IT*), but no (*VT*) or (*IA*)
  (10) (*VA*) and (*IA*), but no (*VT*) or (*IT*)
  (11) (*IT*) and (*IA*), but no (*VA*) or (*VT*)
  (12) (*VT*), (*VA*), and (*IT*), but no (*IA*)
  (13) (*VT*), (*VA*), and (*IA*), but no (*IT*)
  (14) (*VT*), (*IT*), and (*IA*), but no (*VA*)
  (15) (*VA*), (*IT*), and (*IA*), but no (*VT*)
  (16) All four classes

These combinations are logical propositions: the vertebrate
label is the same as saying "This animal has a backbone," and
the invertebrate label says "This animal has no backbone."
The terms terrestrial and aquatic are analyzed similarly. This
reasoning, then, leads to the following proposition: if an animal
is a vertebrate it must live on land. In other words, the child can

make the total of 16 combinations and permutations from this set of data, since each proposition may be true or false. The important point is that the adolescent can make these combinations because he is able to ignore the content of the proposition and deal only with the formal aspects. In this example we see how the adolescent is able to think in terms of propositions and abstract characteristics, treating each of them in isolation as well as in varying combinations. Thought is no longer limited to the reality, but can also be in hypothetical terms, and the ability to think in hypothetical terms indicates that the child no longer needs concrete props or visual stimuli, but can think and reason mentally. To be sure, the individual will use signs and symbols. Thus, the binary combination expressed in the example can be designated by such terms as *VT*, *IT*, and so on. There is no need for more elaborate perceptual cues because the operation no longer requires such concrete supports. The understanding of the logic of 16 combinations in our example is another index of formal operational thought.

Perhaps one way to grasp the difference between concrete and formal operations is to provide a vignette of Piaget's methodology clinique by showing how children at different developmental ages approach a problem—flotation and the law of contradictions.

We shall present some of the key processes involved in concrete operational thought, transitional stages through to formal operations, and finally formal operations by following through on a particular problem. Notice that the same problem is used, but children at different ages respond to it differently. The variations in children's responses cannot be attributed to changes in the problem, but rather to the thought processes available to the child at any particular time.

Flotation Problem

The problem we have elected to present is the discovery of the law of floating bodies and elimination of contradictions. For Piaget, this is one of a number of relevant problems that reveal what logical operations are employed and how solutions vary depending on the child's developmental level. The problem for the child is to discover that objects float if their density or specific gravity is less than that of water (Inhelder and Piaget, 1958, p. 21).

The children are given a group of diverse objects and asked to classify them in regard to whether they can float on water or not. Once the child makes this classification, he is then asked to explain the basis of his classification. Following this procedure the child is asked to experiment and given several buckets of water. Now, the child can check the accuracy of the classification. After this presentation and experimentation the child is asked to summarize his observation. In essence, the summary expected of the child is to explain what happened when he tested his theory.

The value of this experiment for Piaget is that the law cannot be derived only from manipulation or observation of what objects float and what objects sink. For the child to discover "that objects float if their density or specific gravity is less than that of water, two relationships are essential to the solution of the problem; *density* i.e., the relation of weight to volume, and *specific gravity*, i.e., the relationship between weight of the object . . . and an equivalent volume of water" (Inhelder and Piaget, 1958). So, we begin to notice that to solve the problem logically the child first has to construct a category of floating objects and nonfloating objects. Other classes of objects may be constructed such as flotation under some circumstances (like a metal boat, an empty body full of air), or the objects which may remain suspended in water.

Working with children from four- through fifteen-years-old, Inhelder and Piaget identify three stages which we shall discuss separately.

STAGE I. The children at the beginning of this stage do not formulate the dichotomy between floating and nonfloating objects. The children contradict their own statements regarding properties of floating objects. Here is a verbatim excerpt from an actual interview reported by Inhelder and Piaget (1958). As you read note how the child contradicts himself, how he indicates an awareness, a consistent frame of reference toward a particular class of objects.

IEA (four-years-old) says, for example, of a piece of wood that "it stays on top. The other day I threw one in the water and it stayed on top." But a moment later: "Wood? It will swim anywhere." "And this one?" (a smaller piece). "The little wood will sink." "But you told me that the wood would swim." "No, I didn't say so." On the first presentation of a wire, he says, "The wire goes to the bottom" (he has not done the experiment). "And this weight?" (metal). "It will swim." "The wood?" "It will swim anywhere." "The wire?" (third presentation). "It will swim." Finally, for two metal needles of identical appearance he says the opposite: "This one?" "It will float." "And that one?" "It will sink." We must add that although IEA generalizes little, his explanations can be reduced to the format: "The pebble?" "It will sink." "Why?" "Because it stays on the bottom" (p. 22).

Obviously the child is unaware of his contradictions and has not established a single characteristic by which to classify items. Hence, he searches for causes in single events and produces a nonorganized set of observations.

In the latter half of this stage the child does create a dichotomous floating and nonfloating category, but at this stage the child does not achieve a coherent classification because, as we shall see in the example, the child is satisfied with a variety of explanations, such as size, shape, and nature of material. He does not work from a principle. He also, when encountering the problem, may give new explanations which are not integrated into the already existing knowledge and, finally, he is unaware of the contradictions. In effect, the child is heavily influenced by the "moment" of his interaction with materials.

TOSC (5.6 years) divides the objects presented into two classes prior to the experiment: class B (objects remaining above water) and class B' (objects which sink). Class B includes seven subclasses. (A_1) Objects which "swim" or float because it is their nature: boats and ducks ("My little duck that swims like the real ones"). (A_2) Small objects ("little tiny pebbles," tokens, needles). (A_3) Light objects (small pebbles float "because they aren't heavy," and thus belong simultaneously to A_2 and A_3, but an aluminum plate floats because it is light although it is not small). (A_4) Flat objects ("This pebble, because it's so flat"). (A_5) Thin objects (a wooden blade). (A_6) Objects which are the same color as the receptable ("Why will this plank stay on top?" "Because they are both the same color" [the plank and the bucket]). (A_7) Objects which have already floated (a piece of wood "because it stayed up before"). Class B' includes the following subclasses: (A_1) Objects "that don't belong on the water" by nature (for example, a piece of candle: "Where will it go?" "To the bottom." "Why?" "Because the candle doesn't belong on the water." We put it in the water: "It floats. Why?" "Because it swims on the water." Thus the candle is classified parallel to subclass A_1 of class B.). (A_2) Large objects. (A_3) Heavy ones (with the same difficulty in identification and the same interference as for A_2 and A_3 of class B). (A_7) Those that "went to the bottom before."(A_8) Long objects (a copper wire sinks "because it's long"). (A_9) Those which have been shoved (a metal cover) (Inhelder and Piaget, 1958, p. 24).

In this example the child is increasingly confused because he does not have a coherenet framework but rather constructs categories while he is in the experiment, which are not hierarchical or even consistent. He still is unaware of the logical contradiction, for example, when he says that the wire will float because it is thin and then it will sink because it is long. So, length makes it sink and thinner makes it float, yet copper wire is both thin and long.

STAGE II. The children now try to remove the main contradiction, that some large objects can float and some small ones sink. Inhelder and Piaget conjecture that now the child is revising the significance of weight alone as the variable, and begins to seek other explanations such as density or specific gravity. The child does not necessarily have the vocabulary or the technical terms, but the ideas seem to be there. An example of the move away from the contradictions is noted in the following excerpt.

BAR (7.11 years) first classifies the bodies into three categories: those which float because they are light (wood, matches, paper, and the aluminum cover); those which sink because they are heavy (large and small keys, pebbles of all sizes, ring clamps, needles and nails, metal cylinder, eraser); and those which remain suspended at a midway point (fish). "The needle? "It goes down because it's iron." "And the key?" "It sinks too." "And

the small things" (nails, ring clamps). "They are iron too."
"And this little pebble?" "It's heavy because it's stone." "And
the little nail?" "It's just a little heavy." "And the cover, why
does it stay up?" "It has edges and sinks if it's filled with water."
"Why?" "Because it's iron" (Inhelder and Piaget, 1958, p. 29).

In this example *BAR* is creating classes which are attempts
to resolve the contradiction and also create a system of order
among the materials.

Toward the end of this period, when the child begins to *conserve* weight and is able to work with seriation and even rudimentary concepts of measurement, the child recreates new contradictions, but these new contradictions, for example, confusion between weight and volume, are closer to the relevant
variables. To combine weight and volume still poses a problem
since he does not yet have a workable concept such as specific
gravity.

Careful reading of the example, however, does reveal a search
by the child for an internal consistency, but since the child still
has not acquired the competence to combine classes, such as
weight and volume, he cannot discover the laws. This is typical
of concrete operational thought.

STAGE III: The child now uses logical operations to solve the
problem. He is at the stage of formal operations. Below is an
example of a solution to the problem and the kinds of reasoning involved.

JIM (12.8 years) classifies floating or sinking objects according to whether they are "lighter or heavier than water." "What
do you mean?" "You would have to have much more water
than metal to make up the same weight." "And this cover?"
"When you put up the edges, there is air inside; when you put
them down, it goes down because the water comes inside and
that makes more weight." "Why does the wood float?" "Because
it is light." "And that little key?" "No, this piece of wood is
heavier." "So?" "If you measure with a key (= with the
weight of a key), you need more wood than lead for the weight
of the key." "What do you mean?" "If you take metal, you
need much more wood to make the same weight than metal"
(Inhelder and Piaget, 1958, p. 38).

How do Inhelder and Piaget use the type of solution provided by *JIM* to reveal formal operational properties?

First, Inhelder and Piaget acknowledge that knowledge acquired from school learning will be used in the solution but they steadfastly hold that academic knowledge is usable only when assimilated and such knowledge will be assimilated only when it corresponds to the mental structures. The operations involved now, however, are quantitatively different from those previously used. The child now classifies the material on different criteria with greater discriminability and coherence. The contradictions or multiple criteria, which were employed earlier, are no longer used.

Further, the child can separate relevant variables (density) and variables which are not there by direct observation, evolving a set of propositions. The child not only creates a single hypothesis, but also begins to employ verification which during this period takes into account the number of possible combinations. So, while the child at the concrete operational level accumulates facts and does not link them together, the child at the formal operations level is able to do so in the form of an hypothesis. The following final excerpt regarding the law of flotation will illustrate the process.

LAMB (13.3 years) correctly classifies the objects that sink: "I sort of felt that they are all heavier than the water. I compared for the same weight, not for the same volume of water." "Can you give a proof?" "Yes, I take these two bottles, I weigh them. . . . Oh! (he notices the cubes) I weigh this plastic cube with water inside and I compare this volume of water to the wooden cube. You always have to compare a volume to the same volume of water." "And with this wooden ball?" "By calculation." "But otherwise?" "Oh, yes, you set the water level (in the bucket); you put the ball in and let out enough water to maintain the original level." "Then what do you compare?" "The weight of the water let out and the weight of the ball" (Inhelder and Piaget, 1958, p. 44).

Piaget has used a number of other problems to illustrate the changing logical system children employ. By using the same problem with children of different ages, the solution by children at each level exemplifies Piaget's ideas regarding the relationships between the problem to be solved and the mental status of the individual. The child constructs the solution to the problem relative to his developmental level. With this strategy Inhelder and Piaget have been able to characterize thought from concrete operations to formal operations.

Relation between the Formal Stage and the General Pattern of Adolescent Thought

Inhelder and Piaget, however, are fully aware that formal logic is not the gamut of thinking. They address themselves to the issue of how hypothetical-deductive thought is related to the more general pattern of adolescent thought. To demonstrate the relationship between formal thought and the adolescent's general life situation, Inhelder and Piaget take into account the changing social-biological situation of the adolescent. In this period of life, two important things are going on; one, the appearance of puberty, and two, the acquisition of adult roles. The authors do not attempt to relate formal thinking to puberty. They emphasize the relationship between the adolescent's acquisition of formal roles and formal thinking. "The adolescent's adoption of adult roles certainly presupposes those affective and intellectual tools whose spontaneous development is exactly what distinguishes adolescence from childhood" (Inhelder and Piaget, 1958, p. 339). In other words, the ability to think in formal terms enables the adolescent to adopt adult roles.

Inhelder and Piaget describe the intellectual and affective tools the adolescent employs in coming to adulthood and demonstrate how these tools relate to formal thinking. They point out that the adolescent is a system builder. He builds social and political systems as a means of explaining the world he lives in. To do this, the adolescent systematizes ideas. This activity is in contrast to the younger child who does not make such efforts. The building of systems is considered by Inhelder and Piaget to be of considerable import, because "it is vital in the assimilation of values which delineate societies of social classes as entities in contrast to simple inter-individual relations" (Inhelder and Piaget, 1958, p. 340). The adolescent is using an ability to think in terms of propositions and logic to arrive at a system. Further, adolescents are able to introspect and to analyze their own thinking. By virtue of these processes, elaborate philosophical, scientific, and political systems of ideas may evolve.

Inhelder and Piaget take pains to point out that adolescents' thought is not just vacuous logic applied to vague theories. Quite the contrary. Adolescents use their new found skills to develop a detailed philosophy of life and plan of society. They are usually quite certain that their plan for the world will be more successful than that of their elders.

In this sense, the adolescent is still egocentric; that is, he still views the world and the events in it from a personal point of view (Elkind, 1970). They have difficulty taking into account the views of others at times. This reflects a recapitulation of earlier stages of the child's development, when the young child is egocentric. Now adolescents show the same orientation, when they try to adapt the environment to their ego. Quoting from Inhelder and Piaget (1958):

when he begins to think about the society in which he is looking for a place, he has to think about his own future activity and about how he himself might transform this society. The result is a relative failure to distinguish between his own point of view as an individual called upon to organize a life program and the point of view of the group which he hopes to reform.

This form of egocentricity decreases as the adolescent gains in perspective, because of an ability to be introspective and analytic. Social experiences, especially entering into the occupational world, also contribute to the adolescent's change in perspective.

Some Interpretations and Conclusions

We have presented a schematic review of the stages of development, using Piaget's system as an organizing framework. This monolithic and complicated theory is a stage-dependent one in which the child is said to move in an invariant order through major periods and stages, each specifying the necessary operations required. That is, the child moves from sensorimotor intelligence, birth to two-years-old, to preoperational thought, two- to seven-years-old; then into the concrete operations, seven- to eleven-years-old; and finally, at eleven- to fifteen-years-old, into the period of formal operations. Passage through these periods results in transformations, substitutions, and integrations.

The reader may be concerned that these periods are tied to rather specific ages. These ages have been established by Piaget, but he has indicated that they are only guidelines and not to be treated as fixed. The chronological ages can be used only as estimates of when certain kinds of functions may be expected. In fact, children at various ages employ behaviors which are characteristic functions of many of the periods.

Children within these periods do show variations in intellectual maturity. Modes of thought do not "reach the operational level in all areas simultaneously, but rather are subject to horizontal time lags whereby the same intellectual structures are successively applied to different contents" (Laurendeau and Pinard, 1962, p. 251). The children, on some problems with certain materials, will be on a concrete operational level while for others they might be on a logical-formal level. To illustrate, consider integrating items into a class. The success a child has in building classes depends on the extent to which the elements to be integrated are endowed with properties readily accessible to perception or intuition. For example, the integration of the subclasses "boys and girls" into a general class of children is easier to make than that of the subclass "blue beads and red beads" into the class of wooden beads. For the same reason, development of the concept of conservation of mass is grasped earlier than conservation of weight, even though both problems call for operational thinking.

Language is another factor that influences the development of operational thought. According to some theories, language is the key determinant of the developmental sequence of attainment of logic and thought in general. The structure of language influences the system one employs to organize and understand the environment (Johnson, 1962). From this point of view, language acquisition determines how the environment is discriminated, what objects can be integrated, and what kinds of thinking can be invoked. Lacking a name in English for a category encompassing the relationship between two mothers-in-law, English-speakers do not use this category. But it is not so in Yiddish, for example. It follows that organizational concepts of kinship would differ among English-speaking groups, in contrast to Yiddish-speaking groups. Thus availability of categories can even be determined by the language structure (Brown, 1958; Whorf, 1956). Language acquisition during the early periods of cognitive development will be our next topic in Chapter 5.

Educational Implications

Now that we have described the development of concrete and formal operations, the information is available for considering its application to education.

Piagetian theory is highly complex and considerably more detailed than we have presented it. Nevertheless, the argument regarding its relevance for education can be distilled from our presentation. In this section, we shall direct our attention to the later stages, concrete and formal operations, discussing sensorimotor and preoperational stage implications in Chapters 3, 6, and 8.

The relevance for education resides in the three areas we have consistently been concerned with: (1) conceptual scheme for the development of intelligence; (2) organization of curricula; and (3) teaching strategies.

CONCEPTUAL SCHEME FOR THE DEVELOPMENT OF INTELLIGENCE. Recall that the periods of development of interest are concrete and formal operations—two periods which parallel elementary and secondary grades. The point of view derived from a Piagetian perspective toward these grade levels should influence the quality of the educational interaction. Children at the concrete operational period have mastered language and therefore can make statements which often make them appear to be more competent than they might actually be. For example, children acknowledge in the conservation experiment that the deformed piece of clay was in fact the same amount as the non-deformed piece. Yet, their reasoning for the answer may be on perceptual grounds. "I saw you just push it flat." This response does not indicate an understanding of the basis for equality.

This also occurs when children are asked to use verbal concepts, such as, animal. A child in the concrete operational period will not make an error in using the word, animal, but she will not have an extensive category—including all classes that are appropriate. Thus, frequently ducks or fish are excluded, since animals are frequently defined on the basis of the number of legs they have. The point here is that the child's facility with language and apparent correct usage, especially of conceptual labels, are often construed as indicating that the child's concept is congruent with the adult's. To make this determination, the educator must employ strategies similar to Piaget's clinical method. We leave that discussion to the next section, Teaching Strategies (p. 102).

It is sufficient that the Piagetian framework provides a perspective for listening to children as they think and reason. Keeping in mind that the abilities of the child are constructed differently from those of adults, and that the child processes adult communications not in terms of some objective basis but rather in terms of developmental level, the educator should not be surprised at discovering discrepancies between the understanding of the adult and that of the child. Failure to grasp these principles can lead to poor communication and misunderstandings which might be avoided if the adult is sensitized to the way children process information. Though, by the time the child reaches the stage of formal operations, reasoning and thinking are closer to adult skills. The task for the educator is to recognize when this stage has been achieved.

PIAGETIAN THEORY RELEVANT TO THE ORGANIZATION OF CURRICULA: Piaget's interest in studying children is to discover how knowledge is acquired and organized. He has divided knowledge into three broad areas; physical knowledge, social knowledge, and logical-mathematical operations. What he has studied is the acquisition of scientific knowledge and mathematics. Thus, Piaget and his colleagues have investigated thought and reasoning as it evolves with problems in geometry, gravity, time, space, and logic (Inhelder and Piaget, 1958). Each of these areas has been investigated and stages identified and described, suggesting that curricula in these fields might be ordered accordingly. Thus, for Piaget, learning to count before understanding the principle of one-to-one correspondence would be an example of incorrect sequencing of the curriculum. Understanding number or quantity follows an invariant sequence and this curriculum should also be organized accordingly.

Some people argue that this recommendation is premature because the evidence is not yet able to justify Piaget's assertions about the stages in development of knowledge (Sullivan, 1967). Nevertheless, the educator should consider and evaluate various curricula in the physical sciences with a Piagetian perspective.

The basic principle is that knowledge is acquired commensurate with the developmental level. Hence, children cannot learn unless they have the appropriate mental structures.

RELEVANCE OF PIAGETIAN THEORY TO TEACHING STRATEGIES: Piagetian theory has direct relevance for teaching. Perhaps this area is the most directly derived from the theory. Piaget places great emphasis on discovery through activity.

The use of active methods . . . gives a broad scope to the spontaneous research of the child or adolescent and requires that every new truth to be learned be rediscovered or at least reconstructed by the student and not simply imparted to him.

The teacher as organizer remains indispensable in order to create the situations and construct the initial devices which present useful problems to the child. Secondly, he (teacher) is needed to provide counter examples that compel reflection and reconsiderations over hasty solutions. What is desired is that the teacher cease being a go-between, satisfied with transmitting ready-made solutions. His role should rather be that of a mentor stimulating initiation and research (Piaget, 1974, pp. 15–16).

Finally, Piaget contends that "no real intellectual activity can be carried on in the form of experimental actions and spontaneous investigations without free collaboration among individuals, that is to say among the students themselves, and not only between the teacher and the student. Using the intelligence assumes not only continual mutual stimulation, but also a more importantly mutual control and exercise of the critical spirit which alone can lead the individual to objectivity and to a need for evidence" (Piaget, 1974, p. 108).

Piaget summarizes the theory's relevance for education by stating that

the goal of intellectual education is not to know how to repeat or retain ready-made truths (a truth that is parroted is only a half-truth). It is learning to master the truth by oneself at the risk of losing a lot of time and of going through all the round about ways that are inherent in real life activity (Piaget, 1974, p. 106).

We may summarize the teacher's role as the person who identifies the relevant domains for study and who is the organizer, so that the proper materials are available and the classroom arrangement will enable peer exchange. The child's own activities must take priority from that point if learning is to derive from invention. The teacher's role, then, shifts to challenging the new discoveries, forcing articulation of principles, and rethinking of erroneous conclusions while the child experiments.

Summary

In this chapter we have presented the details of two major developmental periods, concrete operations and formal operations.

The concrete operational period (approximately between seven- and eleven-years-old) is characterized by thinking patterns and operations which are still in the process of developing. The children need the concrete observable objects with which to interact. They begin to perform operations of *reversibility* (returning to the original starting point of his thought), *reciprocity* (the principle of compensation), *classification*, and *seriation*. The reason they can perform these actions is due to their increasing decentration. Initially egocentric, the child increasingly decenters and is able to take another point of view. These operations and decentration enable the concrete operational child to make and decide crucial transition-solving conservation judgments. Conservation is vital to subsequent logical thought.

The concrete operational stage transforms into the period of formal operations beginning about eleven or twelve years of age. Formal operations are expressed in the child's ability to think in adult logical terms. During this period the adolescent engages in logical thought, uses propositional thought in solving problems, and can transform these propositions into appropriate logical symbol systems. The cognitive system develops so that the adolescent is capable of combinatorial thinking, the ability to combine diverse operations into a single system.

The cognitive apparatus of adolescents interacts with social and personality aspects of their lives. Because adolescents have developed the ability to employ propositional logic, use symbols, and create coherent systems of ideas, they are able to engage in ideological and philosophical arguments. Such changes involve not only the cognitive system, but also the adolescent's orientation toward the self as a social organism and toward future social roles and career choices. In effect, the adolescent is defining a place in the social world.

The relevance of the Piagetian system for education is at least three-fold: (1) it provides a conceptual system which should aid the teacher in understanding developmental processes; (2) the research literature is replete with implications for curriculum planning, particularly in the physical domain where so many of Piaget and his collaborators' research studies have been conducted in order to investigate the stage sequence in the acquisition of these concepts; and (3) teaching strategies are quite explicitly discussed by Piaget, with many good examples available from the clinical interviews themselves.

Chapter 5 Language Acquisition and the Early Stages of Cognitive Development

The previous chapters have presented a discussion of the intellectual development of children from the genetic or developmental viewpoint as elaborated in the theory of Piaget. We will now turn to the language development of the child and discuss it first in terms of the precursors to verbal production and then in terms of the developmental sequences of child utterances. Throughout our discussion the reader should keep in mind, and try to apply to language development, the previous chapters' descriptions of the processes underlying the growth of cognitive structures. Assimilation (referring to the child's integration of experience) and accommodation (referring to the child's modification as a result of experience) are processes which have been occurring since birth. The fact that language, the acquisition of which is our major concern, does not make any ostensible appearance in the child's own behavior until twelve to eighteen months of age means that we are dealing with a phenomenon in relation to which these processes are not immediately obvious. The child has considerable and varied experiences in the world and undergoes dramatic behavior changes that affect his or her language development even before exhibiting language itself.

The model of development which we have been proposing has *representational competence* at its core. We are now going to consider language as one form of representation. Language embodies all of the aspects of representation which we have discussed thus far: Language is a symbol system; language is a means of presenting and re-presenting experiences to oneself and to others; and language is a tool with which humans can, through symbol manipulation, create and analyze hypothetical situations. These three functions of language as representational thinking are theoretically consistent with what we have already stated. Let us now look at the practical level of language, by considering very briefly some general functions of speech. Perhaps in this way the reader will gain insight into the rationale for the lengthy, theory-based discussion of language acquisition to follow.

To an observer of a class of preschool children it would be obvious that one general function of speech is to promote and help in the maintenance of social and working relationships. Watching children work together, one can observe how cooperative work ventures are facilitated by verbal exchange. Although children of this age often work side-by-side without conversation, even their chatter helps them maintain contact with and awareness of one another. The observer might also recognize the self-monitoring aspect of children's speech as when they represent their actions with sounds or when they use language to comment to themselves on the nature and course of their ongoing play activities. And, one might note yet another social-relation function as the preschoolers use language to assert their rights during play exchanges. By vocalizing with others, by monitoring oneself, and through self-assertion, three major aspects of the social-relation function of early child talk, the child is learning most importantly to make judgments about people and discern others' reactions toward him or her.

In addition to the preschool children's use of speech to maintain social relationships, their language can serve the purpose of *promoting* play activities, a second general speech function. Language may be employed in setting up a play scene where "real" items (for example, horses, cowboys and cowgirls, fire engines, restaurants, and so on) do not exist: While objects can serve as symbols or representations of other objects, pantomime can act as a means of representing, too. Language is another way of *representing* the elements essential to the play theme. Whirring sounds can represent police sirens and whinneys can represent horses. The development of the scene can rely largely upon the language the children use to create play elements where they previously did not exist.

A third major speech function involves information exchange. Language enables recall of past events, recollection of remote experiences, examination of situations which might not recur, rehearsal of past and future events, as well as analysis of situations—new, old, and immediate. In the following dialogue new information is offered and acquired by both participants:

Let us return to more of Mark and John's conversation. They are looking at a shoe box and discussing its suitability for making a garage:

Mark: Well, you know, garages have to have doors.

John: Sometimes they don't.

Mark: Garages have to have doors that will open and shut.

John: My grandad has one and he puts his car in and that hasn't doors.

Mark: But a garage has doors—and you lock the door so nobody can take it—the car you see.

John: My grandad has a car thing and it hasn't doors on. It just keeps the rain off you.

Mark: Oh—well—shall we make a garage or a car thing like your grandad's?

John: Well, I don't know how to put doors on.

Mark: I would think of glue or pins or something like that.

John: No—put it this way up see—and cut it.

Mark: Yes, that might be all right.

John: Right—Mark—right—I'll get the scissors.

Here we see *further uses* for language in addition to some we

have already referred to. Without doubt these two little boys
speak in such a way as to maintain their good working relationship—*considering each other's point of view*, for example.

Shall we make?

I don't know how to put doors on.

That might be all right.

But there is little here that reflects action, in fact it has about
it a very adult-like air of discussion. The question is how to
make a garage. The *shoe box provides an anchor in the present*.
Both boys use language to *express information about past*
experience which has some relevance for the present problem.
Mark's first statement "Well you know, garages have to have
doors" is not accepted by John as a valid conclusion; he has
seen evidence to the contrary, but his "sometimes they don't"
acknowledges that they often do have doors. Both little boys
then endeavour to be more explicit in order to establish their
own case:

Mark: Garages have to have doors that will open and shut.
He cannot envisage a garage without doors for letting the cars
in and out; he persists with his argument:

Mark: But a garage has doors—and you lock the door so
          nobody can take it—the car you see.

Clearly Mark has a very full notion of the purpose for which a
garage serves. But John also must be more explicit; his case is
also a valid one and he struggles to convey to Mark the way in
which a garage without doors will work.

John: My grandad has one and he puts his car in and that
          hasn't doors.

John: My grandad has a car thing and it hasn't doors on.
          It just keeps the rain off you.

Both children here make an effort to reveal to each other the
meaning which each attaches to "garage." *Through the sharing
of knowledge perhaps each extends his own meaning*. John is
presented with the conflict between Mark's argument that
garages have to have doors so that cars can be locked up and
kept safe, and his own knowledge about his grandfather's car
port. Perhaps his later reference to a "car thing" suggests that
he has recognised what the essential characteristics of a garage
are, and that his grandfather's does not qualify as a garage.

Mark, on the other hand, concedes that John has a point, that it is possible to have somewhere to put a car which does not have doors. The argument in fact demonstrates the way in which even the young child's *meanings can be modified by means of a transaction through the use of language.* Mark demonstrates very clearly his acceptance of the possibility presented by John although preserving the distinction between "a garage" and "a car thing." He resolves the slight conflict of views:

> *Mark*:   Oh—well—shall we make a garage or a car thing like your grandad's?
>
> (Tough, 1973, pp. 20–22; author's italics)

Dialogue of this sort serves to break apart complex ideas and clarify issues. Similarly, complex mental activities must sometimes be broken apart for clarification to oneself. When "if . . ." and "because . . ." aspects of verbally transmitted causal information are broken down by the child, the language itself transmits the relatedness and connectedness of the situation. That is, relatedness and connectedness, as expressed in language, show relationships which are not evident in disconnected language.

In summary, we may state that talk functions for children in the following ways:

1. To maintain a social and working relationship
2. To express intentions about actions to each other
3. To exchange information
4. To secure cooperation and coordinate action (see quotation)
5. To defend one's rights of property and status (already mentioned as subcategory of #1)
6. To monitor one's own activity (already mentioned as subcategory of #1). (Derived from Tough, 1973, p. 17)

The major thrust of this chapter will be to detail the development through which the cooing, babbling infant goes to arrive at this point.

Our discussion of child language will fall into three major time periods: (1) the preverbal child (birth to eighteen months of age); (2) a period when language structures are developing in a predictable sequence and remain relatively simple in form (eighteen to thirty-six months of age); and finally (3) a period in which syntactic development becomes the significant, notable change in children's language (from three years of age onward).

First, let us review some Piagetian terminology in order to avoid any confusions that might arise when we discuss the early representational thought and language of the child.

Representation, Symbols, and the Semiotic Function

First, the word *representation* embodies the notion that a thing (object or event) is capable of being portrayed or depicted in some medium or by some mode. The utility of the concept is that representations generally provide an economical way of conveying complex notions. Pictographs, in early writing, conveyed an entire action-sequence, but they were not very economical nor very effective in conveying abstract notions. In contrast, words can economically and effectively convey both concrete and abstract notions. In either form, however, these representations act as symbols—they represent something. Note that the term *symbolic* is not necessarily synonymous with the term *abstract*. Neither does the term *representation* necessarily imply the notion of abstractness. Indeed, the first two years of the infant's life are termed the *pre-abstract* period. Words and simple language, as well as early symbolic (representational) thought appear within, though in the later stages of, this period. The infant's thought, while it can be symbolic, is by no means abstract. An infant who continues to search for an object when it is no longer in view is functioning on the basis of his memory of that object. Based on the way infants function generally, we can assume that his memory is comprised of a literal mental image of that specific object, not some abstract notion of a class of objects or events. Thus, while he is capable of representation, he is not yet capable of abstraction.

The various modes for representing experience follow a developmental sequence, from action to imagery, and eventually, to language. The enactive mode is the basis for representing experience in the early stages of sensorimotor intelligence (action schemes). Experiences may be translated into mental images by ten to twelve months. By the end of the sensorimotor period (eighteen to twenty-four months), language begins to emerge and becomes an additional and very valuable mode for the infant to represent experiences.

A further clarification of terms, especially *symbol*, is essential to a discussion of language. It carries a special connotation in the Piagetian system. Symbol, literally, implies a relationship between two objects or events. For the infant, a mental image is a symbol of the real object or event. If the object is not presented to the perceptual field by physical reality, it is presented to the perceptual field through mental imagery. The mental image, while it is but a copy of the reality which the child perceives, is nevertheless termed a *symbol*. And, although the symbol is an abstraction away from physical reality, it is not "abstract" in the sense that we often use, such as when we refer to the *abstract symbols* a painter employs to depict an idea. For Piaget, a symbol is a translation of reality: The mental image is a symbol of reality.

In language, there is no mental image conjured up when specific words are uttered. Of course, we can think of particular instances of "boy" or "skating," but we do not form a mental picture of the graphemes "B-O-Y." The term "symbol" is not appropriate for words, then; and Piaget, to distinguish the way mental imagery functions symbolically from the way words function representationally, uses the term *semiotic* (see p. 49).

The *semiotic* function of language considers words as *signs*. Signs are symbols different from those we have been discussing by virtue of their arbitrary nature. Words and word combinations carry many meanings determined by the culture within which they occur. Words do not stand for unitary objects or events in the way mental images do. The mental image we conjure up when we think of "walk" is a symbol. But the fact that as a word it could refer to a red brick walk, or to taking a walk, or to the idea "I walk very fast" (the action of the verb)—any of a variety of possible interpretations of "walk"—illustrates the semiotic function of language (Menyuk, 1963). There is no direct resemblance between the words and the objects and events they symbolize, but only an arbitrary connection that has been determined by the speakers of the language.

In summary, we may state that the child can function symbolically, that is, employ primitive representational thought, by age two: but that is not to say that thought is abstract. The child constructs mental representations of reality when the physical objects or events are no longer in the direct physical perceptual field, and in so doing restores the salient aspects to a perceptual field via mental imagery. The mental images are symbols of reality. The language which emerges at this time carries much of the meaning of these mental images, but eventually comes to function beyond the symbolic level; and therefore we say that language is semiotic rather than symbolic. The symbolic or mental image representations are intimately tied to the action-schemes of the child. The semiotic function, in contrast, detaches the thought from the action schemes. We will pursue this point momentarily, when we discuss the action-pattern basis of language.

The Preverbal Child

There is some debate among psycholinguists (Kaplan and Kaplan, 1971) as to whether there is a period during the life of the child which we might label as "preverbal." There are, indeed, some stable prelinguistic stages prior to the utterance of the first word by the child. During at least the first five pre-abstract substages of the sensorimotor period, the child engages in certain vocalizations which psycholinguists segment into three, progressively differentiated categories. The first noticeable vocalizing is fussing, crying, respiratory sounds, gesticulation accompanying feeding, and so forth. The earliest sounds, then, may be labeled generally as organically based sounds. It also has been suggested that babbling, crying, cooing, and other early sounds, all of which every individual infant can produce, may possess distinct vocal properties and may occur in distinctly different situations. Thus, the fact that the vocalizing is organically based does not preclude vocal differentiation nor its differential usage.

A decrease in fussing and crying are accompanied by an increase in cooing (Lenneberg, Rebelsky, & Nichols, 1965). Cooing also changes qualitatively with development and sounds which parents report as attempts at words begin to emerge. Early infant vocalizing does possess acoustical features which make it sound like human speech. As a result, parents' reinforcement of babies' babbling sounds which they detect as "nearly-words" may play an important role in the emergence of the child's initial words and may also contribute to the phenomenon of the "babbling drift," an unsupported hypothesis that language is a direct outgrowth of babbling. The fact remains, however, that because of the lack of muscle development and cortical control, the early babbling sounds are unlike any adult speech sounds (Lenneberg, 1964; Ervin-Tripp, 1966), and do not appear to be directly related to the language which follows.

Evidence for the organic basis of babbling is that it occurs in both hearing and deaf infants. In fact, their babblings are indistinguishable from one another during the first six months. The fact that babbling includes sounds and sound sequences which adults do not use, and thus are sequences which the infant has never heard, precludes direct environmental input or imitation and lends further support to the biological bases of this early vocal output. In terms of our previous scheme for development, we might say that, insofar as the first six months are concerned, the auditory environment is not overwhelmingly important to the child who assimilates very little from it. This is not to say that it is unimportant, however. During the next six months, most likely because of cortical changes and the development of the vocal organs, vocal patterns begin to change (accommodate). Table 5.1 summarizes the relatedness of motor development and language advances.

At this juncture, let us discuss the concomitant intellectual and language developments which occur during the sensorimotor period. As we have seen from the discussions in the previous chapters of this book, the schemata of the first six months of life (incorporating the first three stages of the sensorimotor period) are organically based. In fact, we may say that behavior is essentially organized by innate patterns of action or perception and that schemata are organized with the goal of dealing effectively with the environment. In a fashion corresponding to the adaptations through which the sucking reflex goes, the organically based vocalizing schemata unfold. Though we have stated that representational thought does not begin to emerge until the latter part of the sensorimotor period, the earlier stages do prefigure these later developments. At roughly five or six months of age, when vocalizing begins to undergo

Table 5.1
Correlation of Motor and Language Development

Age (years)	Motor Milestones	Language Milestones
0.5	Sits using hands for support; unilateral reaching	Cooing sounds change to babbling by introduction of consonantal sounds
1	Stands; walks when held by one hand	Syllabic reduplication; signs of understanding some words; applies some sounds regularly to signify persons or objects, that is, the first words
1.5	Prehension and release fully developed; gait propulsive; creeps down stairs, backwards	Repertoire of three to fifty words not joined in phrases; trains of sounds and intonation patterns resembling discourse; good progress in understanding
2	Runs (with falls); walks stairs with one foot forward only	More than fifty words; two-word phrases common; more interest in verbal communication; no more babbling
2.5	Jumps with both feet; stands on one foot for one second; builds tower of six cubes	Every day new words; utterances of three and more words; seems to understand almost everything said to her or him; still many grammatical deviations
3	Tiptoes 3 yards (2.7 meters); walks stairs with alternating feet; jumps 0.9 meter	Vocabulary of about 100 words; about 90 percent intelligibility; grammar of utterances close approximation to colloquial adult; syntactic mistakes fewer in variety, systematic, predictable
4.5	Jumps over rope; hops on one foot; walks on line	Language well established; grammatical anomalies restricted either to unusual constructions or to the more literate aspects of discourse

From E. H. Lenneberg "On explaining language: The development of language in children can best be understood in the context of developmental biology," *Science,* 1969, **164**, 635–643.

accommodation, and cooing and other evidence of the processing of environmental effects on the child become apparent, we notice the precursors to early representational thinking. The process, we cannot overemphasize, starts from the sensorimotor action schemata. The issue which interests us here and which bears on the early concomitant development of language and thought involves the way the action schemata are preserved. There is some evidence that certain of these early, specific actions are translated into representations.

The Action-Pattern Basis of Language

The child's knowledge derives from the early action schemata. The most basic pattern for a schema is

ACTOR—ACTION—ACTED UPON

or, to put it another way,

AGENT—ACTION—OBJECT

This is the simplest way to break up any event for analysis. But even this basic pattern is overly complex for the infant. Although it represents the basic elements which the infant seems to extract from the environment, the objects and events are not so organized, and the relations which we understand to exist between AGENT—ACTION, between ACTION—OBJECT, or between AGENT—OBJECT are not meaningful relations to the infant in the early stages of the sensorimotor period. The patterns of relations which exist for him initially are simply inherited categories of the reflex structures (such as sucking or grasping).

Adult-child interactions account for the way the world is broken up into meaningful units by an infant. The mother's footsteps (auditory) upon approach to the feeding situation, her presence (visual and tactile), the feeding situation itself which leads to the sucking reflex and subsequent oral stimulation of the roof of the mouth by the tongue (tactile, gustatory), and so forth, all evoke specific action schemata. The objects and events are, at first, defined in terms of the schemata which apply to them. Later, they become organized into nameable, generalizable categories through the coordination of two or more motor schemata. These schemes are initially fragmented and sensitive to their context; therefore, the two schemes are not at first related to each other by the child. By the time the child reaches the end of the first year of life, however, these schemes are becoming de-contextualized, and organized knowledge begins to emerge. The sequence is now something like the following:

visual recognition → motor schema → grasping → toy
(the arrows refer to coordination)

The relationship between the early coordination of schemes and the simple analysis of events is no doubt apparent, for both contain the AGENT—ACTION—OBJECT sequence. These three categories are prototypic of other concepts which will emerge as well.

Nelson and Kessen (1974) have pointed out that all prototypic *concepts* start with particulars (a specific "car" or a specific "dog"). Early concepts are aggregates of specific instances of events or objects. The functional utility of these early aggregates is that they help organize thought. Nelson and Kessen report that the categorization of the information carried by the concepts leads to language. Categorization, specifically, is the integration of the action schemata so that relations among objects and events can be organized meaningfully. Nelson and Kessen state that schemes such as the motor and the visual are only gradually organized relative to each other:

Apparently only gradually does the motor scheme (grasp) come to imply the visual (toy) which in turn directs the action (uncover) that reveals the toy. . . . Now we postulate that sometime at around six months the child integrates two or more of these previously separate schemes such as mother's face and mother's voice, in regard to a particular familiar person or object, and thus forms a representation of a *valued particular whole.* . . . When these various schemes that represent parts of a particular valued whole person or object are integrated into a *schema* uniting the components, the contextual schematic relations are not lost but remain as expectations about the possible relations of the *whole* to other objects, people, and events. In addition, moreover, at this time, one *part* of the whole begins to imply the entire; for example, mother's voice comes necessarily to imply mother's face and other aspects of mother. It is at this point, as many have observed, that stranger anxiety appears. When a part of the presentation of the stranger (voice, face, movement) seems to imply the mother schema but the implication is not borne out, anxiety results (Nelson & Kessen, 1974, pp. 11–12).

Piaget states that as these action schemes become generalized, they not only prefigure later classification behaviors but constitute kinds of classifications in themselves. The logic of the relations develops later, when the child is capable of representational thought. We may say, then, that knowledge of the categories emerges prior to knowledge of relationships among these categories.

The relations which Piaget says grow out of the early coordination of the sensorimotor schemata prefigure (1) *conservation* and (2) *operational reversibility*. The elementary form of *conservation*, discussed in previous chapters, is the concept of the permanent object. That is, as the context or contextual conditions change, the object remains unchanged. The concept is built upon awareness of *location*, an important feature in the child's early receptive language. Prior to language, then, there is a *logic to relations*. This logic of relations is a key to later language. Language is not understood or produced in random order; rather, it follows a sequence which has some logic to it— the logic of the relations of the elements. Although this logic of relations develops later when the child is capable of representational thought, it follows the *logic of actions* of the sensorimotor schemata. This knowledge of the relations among language elements—the relationships among AGENT, ACTION, and OBJECT—is what Lenneberg (1971) views as the underpinnings of language competence, a capacity much more fundamental than merely producing the elements of a sentence in correct sequence. The basis for later language competence is found here in *sensorimotor intelligence*, in which the child's own action schemata provide the information about actor and action (stage 2) and about actor and effect (stage 3). We must caution, however, that we are talking about *logical relations*, not *grammatical relations* (not subject-verb-object).

Recall that during the second, third, and fourth stages of sensorimotor development, *circular reactions* play an important part of the child's action schemata. The *primary circular reac-*

tion of stage 2 involves the repetition of the innate action patterns; the actions (responses) are the stimuli to repeat the body movements (for example, the sucking response is stimulating to the roof of the mouth, resulting in a continuation of the action). *Secondary circular reactions*, as opposed to primary circular reactions, are repeated more for their effects (outcomes) than for the actions themselves. However, the actions continue from the child as the source at the third sensorimotor stage. The *tertiary circular reactions*, Piaget points out, are continuous of previous, repetitive action patterns. The repetition now, rather than occurring for the simple effect as in the secondary circular reactions, occurs for the purpose of "making interesting sights last" (Piaget, 1952a, Ch. 3). As a milestone in the development of language, Brown (1973) points to the early linguistic expressions of *recurrence* and regards them as outgrowths of the tertiary circular reactions which cause events to recur so that they "last."

For language development during this period we may say that the first *meanings* are extensions of sensorimotor intelligence. The evidence for this statement comes from the behaviors which occur at this time and the language which follows. The abilities which develop in the stages of sensorimotor intelligence include recognition, nomination (labeling), recurrence, location, object permanence, plurality, anticipation, and the notion that a single space can contain self and others. Nomination or labeling and recurrence presume recognition, the ability to recognize objects and actions. On the basis of the following evidence presented by Piaget, Brown (1973) says that recognition, or more particularly motor recognition, is the precursor of nomination. At stage 3 (four to eight months), the child sees the familiar object and reacts to it by performing the old, well-developed action schema associated with the object, but in abbreviated form. We can see the scheme for this "recognitory assimilation" in the following diagram:

$$\text{action schema} \rightarrow \text{grasping} \rightarrow \text{toy}$$
$$\text{(visual)}$$

Recognition is a requisite infant ability for the enactment of this scheme. The motor recognition of which Brown speaks is this recognitory assimilation, a taking in of the familiar, which for infants of this age consists of taking in via an action mode or motor activity, knowing through action. Nomination, a precursor of language development, can be an outgrowth or extension of recognition through action, "an action of articulation" (Brown, 1973, p. 199). The difference between nomination and recognition, Brown points out, is that names are associated with objects by social convention for the verbal behaviors, rather than through the accommodation of the reflexes for the motor behaviors.

The location of objects in the not-present physical, perceptual field presumes object permanency, or to use Brown's term "object durability." The concept that objects are not "unmade" when they go out of sight, but are simply displaced to new locations presumes knowledge of location. Search strategies for these not-present entities further imply anticipation of objects and actions.

The concept of more than one, that is, plurality, also appears at this time. A study illustrating children's knowledge of this concept prior to their ability to express the concept linguistically was reported by Carlson and Anisfeld (1969). A twenty-one-month-old boy, who had final sibilants ("s" sounds) in his speech used the "ree-roar" of "one, two, three, four" to express plurality, rather than the conventional /s/ morpheme at the end of the noun. Hence, one boy, ree-roar-boy; one dog, ree-roar-dog. This example clearly illustrates that children may have a conceptual awareness (the difference between oneness and more than one) but not yet have the linguistic rule for expressing the concept.

Of the operations growing out of the preverbal period nomination (labeling), nonexistence, and recurrence are predominant. The child's productive language by the end of this period can express the presence of an object ("doggie"), its nonexistence ("allgone doggie"), and its recurrence ("more doggie"). In addition, concepts of possession and location are expressed through a simple juxtaposition of the labels by the child rather than by the language markers employed in more mature speech. Thus, location, which is expressed in adult language by the use of a preposition, is expressed by the eighteen-month-old child as "pencil cup" to designate that the pencil is in the cup.

"Mommy dress," similarly, expresses possession by juxtaposition, while omitting the possessive inflection. The point is that even though the language of this period may not possess some of the linguistic markers characteristic of later language use, the juxtaposition of words which the child uses strongly suggests that he *knows* the relationship between cup and pencil. The expression is not produced as "cup-pencil," which would imply that the child is merely ennumerating the objects in his perceptual field. Rather, it is produced as "pencil cup" in order to express a relationship, that the location of the pencil is *in* the cup. The child's words are produced in the order of the intended relationship, not in spurious order.

The early aspects of language development which significantly relate to thought, then, are those which concern language comprehension: together, language and thought comprise the comprehension process for the infant. The assumption underlying this discussion has been that the child's thought, at this time, is more advanced than language *production*, but that it is part of language *comprehension*. Prior to being able to verbalize and comment on the world, the child makes observations, shows evidence of simple classifications of the objects and events of the world, and establishes some notion of a personal effect on the objects in this world (Sinclair-de-Zwart, 1969).

The mental life of infants consists of perceptions and movements, that is, what they perceive and their own actions. Both the early knowledge of AGENT—ACTION—OBJECT, and the corresponding early receptive language, are tied to the perceptual immediacy. Labeling, represented in words (productive language), depicts a disjointed sequence which, undoubtedly, corresponds to the pictographs of the child's mental life, the mental images. The child is still not liberated from perceptual exigencies, and verbal labels do not transcend time and space as they do for adults (Piaget, 1954). In other words, the early stages of the sensorimotor period are prerepresentational. By twelve months of age, however, we see the emergence of behaviors such as the search for an absent object, an indication that objects, even in their absence from the physically perceptible field, may continue to form a part of the child's mental life. The actions employed in searching for the object recapitulate the actions employed when the object was present. These behaviors are taken to mean that the child is responding to mental images in much the same way the child responded to the physically present object, and that thought about familiar objects and events is becoming "representational." The child's intellectual functioning is at the level of reality or mental images of previous encounters. Piaget's term, "figurative knowledge," denotes that the child's knowledge centers on present or re-presented images.

The language which the child understands appears to be more advanced than what is uttered. Comprehension (or "receptive language," to distinguish it from "productive language") is a focal feature in the relationship between language and thought during this first period.

The development of receptive language follows the appearance of image formation, after the appearance of symbols. The receptivity to language depends upon the development of images because the child is still in a world of "figurative" knowledge. Although functioning in the absence of "real" objects, the child still needs them present in the perceptual field. Receptive language is denotative language of these mental images.

The early productive language of children at this period is generally termed "holophrastic speech," to indicate that language is mostly limited to one-word utterances. The one word may be a noun or a verb; it may denote a desire or a command. In short, the holophrases are one-word "sentences."

Summary

Children bring with them biologically inherited reflex structures and sensitivity to sounds as they encounter the linguistic world during the sensorimotor period (stage 1). The primary (stage 2), secondary (stage 3), and tertiary circular reactions (stage 4) show reflex coordination, effect on the environment, and intentionality or purpose, respectively. The period ends with the child's being able to represent reality and to deal with the symbols of reality (eighteen to twenty-four months). Brown points out that probably the first sentences which children utter are constructions proceeding directly from sensorimotor intelligence. The information which has been acquired through motor intelligence—information about objects and the immediate world, the action schemes, notions about location, recurrence, object permanence, and so forth—do not need to be learned all over again as the child begins to speak. Brown says that representation starts with the skills learned in the sensorimotor period and takes that intelligence beyond the sensorimotor level by applying them to new domains of thought. "Representation is a new level . . . which quickly moves to meanings that go beyond immediate space and practical action" (Brown, 1973, p. 200).

The context is a critical variable in early representation; it provides for a literal re-presentation of the familiar object in the context of the familiar. The object, first recognized in context, is later re-presented mentally, *in context*; until, finally, there is a re-presentation of the object outside of the familiar context. The developmental shift is from the specific to the more general, and this eventual representation of objects independent of context is the first sign of the process of generalization, an important process by which children later learn syntactic rules.

From Action Patterns to Verbal Meaning: Early Semantic Development

The period (birth to eighteen months) just described for the development of language and thought in the child has been termed preverbal. While it was acknowledged that language does not actually appear during this period in the child's development, the action patterns characteristic of sensorimotor intelligence prefigure later language behaviors. The nomination (labeling) behaviors which appear during this early period follow the AGENT—ACTION—OBJECT analysis of events. The learning of the logic underlying the relationships expressed in this paradigm, beyond the initial Agent—Object (mommy sweater), Agent—Action (baby go), or Action—Object (see truck) language of stage 1, represents a significant development of the second period (eighteen to thirty-six months), our present topic. The action basis of meaning approaches the representational level by the end of the preverbal period, until eventually the child is capable of functioning at a symbolic level through mental images. The images are labeled and the former holophrastic speech (one-word sentences) becomes two- and three-word utterances which directly relate to the AGENT—ACTION—OBJECT elements.

This second period, then, is a period during which *meaning* develops. The meaning which develops is not only lexical meaning (word meaning) but the meaning of word relationships appears at this time. The logic of these relationships is the key to the child's thought as expressed through language. The relationships which develop at this time, then, can be between one word and its referent (dog—four-legged animal that barks), as well as between two or three sentence elements ("Tommy runs"—a specific person whom he knows as Tommy is performing an act which he knows as running.) The second relational aspect conveyed by the *order* of words is central to the issue of the logic of word relationships.

In the previous section we discussed the sequential order of the child's use of words and stated that the words do not, even initially, appear in random order, but rather follow the sequence of the intended relationship, such as "pencil cup" to express location. We wish, now, to pursue the sequence of words further and to examine how it relates to both the action pattern basis of language of the first period and the relationship between language and thought of the second period. The second part of the development of language and thought occurs roughly between eighteen months and three years of age. During this time the relationship between cognitive structures and verbal representation is more marked then ever. From the standpoint of language it is a period of semantic development. In terms of cognition, it is a period for the development of meaning.

The evidence for stating that the child's early use of language (both in the sense of *comprehending* and "making use of" what others say and for *producing* utterances) depends upon a *meaning* base derived from that early period when the child's thinking abilities were more developed than the language abilities. Early "language" learning primarily involves learning the names for objects, and "language," is at this time narrowly defined by the child's vocabulary. Names for conditions, activities, and states ("sick," "play," "happy") come fairly early, too. But the meaning component of language comes only later. During this period of learning, the child is utilizing the semantic information which is available to her from the linguistic environment and which she had previously ignored. This further serves as a reflection of her intellectual state. As an example let us consider the referent class of pronouns which begins to develop at this time. The child is always addressed in the pronoun "you," and yet learns to use the pronoun "I" when referring to the self. MacNamara (1972) suggests that the child uses the semantic force to guess the meanings, initially. *Semantic force* means that the relationship between the pronoun and the referent is so clear that the situation provides very forceful clues to enable the child to guess the meaning. The point is that the child is now excrcising capacities for language and thought and is not mimicking what is heard. The strategies employed to convey meaning will constitute the *thought* aspect of this section on language and thought.

Clark (1974) has pointed out that we must be careful not to overlook the cognitive phenomena which strengthen language. She has stated:

the child will first learn those aspects of language that are within the scope of his current cognitive development, so that as the child develops cognitively, he will gradually learn to use more complex linguistic formulations. In other words, cognitive development provides the basis for language acquisition, and the order in which certain linguistic distinctions will be acquired can be predicted on the basis of their relative cognitive complexity (Clark, 1974, p. 106).

Consistent with our formulation of sensorimotor intelligence, Clark hypothesizes that word meanings develop through children's acting as if a "word" is defined by the most salient perceptual characteristics of its referent (the object referred to), and that this strategy works until the child experiences sufficient counter-evidence to learn that this is an untenable hypothesis. Clark says that the components of meaning that the child appears to use derive from the salient perceptual input from the object or event, including touch, sight, smell, hearing, and so forth. After attaching meaning to these words, then, the child *overextends* the meaning. This is due to the child's use of less than the full set of features of the category which he is defining. Thus, an eighteen-month-old toddler might call out "birdie" when watching tropical fish swim in an aquarium. The problem is that children's early word meanings are based upon only one or two perceptual features. Clark (1974) states that the principal characteristics that form the basis for overextensions can be sorted into six major categories based on shape, movement, size, sound, taste, and texture, with visual perception playing the principal role. Clark lists the categories that promote over-extension as follows:

1. Shape: visual, tactile
2. Movement: visual, auditory
3. Size: visual, tactile
4. Sound: auditory
5. Taste: gustatory, olfactory
6. Texture: visual, tactile

Many research studies have been conducted to determine when the infant first detects sensory input. Table 5.2, derived from the review by Clark (1974), presents a summary of the studies which have investigated the age at which the various perceptual dimensions become meaningful to the infant. These demonstrations are essential to the concept of overextension which has its beginnings in the first period of language development.

It might appear, at this point, that we are suggesting two, opposing systems for the acquisition of meaning: Piaget's reliance upon action-based sources of information, and Clark's suggestion that perceptual saliency accounts for first meanings. Actually, it would appear that both processes are operative. Since Piaget's model postulates *construction* of meaning out of experience, the child's actions probably prefigure the organization of information into perceptual categories (shape, texture, and so on).

The single words from the sensorimotor schemes, through the process of assimilation and generalization (overextension), come to express a variety of desires and emotional states for the infant. What marks the transition into this second, meaning-based period of language development, are the short sentences and the various meanings which are expressed through the child's peculiar word combinations. Let us consider an adult-child sequence from the transcripts collected by Roger Brown (1965). The sequence conveys the point that these early productions are *conservative* in that they convey the *meaning* while

Table 5.2	Summary Table of Research Relating to Infants' Abilities To Attend to Sensory Information		
Dimension	Aspect	Age of Infant at Appearance	Investigators
Shape	Vertical		Salapatek and Kessen, 1966; Kessen, Haith and Salapatek, 1965
	Brightness	1-5 days	Hershenson, 1967; Fantz, 1961a, 1963; Fantz, 1961a,
	Complex patterns	1-15 weeks	1963; Bower, 1966; Fantz, 1967a, 1967b;
	Shape or contour	first months	Fantz, 1961b; Fantz and Nevis, 1967
	Three-dimensionality	1-6 months	Ricciuti, 1963, 1965
	Shape dominance in sorting tasks	12-24 months	
Movement	Motion	2 weeks	Bower, 1967b; Bower, Broughton and Moore, 1971
Size	Size constancy	8 weeks	Bower, 1965a, 1965b
Sound	Auditory stimulation	soon after birth	Wertheimer, 1961
	Distinguishes voices from other sounds	2 weeks	Wolff, 1966
	Distinguishes affective quality of voice (e.g., anger)	4 weeks	Wolff, 1966; Kaplan, 1969
Texture	Shading and pattern due to texture	1-6 months	Fantz, 1963, 1965
	Tactile textures		Piaget, 1954, 1962

Note: This table was derived from Clark's (1974) review of the sensory basis of overextension.

utilizing the minimal necessary information. The child's speech is telegraphic, retaining only the *content* words while omitting words which express *functions*. The developmental period which we are discussing occurs between eighteen and thirty-six months of age. The speech sample (Table 5.3) cited by Brown (1965) was produced by a twenty-seven-month-old boy and is, therefore, representative of the midpoint of this time period.

The notable features which Brown discusses in detail are first, that the adult-child verbal exchanges are not typical of the dialogue between two adults. Second, the discussion is contemporaneous present, referring not to events displaced in either time or in space, but rather to contemporary events, to the present. Third, the speech the mother directs to her child (as opposed to that she employs with other adults) is characterized by short, simple sentences, which, however short they may be, are grammatically correct. (We shall return to this point later with respect to the third period in the development of language and thought, but for now let us say that these short, simple sentences are much like those the child produces a year later when beginning to produce grammatical constructions. Brown says that it is unlikely that children would be able to

Table 5.3
Dialogue between a Twenty-seven-month-old
Boy and His Mother

Adam	*Mother*
See truck, Mommy.	
See truck.	
	Did you see the truck?
No, I see truck.	
	No, you didn't see it?
	There goes one.
There go one.	
	Yes, there goes one.
See a truck.	
See truck, Mommy.	
See truck.	
Truck.	
Put truck, Mommy.	Put the truck where?
Put truck window.	

master correct syntax if they heard only complex, compound, and often incorrect adult speech.) Fourth, it is important to note the repetitive nature of the dialogue. Simplified, repetitive speech may play a critical role in the child's developing ability to produce language. And finally, the imitative aspect of Adam's speech reflects the limitations as well as the achievements of both his language and his cognitive development; for while Adam immediately says "there go one" after his Mother has said "there goes one," the verb inflection is omitted. The language is not morphologically developed ·(that is, it does not include inflections, contractions, and so on in the word formation), nor is the child's intellectual capacity to imitate perfectly.

The imitations which children produce during this period preserve the word order, which we have stated reflects a basic, relational achievement of early, action-based development. There are also certain other notable regularities to early attempts at verbal imitation: First, they omit certain classes of words and, second, the forms which are retained are predictable. Forms which are likely to be omitted include function words— the possessives, contractions, auxiliary verbs ("will"), progressive "-ing" endings, prepositions, and articles ("the"). Forms which are likely to be retained are nouns, verbs, and sometimes adjectives. The forms which the child retains and uses, therefore, are those expressing semantic *content* and derive from the action pattern basis of Agent—Action—Object. The "contentives" *represent* something, while "functors" express grammatical functions. Intonational stress and pointing are also ways in which adults convey meaning to children, helping to account for the sequence in which verbal expressions are made as the utterances extend beyond two or three words, when the Agent—Action—Object scheme must be extended.

Meaning and Word Sequence

The paradigm which we have been using for the child's analysis of events since the preverbal period has been the Agent—Action—Object sequence. We will now extend that paradigm to allow for analysis of verbal expressions and to illustrate that when the verbal analysis does not coincide with this prototype which has been used for so long, the child at first becomes confused and then later searches for an alternative to the old strategy in order to achieve an understanding of the situation.

Semantic Level:	AGENT	ACTION	OBJECT
Syntactic Level:	Subject(S)	Verb(V)	Object(O)
Verb Type			
Reversible	The boy	chases	the girl.
Nonreversible	The girl	waters	the flower.

The sentence which is easiest to understand is the one in which the Agent—Action—Object elements are clear—in which it is explicit who is performing the action and who or what is acted upon. Adults' intonational stress and pointing, accompanying their verbalizations, can help children learn meaning and the proper sequence of elements in a message. The regularity of the adult-originated language input to the child in the form of simple declarative sentences such as those used by Adam's Mother suggests that the first strategy the child employs in gleaning the meaning from others' speech is its characteristic Agent—Action—Object sequence [grammatically, Subject—Verb—Object (*S-V-O*)]. Language comprehension studies provide evidence that the child's thought is limited to a sequential processing strategy by holding constant the semantic input (meaning) to the child while altering the way in which the statements are made. For example, experimenters may offer a simple, active, declarative statement such as, "The girl waters the flowers," and contrast the child's responsiveness to it with his response to a semantically equivalent statement in the passive voice, "The flowers are watered by the girl." The meaning remains unchanged while the presentation of the meaning differs.

Verbs used in the passive voice may express reversible or nonreversible actions, both of which differ in complexity and, therefore, in comprehension. It is referred to as the *semantic reversibility* dimension of the sentence. For example, "The girl is watering the flowers" contains a verb which makes it a nonreversible sentence, while "The boy is chasing the girl" may be reversed. The action (verb) in the reversible sentence *possibly* can be performed by either Actor or Object. This is not the case for nonreversible verbs. The sentence which is easier to understand is the nonreversible one in which it is clear who or what is performing the action and what is acted upon. Refer again to the diagram which presents both the Agent—Action—Object and the Subject—Verb—Object sequences. It is important to ask what the word order does to the meaning in Subject—Verb—Object (*SVO*) relationships; that is, does the sequential ordering of these syntactic features alter the semantic (meaning) component?

Menyuk (1971) proposes that the strategy that children use in interpreting (comprehending) sentences is the actor—action—acted upon sequence, and when this plan does not lead to comprehension, the child requires additional time to change to a new strategy and shift the subject—object order in the sentence in the hope that it will describe the situation. It is important to note that during this second period of development, if one reverses the subject—object (actor—action—acted upon) order in sentences containing reversible verbs by changing to the passive voice, the child responds as if nothing has been changed. Such shifts from active to passive illustrate how the sequential order to syntactic items in the sentence does contribute to the description of the situation that the child is attempting to understand. Although the child may understand the sequence "The boy chases the girl," when the information is presented in the passive voice, "The girl is chased by the boy," she tends to respond to the second situation as follows:

	Agent	*Action*	*Object*
Active	Boy	chase	girl
Passive	Girl	chase	boy

The thought of the child at this time, therefore, appears limited by the use of strategies (a *word order* strategy here) which derive from the action pattern period of language and perhaps by the simple format used by adults when talking to children as well. In Piagetian terms, we may say that the child who treats the two identical meaning situations as if they were different is not *conserving* the semantic relationships.

The semantic constraints of the sentence, then, are not always meaningful to children, and their differential responding may be studied by analyzing their responses to reversible and non-reversible verbs in Subject—Verb—Object order relations to which the passive transformation has been applied. Semantically, "The pony is ridden by the girl" is permissible, but although it may appear as a possible syntactically correct statement, "The girl is ridden by the pony" is not meaningfully permissible. The actor—action—acted upon relation in the sentence is nonreversible. On the other hand, "The girl was chased by the boy" and "The boy was chased by the girl" are both permissible, and so the *S-V-O* relation is termed reversible. If a child has a strategy that can be applied to a sentence from which the child is trying to extract the meaning, one would expect that a statement which contains fixed markers that help keep these relations straight (such as the word order) would be easier and more quickly processed than one which has two possible forms. That is, nonreversible verb forms ought to facilitate comprehension. McNeill (1970b) found that a child, given the nonreversible statement above, judges the falsity of "the girl is ridden by the pony" on internal semantic grounds and that the semantic constraints seem to simplify the verification (p. 1025). But, the Agent—Action—Object sequence is responded to similarly for the active and passive sentence constructions where the verbs in the sentences are reversible. Consequently, when failing to process a reversal in the sequence of the information when its presentation changes from active to passive, the child errs. Reversal through transformation from active voice to passive voice when the verb of the sentence is a nonreversible verb, however, does not lead to error. While it is difficult to keep the relationships of Actor—Action—Object straight if two options exist, when "girl on pony" is the only option which exists *in reality*, the speaker could probably utter the content any way he wished and the child would process it correctly because he has no other reasonable alternatives from which to choose. Nonreversibility lends a "fixedness" to the sequence which follows the Actor—Action—Object paradigm of the earlier stage of development and in so doing seems to facilitate comprehension.

McNeill has cited some unpublished studies which explicate the development of reversibility. A study by Bever, Mehler, and Valian (cited in McNeill, 1970b) reported on the comprehension of reversible and nonreversible statements among two- to four-year-olds. Bever et al. found that the semantic constraint of nonreversibility does not always aid comprehension in children. These researchers discovered that while the four-year-old children had improved in their comprehension of nonreversible passive sentences, at the same time it appeared as if they had become worse in their performances on reversible items. Thus, at three years of age, children treat reversible and nonreversible situations as if they are alike, and at about four years of age, they begin to treat the situations differently.

McNeill's explanation of this apparent regression in passivization comprehension competence is based on a model similar to that of Menyuk cited earlier. With regard to the time lag one witnessed when children process statements which require transformations from the active voice to the passive voice, Menyuk noted that, at that time, the child seems to be applying an *S-V-O* strategy to the statement, and that, when this strategy does not fit the situation, additional time is required to explore the other relations. McNeill (1970b) lists the strategies:

1. Assume that noun—verb—noun stands for actor—action—object;
2. If this is implausible, assume that noun stands for object—action—actor (p. 1126).

Using these strategies, the reversible passive sentence is construed as an active statement, even though the passive transformation has been made by the child. "The cat is chased by the dog," when subjected to this strategy, becomes: cat (actor), chase (action), and dog (acted upon) (McNeill, 1970b, p. 1126). McNeill says that "the semantic coherence of a cat chasing a dog leads to a reversal of grammatical subject and object." Once children have a semantic strategy and expect semantic coherence, however, they reject pony (actor), ride (action), and girl (acted upon), so that "the pony is ridden by the girl" is correctly understood. McNeill (1970b) concludes:

Young children without a semantic strategy treat reversible and nonreversible situations alike and sentences describing both are open to the same confusion. (p. 1126).

Thus, it is with age and cognitive development that new strategies develop. Oftentimes, however, the newly acquired skills interfere with rather than assist the child's efforts to comprehend events in the world, causing an apparent regression in thought and language. Parents often report that their children are making errors in their speech which they did not make when they were younger. When new rules hamper performance, parents often view their children's intellectual ability as regressing rather than advancing to new strategies. For this reason we label the children's errors as apparent regressions though, logically, the errors represent advances in development.

This explanation is similar to Beilin and Spontak's suggestion (1969) that language subsystems are established by sets of rules which operate as "linguistic algorithms"; they provide a model or a template for processing the input and if the data are isomorphic with the template, they are coded or integrated correctly. In the case of nonreversible verbs, it is not necessary to have the knowledge of reversing the Agent—Action—Object sequence. Rather, the child can use the old and familiar prototype of S-V-O. But to process reversible input of the noun—verb—noun variety requires a different rule.

Jacobson (1960, cited in McNeill, 1970a,b) says that the expectations that children have concerning the actor—action—acted upon sequence are a function of but one of a group of many hypotheses they generate about language. He says that they are comparable to the hypothesis, for example, that all words have a rhyme. Jacobson refers to children's hypothesis-generation as the "metalinguistic" function of language. McNeill says that young children are insensitive to semantic coherence, that is, to strategies which are based on meaning rather than the relative positions which words occupy in sentences. The pervasiveness of the actor—action—object strategy with respect to other child behaviors is discussed by McNeill (1970a,b); Huttenlocher, Eisenberg, and Strauss (1968); and Huttenlocher and Strauss (1968); it is not unique to language.

The development of strategies appears late in the second period and is the indicator of the coming transition to the third period, when language itself evolves into a developed system. In order to discuss this transition, we must first consider learning which antedates the appearance of these strategies. Let us look briefly at the child's ability to comprehend the simple, active, declarative sentences of the mother, and the shift involved in the transition to comprehending passive sentence constructions containing nonreversible verbs.

We have stated that the child, early in this period, does not conserve the semantic content when a statement is transformed from the active voice to the passive voice ("The girl chases the boy" → "The boy is chased by the girl.") The clue to the action pattern basis of the language at this time comes from research which investigated the degree of comprehension in "transformed" statements. The data also suggest the status of the child's representational thought at this time. It is closely linked to the mental images of agent—action—object.

In a study by Cocking (1972), two methods of language comprehension were assessed in three-year-olds. The first kind of comprehension, assessed by the technique devised by Bellugi (1971), is the understanding of a complete sentence. The procedure involved presenting a different array of manipulable toys and objects for each of a series of different language structures. The child was to perform a task according to the statement an experimenter made about those objects. For a preposition item, the child was told to put a ping pong ball under, behind, next to, and on top of a paper cup. For the passive structure, the child was presented with two small dolls, a boy and a girl, and the experimenter demonstrated the verb "chase" in the active voice. The child was then asked: "Show me 'The boy chases the girl,' or 'The girl chases the boy.'" The toys were placed in the original positions and then the child was asked to perform the same action; that is, the semantic content remained unchanged, but the experimenter made the statement in the passive voice: "Show me 'The girl is chased by the boy,' or 'The boy is chased by the girl.'" The child is always asked to perform the action in the active voice first so that one could be sure that the child understood the basic content of the task. The first assessment of children's comprehension, then, involved the child responding to a *complete sentence* structure by manipulating the objects in the way that statement was understood.

The second way of assessing comprehension was to probe the child's understanding of the *elements* of a statement. For the passive construction, the child was asked, "Show me 'The boy is chased by the girl.' " After replacing the objects in their original positions and repeating "The boy is chased by the girl," the experimenter asked the additional questions about the agent and the object of the action: "Who chases?" "Who is chased?" and "Who gets chased?" The "got" form was included as an immature passive form which children use and which, it was thought, might also be understood before the true passive form. This second procedure for assessing comprehension of the Subject—Verb—Object (*S-V-O*) or the actor—action—acted upon focused upon *components* of the same sentences in contrast to the Bellugi procedure's focus upon the connected sequence comprising the stimulus-statement.

The first form of assessment reflects the child's ability to comprehend *sentences*, while the second inquiry procedure parcels out the Agent, Action, and Object one-at-a-time. Children who demonstrate the capacity to understand the content of the active, declarative *sentence* but who do not "conserve," that is, do not continue to understand the same statement after its restatement in the passive voice, are nevertheless capable of correctly answering questions about the Agent—Action—Object *elements* of the passive voice statements. The child seems to be able to process the unitary elements when they are disembedded from the sentence and presented singly, but the elements in combination, as in the task of sentence comprehension, are not responded to correctly at this age.

Although inquiry-probe procedures provide a means of measuring the child's comprehension of both syntactic and semantic *elements*, the grosser measure reflected in whole-sentence comprehension tells us what the child is capable of processing when the elements are integrated as a string of elements. The *sequence* of the string of elements for the passive syntax is different from the sequence for the active string. Semantically, however, the situations are identical. Therefore one might say that the issue is not one of the *string* versus the *elements*, but rather the *order* of the string of elements. The child who shows evidence of semantic but not syntactic comprehension responds to a string of elements, but in the active string order. The child at this time appears to have a *representation* only of the active string; that is, a representation only of Agent—Action—Object.

At the heart of the problem, Gough (1971) suggests, are the *different* ways in which comprehension may be *represented* or mapped by the child. He has said of H. Clark's model:

in each instance, the subject's response is based on a comparison of his representations of the sentence and the information demanded by the task (Gough, 1971, p. 15).

Clark's stages of comprehension are:

1. A representation of the sentence. This means that the basic content of the simple, active declarative sentence is understood. It corresponds to the knowledge the child brings to language from the action-schematization.
2. A representation of the *information* in the task, referring both to its meaning and its transformation.
3. A comparison of the representations in steps one and two.
4. A response.

For our purposes, the important stage to focus on is step 3. Of it, Gough (paraphrasing Clark) has said:

Clark proposes that comparison proceeds in accordance with what he calls the *principle of congruence*. This principle states that comparison is based on *identity*; if the representations being compared are not congruent, then they must be made so. The operations which accomplish this take time: The more operations required, the more time required for comparison, and the longer the comprehension task will take (Gough, 1971, pp. 15–16; authors' italics).

The model applies to observational data obtained from administrations of the sentence comprehension test. The children (looking at the experimenter) wait for the directions; they pick up the object, stare at it, scan other objects in the array, and hold the one object for a time before continuing; and finally some response is executed. But what is more important for explaining what occurs during inquiry-probe measures of comprehension is the issue of degrees of *knowing*. As an illustration of Gough's analysis, we may say that the children in Cocking's study had a representation of the active sentence ("The girl pushes the boy"), but not of the information required by the task when transformed (Show me "The boy is pushed by the girl"). The match between the mental representation of which

Piaget writes and the language representation depends upon an active-sentence sequence representation. The passive sentence sequence is incongruent with the mental representation or mental image which the child has of the events. Thus, the child's representational thought at this time seems to be closely linked to the mental images of an Agent—Action—Object sequence.

Context and Meaning

We have noted that during the development of sensorimotor intelligence one of the important milestones for the infant is the liberation from context-specific activity. The development of early representational thought is indicative of this achievement: Whereas the children at first treat each encounter with an object as a discrete, new event, they eventually become capable of recognizing the object in new contexts (recognitory assimilation) and finally form mental images of the objects and events outside of the *familiar* context. The development of linguistic meaning also follows this pattern. The principle of decontextualization provides a statement of the child's cognitive functioning. Even after considerable experience, children do not understand certain linguistic (semantic) situations out of context. Fillmore (1971) reports research on *deixis*, a dependence upon the anchors in the social context for full comprehension. Cohen (1973) has pointed out that context provides spatial relations cues about relative positions of speaker and hearer, themselves possibly tied to the child's prototypic Agent—Object relations derived from the action schemata. The notion of the location of objects, which develops in the child's thought during the first period we have outlined, is apparent in the child's ability to identify the position of objects ("pencil cup" to locate the pencil *in* the cup). The child has difficulty during the second period, however, when speech is comprised of more than one element and when a judgment must be made about the *relations*, about the *relative locations* of objects, or about the position of someone else *in relation* to the self. Decontextualization proves to be a problem because the child does not have the ability to *represent* perspectives (that is, to decenter). We conclude, therefore, that linguistic meaning at this stage of development is very context- and referent-dependent because of the child's inability to employ symbolic representation in the realm of spatial relationships.

A Summary of Semantic Development and the Phase of Preoperational Thought

Let us summarize language growth, now, in terms of our discussion in Chapter 3, in which we presented the model of psychological development in children. The linguistic and thought evidence presented in this section reiterates Piaget's observations but covers a time span somewhat longer than the preoperational period outlined earlier. We have considered eighteen to thirty-six months of age as a critical period for the development of linguistic meaning, as opposed to the span from twenty-four to forty-eight months which Piaget refers to as the preoperational phase of thought. However, the language of this general period reflects the egocentric, perceptually dominated thinking which Piaget says characterizes the child's thought at this time. The child's language and thought are self-centered: No attempt at taking another's perspective is evident. Not until the child can decenter is there a breaking away from the perceptual features (physical or mental) of the situation. And until decentering is a part of children's thought, we shall continue to witness their inability to incorporate phenotypic changes (transformations) of objects into the previously learned concept of object durability (conservation). We shall observe errors in reversing situations and activities (reversibility) such as $A > B$ and $B < A$ (for example, John is taller than Bill and Bill is shorter than John). The children will expose errors in judgment of the meaning of a situation because of a still egocentric perspective (with perspectivism or spatial relations yet unachieved; for example, What I see is what you see even though we are each standing in a different location). Children will reveal an inability to use comparative strategies in making judgments about sameness and differences (identity) that would enable them to understand that white crows are both crows and birds. (The child at this time erroneously concludes that other white birds must be crows and that black birds cannot be crows.) The perceptual dominance and the children's exclusive reliance upon mental imagery (figurative knowledge) encapsulate them.

They conceptualize on the basis of salient features during this period. In so doing, they preclude the objects' being the same and different on various criteria simultaneously. The transductive thinking of this period (for example, if *A* is like *B* in one respect, it is like *B* in all aspects) is no doubt an early thought strategy in analyzing the meaning of linguistic statements; if Subject—Verb—Object is a workable solution, it must be the "rule" to linguistic understanding. Therefore, we see children applying the active sentence sequence (Agent—Action—Object) when trying to make sense out of the passive sentences he hears [the ball (Object) is thrown (Action) by the boy (Agent)]. Other metalinguistic functions are transductive: Some words have a rhyme, and therefore all words must have a rhyme; words that have the same sound (rhyme) must have the same meaning; and so forth.

We might point out that the strategies for processing linguistic information, based on Cocking's work, imply a one-to-one correspondence strategy between grammatical and logical analysis; for example, (Agent—Action—Object) = (Subject—Verb—Object) = (Noun—Verb—Noun). The processing in sequential order rather than by logical placement of elements might be a function of the emerging seriation behaviors in children.

The cognitive operations which delimit the child's speech at this time appear to be the limited understanding of conservation, reversibility, seriation, identity, and spatial relations (perspectivism). We do not mean to imply that identity, for example, at the early stages of emergence operates at the sophisticated level of the child's being able to employ mathematical operations of identity.

Though these logical operations are not developed during this period, they do figure into the language which begins to appear. Language is not a developed expressive system at this time. However, the language development which occurs through comprehension illustrates that the initial slowness with which meaning develops is due to the lack of a development in the general cognitive functions. Linguistic development expands in concert with these cognitive skills. The difficulties encountered in passive reversible-verb constructions are an illustration of how children learn an alternative to the active, declarative sentence strategy for understanding the passive transformation, and then become confused when required to apply a second, new strategy simultaneously in order to handle a special sub-class of verbs. The language during this second period can be seen, therefore, as corresponding to the development of thought in the child. The next section will focus upon a third period of language growth. We shall discuss how thought development progresses sufficiently to allow for language to become an independently developed system.

The Child as a Grammarian

The third and final period for our discussion of the development of language and cognition begins when the child is roughly three-years-old. The child is beginning to learn the tools of producing a language to express relationships at this time. The way in which the child learns language and modifies imperfect attempts at expression are reflections of the thought structures at this time. This is the final point for our discussion of the language and cognitive systems, because at this time a clear distinction between language and thought begins to emerge. The cognitive structures continue to develop in universal stages toward concrete and formal operations, as outlined in the theory of Piaget. Language, on the other hand, develops in complexity and specificity within the constraints of the structure of the native language. As might be anticipated from the previous two sections, in which the development of meaning and sequential ordering of elements have been shown to grow out of sensori-motor intelligence, the discrepancies which emerge between language and thought are much less pronounced for semantic development and lexical organization than for the later-developing system of syntax.

Precursors to the Development of Syntax

During the second period of language growth linguistic meaning becomes developed. In our discussion, we emphasize the meaning base of linguistic expression and have pointed to examples of children's inability to grasp meaning relationships when changes in certain structural features of the language are imposed. This does not imply that structure is basic to meaning. On the contrary, basic meanings develop in children before they can incorporate the structural aspects of the language. Even when the children are miscued by the structure of the language we have seen that they continue to exhibit knowledge of the Agent, Action, and Object elements in responses to tests of comprehension. And even though the child cannot conserve the semantic relationships when presented with structural transformations, the comprehension or meaning base of language is retained. Comprehension, therefore, must be regarded as a very basic aspect in the development of language as a system of relationships.

Evidence for the fundamental nature of language comprehension comes from a study by Katherine Nelson (1973). She found that comprehension appears before language production and that it is predictive of the child's rate of language development. Better early comprehenders, Nelson found, became better early speakers. Nelson's comprehension measure tapped the child's understanding of syntax. The Cocking study (1972), cited earlier, compared the relative efficacy of two types of comprehension in predicting a child's facility for learning to produce new language structures which were not yet in the child's grammatical repertoire. The results were consistent with those reported later by Nelson: Performance on new language production tasks was a direct function of comprehension as measured by the child's knowledge of syntax. To reiterate our earlier discussion, syntactic comprehension reflects *sentence* comprehension, whereas inquiry procedures parcel out knowledge of Agent, Action, and Object elements. The child is able to process the unitary elements when they are presented singly, but when the elements are presented in combination, in a sentence like those in the syntactic comprehension task, the child has considerable difficulty in understanding a statement. Although the inquiry-probe procedures are effective in determining the child's knowledge of linguistic elements, the grosser measure reflected in the syntactic comprehension test tells us what the child is capable of processing as a sequence of elements. And what the child is capable of processing as a sequence is what relates to performance on new language learning tasks.

Some psycholinguists would add "the ability to imitate" to

the list of precursors to syntactic development. Fraser, Bellugi, and Brown (1963) used a repetition method of studying language imitation in three-year-olds and they concluded from their research that in the acquisition of certain syntactic structures, the capacity to imitate emerges first, followed by the capacity to comprehend, and finally the capability to produce. Menyuk (1971), however, has pointed out that both comprehending and noncomprehending imitation may occur, depending upon the sentence length and its *structure*. Ervin's data (1964), which indicated that children imitate only what they spontaneously produce, also suggests that performance is related to comprehension. Therefore, it is quite possible that repetition-imitation is dependent upon comprehension, rather than the other way around. If one uses a social learning theory definition of imitation, whereby the child's approximations of the correct *form* rather than direct *mimicries* are considered criterial performance, the evidence for the prior emergence of comprehension before production is quite clear (Cocking and Potts, 1976).

In summary, we may state that the meaning base of the second period of language growth, what we call Stage 2, is critical to language comprehension, but at Stage 3 the knowledge of linguistic elements in themselves is not a sufficient predictor of grammatical expression. The emerging knowledge of the *sequence* of grammatical elements in the context of a sentence, that is, syntactic comprehension, is predictive of the child's rate and age of language production. Let us now consider some of the features of child language as it evolves into an expressive system.

The Emergence of Syntax

The model which we have presented for intellectual development in children derives from Piaget's theory which proposes that the individuals *construct* their world out of the elements (experiences) and tools (mental operations) available at any given point in their development. Hence, the relatively undifferentiated biological being of an infant constructs a world of need satisfaction out of innate patterns and life experiences; the nonconserving, egocentric four-year-old constructs a world of other persons who share the child's world perceptions and experiences;

and the teenager potentially understands the logic of abstract principles of an argument without resorting to a particular case in point in order to grasp the meaning of what is being said. Our model for grammar is a comparable system, whereby each structure derives from basic operations and functions at the developmental level of the user (that is, according to the operations which the individual can employ). The following diagram is of the *generative model* (Menyuk, 1963).

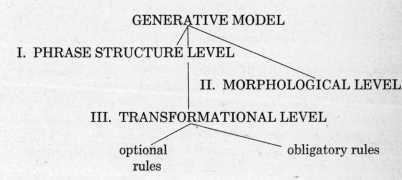

We will refer to the phrase structure level as the *base structure* level, for it is the level at which the simple, active declarative sentence is generated. The *morphological* level includes the systems of inflectional rules, the systems of word endings used to express certain kinds of meaning, such as the /s/ morpheme to express plurality, /ed/ for the simple past tense, and so forth. The third level, the *transformational* system, includes the systems of rules for generating linguistic expressions more complex than the simple, active declarative statements. This level is divided into two sets of rule systems: the *optional* rules are chosen by the speaker to convey what she wishes to say in a way she chooses; and the *obligatory* rules which follow after the speaker has exercised her option. That is, once the speaker has chosen to say something for which the sentence subject is the third-person singular pronoun, she must comply with the linguistic constraint of inflecting the verb to agree with the sentence subject; for example, he *goes*, as opposed to the uninflected verb form "go" required by first- or second-person pronoun ("I" or "you") subjects.

The generative model involves more than taking the three

separate systems and employing them independently of one another. For instance, we noted that toward the end of the first period of language development the concept of plurality was a cognitive achievement, and that sometime soon thereafter, the rule of pluralization, using the /s/ morpheme, develops. Morphological development is essential to the generative model of grammar, but this early achievement is a linguistic expression out of sentence context. During the third phase of linguistic and cognitive development, we witness a *coordination* of the separate rule systems in order to produce the transformational level. This cognitive achievement is much more difficult than adding the /s/ morpheme to a noun. It means that now the inflectional rules which the child has been learning must be applied to Agent, Action, and Object simultaneously.

We should look first at the base structure level. Menyuk's research (1969) presents a picture of children's language in which failure to observe base structure properties and redundancies predominates. For instance, children commonly ignore certain verb properties at the base structure level ("take a haircut"), and redundantly employ certain other sentence markers ("She put on the dress on"). These explanations, Menyuk suggests, represent an early device children employ in order to insure that sentences are understood. Menyuk also points out that when a child says "A leaves fall from trees," this does not necessarily mean that the child does not understand the properties of singular and plural, but that the child does not always observe the linguistic restrictions.

In her study of phrase structure development in children, Menyuk was particularly interested in learning if most children employ the same rules in generating sentences and if so, what the developmental patterns of the deviant rules look like in their approximations of well-formed grammar. The regularities she found at the phrase structure level involved, initially, a failure to use a marker such as the /s/ morpheme to indicate the third-person singular (for example, "She run"). The *omission* was later followed by the *substitution* of some alternate rule which they had derived from their language experiences (apply the regular verb /ed/ to irregular verb—"runned"). The third and latest developing deviant rule system before the structure was used correctly was that of *redundancy* according to which the newly acquired correct rule is employed in conjunction with the former, incorrect rule; that is, both rules are present ("She ranned").

We have stated already that the strings of elements which are first produced as sentences come from the Agent—Action—Object string. The sequences, therefore, are formed by the base structure rules. Since the linguistic expression is in the direction of greater definition of meaning, the expansion of syntactic rules is apparently motivated by the need to convey more specific information. We shall pursue Menyuk's analysis momentarily, to show that the child begins to utilize the transformational rule system to achieve greater economy in speech, since the number of rules and hence the memory strain are reduced by this system. This does not occur until the child has mastered the base structure rules, however. Before discussing the transformational level, let us look at the morphological level and compare the development of these rule systems with those at the phrase structure (base structure) level.

At the morphological level, Menyuk found that the rules were generally present in all nursery school and kindergarten children. However, when errors did occur, the idiosyncratic forms to appear first were "omissions of restrictions." Once the optional form had been selected the child did not observe the obligatory rules. For example, the child may optionally choose to use a third-person singular subject such as "he." But in doing so the child must follow certain restrictions: in providing an appropriate verb to use with the auxiliary and /ing/ form (for example, He is running), the child must, obligatorily, remember the auxiliary rather than saying "He running." *Omissions* were the most frequent errors that Menyuk found in her study. Errors of *substitution* followed omissions: When the context required /ing/, such as in completing the statement "He is _____," the child often substituted /s/ for /ing/, which resulted in "He is *runs*" rather than "He is *running*." Again, it would appear as if the child were treating the two forms as if they were interchangeable (which, in terms of conveying information, they are) and therefore ignoring the restrictions imposed by the auxiliary verb "is." With decreasing frequency, *redundant* constructions in Menyuk's study were employed later in development. The somewhat older children produced constructions such as "he ranned" and "Nobody don't do that."

At both the phrase structure and morphological levels, then, children demonstrate errors of omission, of substitution, and of redundancy with decreasing frequencies. Menyuk characterizes child-grammar as a system which optionally chooses a structure, then omits or changes by substitution or redundancy the obligatory rules.

In attempting to express more specific information, the child begins to generate rules, building upon the base structure rule system. Menyuk (1963) reports that certain transformations, though not completely acquired even among her first-graders, are used significantly more by the older children than by nursery school children, but that the reverse was never true. Thus, there appears to be evidence for the developmental sequence from base structures to transformed structures. The major developments which occur in the generation of sentences from the new rules are:

1. conjoining sentence elements
2. development and elaboration of subject and predicate
3. expansion of the verb phrase
4. embedding (clauses)
5. permutation of elements within the string (rearrangement) (Menyuk, 1969)

Although errors in producing these constructions decreases with age, deviations of two general sorts do occur while acquiring the transformational system: first, the nonobservation of the obligatory rules and second, the use of alternate forms ("She *got* hit by the boy" rather than the passive verb transformation of "She *was hit* by the boy" or simply "The boy hit her"). While older children will apply generalizations as they acquire new structures (that is, they try to approximate what is required), younger children will generally omit the rule. Hence, the developmental sequence is omissions, substitutions, and redundancies.

We may conclude, then, that errors occur at all levels. At the phrase (base) structure level, sentence elements are sometimes omitted or used redundantly. At the morphological level, omissions and redundancies of rules occur, as well as substitution of the child's own rules. At the transformational level, the child, having chosen a particular structure, sometimes fails to observe the linguistic constraints of that form. During this time, the child's grammatical development is marked by the appearance of certain language features:

1. The base structures become expanded.
2. There is an increase in the number of *types* of structures used.
3. The frequency of usage of structures also increases.
4. The approximations to correct structures are gradually eliminated as the correct forms emerge.
5. The selectional constraints of linguistic expressions are gradually observed more often.
6. The syntactic operations of addition, substitution, and permutation are applied in generating grammatical statements.

The cognitive operations which accompany this grammatical development (roughly between three and seven years of age) are implied by the grammatical operations which are employed. First, at the base structure level we have already pointed out that the characteristic deviations are due to nonobservation of multiple levels of linguistic constraints [supplying either the plural/s/ marker for the noun (morphological level) or the plural verb form (phrase structure level), but not both simultaneously]. Second, a certain amount of recursiveness in marker utilization once the child has grasped the notion of particular rules is also prevalent (for example, "I live in the city" and "I live in *the* Chicago"). Third, the accommodative process is probably the most notable feature. The strategies that children employ in conveying their verbal messages may be traced to their linguistic environments. The rules which they extrapolate from that environment, however, are not direct copies of what they hear, but frequently are changed by the children. Lexical meanings are often juxtaposed: "refrigerator" and the notion that it is for the storage of food is rendered as "fooderator." These productions indicate that rules and meanings are accommodated to fit the child's present linguistic and cognitive status. A few years ago, Jenkins (1965) reported some examples of child speech which were clearly generalizations the child had made. One of the quotes was "come out and higher the swing." An adult would have said something like "come out and raise the swing" or "come out and lower the swing." It is unlikely that the child had ever heard the construction "come out and higher the swing," and yet the form, as Jenkins pointed out, was understandable both with respect to meaning and derivation. The conclusion to be drawn from child language of this sort is that the child generates constructions to meet the *situational* and *grammatical* demands. Since children never hear grammatical forms of this sort, the implication is that these constructions are analogous to constructions they have heard. Learning by analogy implies, further, that the construction is modeled after speech which the child hears in the environment. Learning through modeling can occur even at the transformational level, but it is limited to structures which the child comprehends, as pointed out in our discussion of the development of meaning at Stage 2 (Cocking, 1972). Finally, language begins to show evidence of the child's intellectual capacity to include others' viewpoints in the child's world view. This reduced egocentrism is by no means totally listener-oriented. That the child as speaker reiterates grammatical features which he believes convey the message ("the football is *in* inside the house") is a clue to the child's attempt to be heard and understood. Previously, he would not have guessed that someone could not understand his message.

The indicators of the child's level of cognitive functioning accompanying the transformational level of language functioning are implicit in the operations necessary for the linguistic structures that emerge. Let us consider a few sentences as examples and then look at the operations necessary to derive these statements from the base structures.

I. Declarative Sentence:
    a. The time is four o'clock.
    b. [(It) is four o'clock.]
    c. [(What) time it is.]
    Transformed (question): What time is it?
    1. add /*wh-*/ word
    2. reorder pronoun and verb (b)
II. Declarative: a. The girl waters the flowers.
    Transformed (passive): The flowers are watered by the girl.
    1. substitute auxiliary verb (*are*) for present tense (*waters*)
    2. add past participle verb form (*watered*)

3. add agent function (*by*)
4. reverse object—subject positions
III. Declarative: a. The boy waters the lawn.
   The boy mows the lawn.
   The boy weeds the lawn.
Transformed (conjunction): The boy waters, mows, and
                             weeds the lawn.
1. add conjunctions to make one statement
   b. The boy waters the lawn *and*
      the boy mows the lawn *and*
      the boy weeds the lawn.
2. delete initial conjunction (*and*)
   c. The boy waters the lawn,
      the boy mows the lawn, and
      the boy weeds the lawn.
3. delete redundant noun phrase elements (*the boy*)
   d. The boy waters the lawn, mows the lawn, and weeds
      the lawn.
4. delete verb phrase redundancies (*the lawn*)
   e. The boy waters, mows, and weeds the lawn.

Note: Roman numerals refer to examples, lower case letters to sentences, and numbers to operations.

Example I employs both of the operations of addition (the /*wh-*/word) and resequencing in order to obtain the question form. Notice that the step just before obtaining the completely transformed statement (I-c: "What time it is") does not show both operations being employed. This is exactly what is produced in early attempts at question formation; the attention is upon adding the new element, while the word order remains unchanged. Example II illustrates usage of the operations of substitution, addition, and resequencing of elements. The first important substitution requires the knowledge that the time concept can be expressed in two different ways (present tense auxiliary + participle or the simple present tense of the verb). The operation here is that of identity, albeit implicit. Substitution of new forms also requires the speaker to *delete* the previous form, otherwise the verb would be expressed twice ("The girl *waters* the flowers get *watered*").

Finally, example III illustrates several levels of deletion and substitution, while at the same time the verb phrase is constantly expanding. A later development in the operations which are employed is further elaboration or permutation of these noun and verb phrase elements. In summary, the operations for all three examples at the transformational level are the ones which predominate at ages four through seven: addition, substitution, and permutation.

Other cognitive operations continue to puzzle the four- to seven-year-old child and correspond to difficulties in linguistic expression. Causal relations, for example, are frequently expressed simply by juxtaposing linguistic statements, rather than making explicit the causal relations, as Piaget's research (1928) on causal conjunctions has shown. These relations follow our earlier claim that the sequence of language elements is the most basic form of expressing cognitive relations; that is, *causal relations*, in this instance, are changed into *consecutive relations*. One of Piaget's sentence completion tasks evoked the following response from a six-and-a-half-year-old (italics is the response): "I teased the dog, because *he bit me.*" Although he meant "first, I teased the dog and then he bit me," the causal relations become lost in his consecutive relations analysis and mode of linguistic expression. How are we to be sure that the difficulty does not lie solely at the expressive (language) level and that cognitively the logical relations are straight?

One source to which Piaget likes to look for children's awareness of relations is drawings. Generally, Piaget concludes that certain characteristics of drawings represent the same problems as the language gaps: Both lack a *synthesis* of elements. Casual relations, even in the child's drawings, are depicted as consecutive events, indicating that the analysis is in terms of a discrete set of elements, rather than as one event in which the elements are synthesized. The six-year-old's drawing of a bicycle, for example, contains most of the essential details. However, the frame, two wheels, pedals, chain, and cog-wheel are juxtaposed without any order: the chain is drawn alongside the cog-wheel, and the pedals are left unattached. The relationships among elements are not made explicit; the elements are depicted as "they go together," and the relations do not extend beyond the explicit details (Piaget, 1928, pp. 17, 58).

The following two figures illustrate examples of enumeration of elements and of synthesis of elements in children's drawings.

The task was for nursery school children to draw (represent) a specific activity of the nursery school day (juice and cracker time). The teachers queried children about their drawings and labeled them as the children told what each graphic representation symbolized. As seen, each of these children has depicted all of the elements adequately. Figure 5.1 even contains the juice pitcher, as well as the glass into which the juice was poured. The relationships among the picture elements are not made explicit, however, as they are in the second child's drawing. While Figure 5.2 does not contain the juice pitcher, it does add the chair and a person to the scene. So while Figure 5.2 relates elements (crackers and glass *on* table, person *on* chair *at* table), it also adds another feature, the *participant* in juice and cracker time. Interestingly, the person depicted at the table is not the artist, as might be expected of a truly egocentric child. The objective reality of another person's sitting at a table eating crackers and drinking juice are synthesized in Figure 5.2.

Let us summarize the third period of language and thought

Figure 5.1
Enumerated elements in a child's drawing

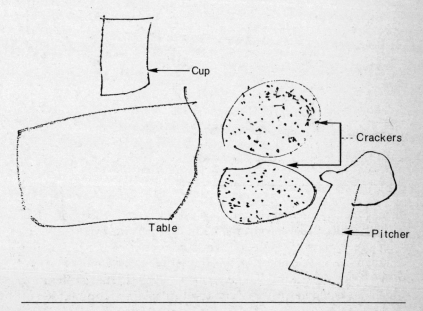

Figure 5.2
Synthesized elements in a child's drawing

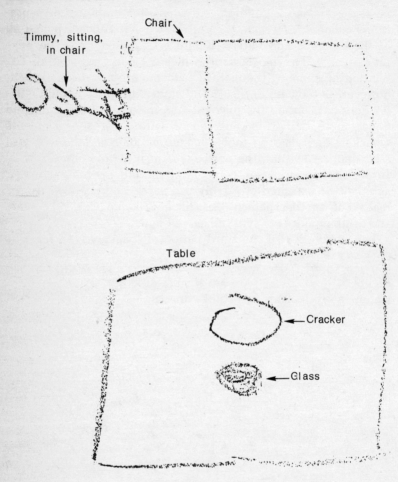

development and then briefly discuss the implications of what at first appear to be convergent, but which are eventually revealed as divergent, systems. We have presented our discussion of language and thought in the format of a developing system, rather than presenting language as a fully acquired system for which we could retrospectively try to explain the processes of linguistic comprehension and production. The developmental format was intended to clarify the evolution of linguistic and cognitive systems. First, the difference between language and other symbolic functions was pointed out. Images as symbols may be linked by common referents, but they do not form a structured system as language does. Also, we pointed out that language is a way of representing what is known, but as Sinclair has emphasized, language is "itself an object to be known" (1971, p. 24). In terms of the child's strategies in learning language, we have discussed the ability to tune into a linguistic environment and to extract the regularities from the speech of others, thereby inferring rules. The emergence of comprehension and the ability to generate sentences are aspects of this system which become the object of study; the way in which the child goes about learning language and constructing sentences provides a means of studying the development of thought and the evolution of knowledge.

Language Development in the School Years

It may seem obvious to the reader that language development continues beyond the periods we have outlined. Yet, as recently as 1963, researchers were still reporting that "all the basic structures used by adults to generate their sentences can be found in the grammar of nursery school children" (Menyuk, 1963, p. 419). Our goal in this chapter thus far has been to follow the major growth and transition periods for language and cognitive development and discuss the ways in which the two coincide. An additional goal is to extend principles of development to educational theory and practice. To this end, we will now highlight the changes which occur in children's language during the school years, for changes do indeed occur. Since language, by this time, involves an extremely elaborated symbol system, our brief analysis will be of three components of language: phonology, syntax, and semantics.

Phonological Development

One of the most neglected areas of language development in children has been the study of the development of the rule systems for learning to combine speech sounds. Research of recent years illustrates that this learning is not well developed even by age five (Templin, 1957). The first major phonological development period is from three- to four-years-old, followed by a plateau from four- to five-years-old, followed by another developmental spurt from five- to seven-years-old, with children's articulation abilities achieving a similarity to those of adults by age eight. While the child may actually possess the complex system of phonological rules by age seven or eight, she still lacks basic information about her language system such as information related to abstractions or the relation of units of sound (phoneme) and units of meaning (morpheme). For example, the "s" sound signifies plural and the /s/ marker on words is the graphic signifier of plurality. While this example is very simplistic, it represents the problem of relating sound units to units of meaning in language growth. Children cannot break up the word unit; contrary to adults, children have not developed the conceptual ability to abstract the phonemes from the word unit (Palermo and Molfese, 1972). It must be remembered that the child who does not perform certain sounds cannot automatically be labeled as learning-impaired, for it is not so obvious as formerly believed that the child at age six, for example, has a fully developed phonological system. In fact, we know that certain articulatory difficulties (such as /s/, /sh/, /l/, and /r/) are to be expected at various ages. We also know that certain phonological characteristics are typical of subculture populations (dialects), including lower-class, white, English-speaking groups. The differences do not reveal a learning disability for a particular subcultural population but rather a normal language development that happens to be specific to that dialect.

Syntactic Development

While in 1963, psychologists were writing that most of basic grammatical structures are developed by the nurseryschool years (Menyuk, 1963), current data suggest that very important syntactic advances (that is, rules for combining words into sentences) occur long after five years of age. Longitudinal studies (Loban, 1966) show increased speech performance with age, more complete syntactic structures in the speech of children, more complex structures in speech, and greater variation in structures and in vocabulary. O'Donnell (1967) showed that the greatest periods of syntactic development after the initial three to five years of age growth period occur between kindergarten and first grade, and then again between fifth and seventh grades. During these two later growth periods, two principal kinds of changes are observed: (1) increase in new grammatical constructions and (2) increase in frequencies of formerly infrequent grammatical construction (Palermo and Molfese, 1972). Menyuk has shown that specific kinds of changes involve fuller development of auxiliary verb forms (*have*) and better control of conjunctions such as *if* and *so*. She also documented about 17 grammatical transformations which were restricted in children's development as compared with adult forms, as well as identifying forms which are used almost exclusively by children. An example of the latter is redundancy within grammatical structures, such as "She took it away the hat." It has been suggested that in the development of indefinite forms of reference (such as the indefinite pronoun *it*) children include both pronoun and noun forms to ensure communication of the message.

Studies which have separated comprehension and production aspects of language development, as we did in our analysis earlier in this chapter, have also reported developmental trends among six-, eight-, ten-, and twelve-year-olds for *comprehension* capacities in various syntactic structures, for example, passive voice, negation, and so on (Slobin, 1966). Also, *production* performance changes significantly on reversible-passive constructions between four and nine years of age (Turner and Rommetveit, 1967a,b).

Katz and Brent (1968) have looked at another kind of syntactic development which appears to extend beyond the three- to five-years-old period. They were concerned with the different interpretations of relational concepts as used by children throughout the age range from first through sixth grades. The data clearly suggested that the meanings of *because*, *then*, and *therefore* change between first and sixth grades, although all children in the range used all the words. Among first-graders, the temporal relationships expressed by *because* are better understood than the causal relations. The younger children appear to have no more than a sequential (as opposed to a causal) meaning for *because*; among the younger children, all three of these words are used as if they mean *then*, with no understanding of them as indicators of causal relationships. Similar studies were carried out for other relational terms such as *but, although, except,* and *unless.* The results of syntactic development studies point to a continued, close interrelationship between general cognitive development and the comprehension and production of syntactic forms; while all forms are used, their meanings differ as the individual becomes more psychologically differentiated. Such differentiation is not complete among nine-year-olds nor among high schoolers. Confirmation with respect to language development may be found both in studies which report that nine-year-olds interpret relational terms such as *unless* as if the word *if* is being used, and in the research which shows high school students having difficulty understanding (comprehending) the term *or.* Palermo and Molfese (1972) state that such evidence suggests that "syntactic and/or semantic development extends over an unexpectedly long period" (p. 421).

The major changes which appear in syntactic development during the school years, then, occur between five- and eight-years-old, and again between ten and thirteen years of age. What are the cognitive changes which were pointed out in Chapters 3 and 4 as appearing during these ages? The reader is encouraged to look again at these discussions, for Piaget has stressed that it is no coincidence that language and cognitive development have comparable developmental and transitional periods.

Semantic Development

The third area in which significant development occurs is in semantics, the study of meaning in language. Additions to the vocabulary are made throughout the life span. However, this is not of concern here. While vocabulary growth is a gross measure of semantic development, of more importance here is the change in features which mark *meaning* differences among words. For example, *wish* and *want* are nearly synonymous, but there is an expansion of the semantic system which occurs during the later period of language development which leads the individual to know that she can say "The girl wishes that he would go home" but not "The chair wishes that he would go home," or "The girl wants that he would go home." The expansion of the semantic system involves both extensions of individual word meanings, and more importantly, the interrelations of words with other words. Studies have consistently shown that children around five or six years of age may use words (such as sweet, cold, or crooked) but that they use them exclusively in the physical domain. Not until around age eleven or twelve do children fully see that words can have multiple functions, that is, that physical-descriptive words can be applied in the psychological sense (cold person, crooked person, sweet person). Asch and Nerlove (1960) conclude that children first master the object reference aspect of double-function words, then the psychological aspect of terms (still keeping the two systems completely separate), and finally the dual relational aspects of the words. They suggest that the two related meanings of the words are acquired independently by the children first, and that only later are the common features of the meanings integrated (Palermo and Molfese, 1972). Considerable evidence exists to further corroborate that concrete and functional definitions of words do not give way to abstract definitions until ten to twelve years of age. Palermo and Molfese point to such research as evidence for the relation between "semantic development and general conceptual development" (p. 424). The relationship appears to be especially evident as children move from primarily concrete operational thought to more abstract thought at eleven or twelve years of age.

Language and Knowledge

The principal parts of this chapter about language and representational thought have been organized around action-based learning between birth and five years of age. We did this not only because Piaget has said that the verbalizations which accompany thinking remain centered upon action until ages eleven or twelve (Piaget, 1962), but also because research data dealing with the major significant advances at this time support this view. Considerable language growth persists beyond the initial learning period, but this development is closely related to precursors outlined in terms of three major periods of early language change. We outlined the action basis of language learning in the preverbal child and then discussed how meaning or the semantic base derives from the action patterns of sensorimotor development, focusing principally upon meaning and its dependence upon word sequence and contextual bases. Early semantic development relates directly to Piaget's model of preoperational thought in children (see Chapter 3). From that point on, we took a more structural approach to language learning and looked at the evolution of the language children begin to utter, centering our discussion upon the precursors to syntax (rules of word combination) and the emergence of speech forms. Language was then discussed in terms of the development which continues through the school years, and in that section it was shown that most of the growth is an elaboration of development which occurred during the preschool years. As an epilogue, we should now like to consider the relationship between language and knowledge.

One of the important developments to come out of the first stage of language (see p. 112) is the nomination or labeling function. Children, at this time, learn that a name refers to an object or an event. What we emphasized in that discussion is that labeling is a very narrow language function, always occuring in the immediate present and functioning as an apparent behavior. In effect, nomination is not operating beyond the enumeration of the perceptible environment or the child's mental images: it is not *re-presentational* in any semiotic way at this time. As Lenneberg (1971) has pointed out, knowing the name of something does not imply knowledge of the underlying principles for constructing the class to which that object belongs. Lenneberg wrote: "Knowing that a certain man is called Pablo Casals is no indication that the knower can understand the class *cellist*, or the class *man*, for that matter" (p. 165).

The important feature of the second stage, during the development of meaning, is partly the extension of this nomination function, the assignation of labels to the Actor, the event (Action), and to the Object. What we stress as the critical feature, however, was the *relationships* mapped among the elements at this time. Word order is an important feature in marking these relationships. Knowing labels and names is not sufficient for knowing how language works. The word order relationships are the critical missing feature of ape sign language (Brown, 1973). Although the chimpanzee "language" of which we read so much today indicates that primates other than man are capable of signing many events and even of adding signs to express relatedness of events, the results of one study (Gardner and Gardner, 1969) indicate that the signs occur in random order and do not imply that the chimpanzee has knowledge of specific relationships among *sentence* elements: the elements all go together, but the signs do not specify *how* they go together. All the appropriate signs for *baby, cup*, and *drink* might be present, but the relatedness of these signs cannot be inferred from the mere sequence of their expression. For example, *baby, drink*, and *cup* can be interpreted in the Actor—Action—Object paradigm which we have used in our discussions. The relationships here are, then, that someone (*baby*) is doing something (*drink*) which involves the object (*cup*), baby—drink—cup. However, the same signs from the chimpanzee might also be used to express a possessor-object relationship (baby's cup) and action (drink). Lenneberg extends this criticism to animal responses to stereotyped verbal commands. An animal's response to "beg" or "heel" is analogous to a child's response to a proper name: The verbalization is very specific and the response is stereotyped. Consequently, Lenneberg states, the most important function of language is missing; no *relations* are mapped which would allow for either generality or productivity.

Language, as it develops during and after the third stage, is marked by the emergence of the linguistic system of *syntax*. Syntax is concerned, principally, with the tools for expressing *relationships*, but we do not wish to imply that it is the only means of expressing relationships verbally. On the contrary, we stated that the early knowledge of Agent—Action—Object was a primitive expression of linguistic relations. The lexicon also expresses relations: "infant" stands for "young being," "inexperienced," and so on (Lenneberg, 1971, pp. 166–167). But the structured system for generating a productive language is contained in the functional units of syntax.

Our discussion of a transformational grammar and a structured system that the individual employs for constructing or

generating numerous linguistic expressions has implied that
language must be understood in terms of *operations*, rather than
as a *product*. The cognitive system also has been presented, in
this and previous chapters, as constituted of *processes* rather
than products. It is not feasible, as Lenneberg points out (1969),
to consider language and cognition as isolated processes: Both
are capacities for perception, storage, and retrieval in cognition
are not isolated from perception and memory processes of language. The divergence in these two systems illustrates how
language develops out of sensorimotor intelligence into a system
for expressing relationships. The semiotic function of language
extends beyond the symbol level of images, and even beyond
the mapping of multiple relations among words ["the word *is*
may indicate (1) prediction-attribution, (2) similarity, (3)
equality, (4) identity, (5) equinumerosity" (Lenneberg, 1971,
p. 168)]. It is the structural system which allows language to
become *prepositional* and to organize thought into a system of
logical relations.

Education during the school years extends language beyond
mere labeling by extending definitions beyond the concrete or
functional attributes to include categorical information which
relates one object to others and inferential aspects which extrapolate critical information about objects. We would not be so
vociferous as Kohnstamm (1970) who has said that "the truly
pedagogic adult should keep his mouth shut, except for asking
the child diagnostic questions" (p. 371). In fact, the adult aids
in rendering language representational by helping (*not* showing) the child discover relationships and by helping to map
those relationships through language functions. Teachers can
facilitate the understanding of class-inclusion concepts, for example, as they guide the child's understanding of verbal directions which stipulate "everyone but X should be in the circle
for this game" as opposed to "everyone including X should now
be in the circle." The child is thereby guided in learning to
present thoughts and to re-present experiences so that the sequences and relational terms convey the child's logic and become
increasingly understandable to other persons. Ultimately the
tutor can aid the child in learning to manipulate language
symbols mentally in order to hypothesize about what might be.

Chapter 6 The Development of Representational Thought: A Special Conceptualization– The Distancing Hypothesis

Introduction

The previous chapters have described Piagetian theory of cognitive development in some detail. It has probably become evident by now that Piaget has produced a most extensive statement touching on virtually every aspect of the development of intelligence. He has provided new insights, particularly regarding the early development of representational thought.

Recall that when Piaget describes the semiotic function, he is describing a most critical shift in the child's thought from sensorimotor to representational thinking. This thought process depicts a central function that enables the child to begin the process of thinking in symbolic terms, to re-present previous experience and to begin to anticipate the future.

While Piaget identifies the remarkable transition from sensorimotor to representational thought and acknowledges the significance of social factors influencing the course of this transition, he has not yet documented or investigated the particular experiences important for the growth of representational thought.

The Problem

In this chapter we wish to address this question: what classes of social behaviors foster the development of representational thought? We propose that the class of behaviors which require the developing child to think in terms of the nonobservable, nonpresent, in terms of symbols and/or signs, are those behaviors used by significant others which require the child to separate self from ongoing present to create mental representations of physical, social, and personal reality. We shall refer to this class of behaviors as *distancing behaviors,* and the proposition that the extent to which they do foster the development of representational thought leads to the *distancing hypothesis* (Sigel, 1970).

We shall discuss this class of behaviors in more detail by showing the empirical basis for an idea which eventuated into a theoretical problem, then led to the translation of these ideas into a practical educational program.

Background of the Problem

In 1954 in a paper entitled "The Dominance of Meaning" Sigel reported that young elementary school children (ages seven, nine, and eleven), when presented with groups of items varying in level of symbolization (toys, black and white photographs, words), sorted the items similarly. For example, when the children were presented with a group of pictures or with three-dimensional miniature objects and asked to classify them in any way they wished, the same categories were used whether the stimuli were pictures or objects. It was concluded that the children established a meaning for the object and this meaning influenced the classifications in spite of differences in media or levels of symbolization. Similar results were found in their classification of a word list enumerating the objects. Thus, three-dimensional objects or the pictures or the words would be grouped similarly, ignoring differences in mode of representation (Sigel, 1954). These results made sense since children do recognize and identify pictures of objects in books, magazines, and other sources. The validity of these findings was shattered, however, when a picture task was used with a group of impoverished six-year-old black children. The impoverished children did label the pictures correctly but surprisingly had difficulty in grouping them on the basis of any obvious similarity. Often the children did not create any groupings. More frequently the children linked one picture to another using a theme. For example, the picture of the cowboy and the picture of the horse were linked together "because the cowboy rides the horse"; then another item would be added which would have no relevance to the cowboy, only to the horse. For example, "The horse goes with the stagecoach—you need a horse to pull it, and the man goes with the stagecoach to drive it"; and so a new item is added as a link in a chain. Hence the term "chaining" describes this type of classification behavior (Bruner and Olver, 1963).

Thus, contradictory results emerged. One group of children did treat all the items irrespective of medium of presentation equivalently, but the second group did not. Why not? The fact that the poor children could label the items correctly but chained their responses suggested that they had difficulty in forming classes, but not because they did not recognize the pictures. Did this reflect difficulty in classifying or difficulty working with pictures? Why did they not treat the pictures as pictures of something? So, the first order of business was to determine whether the difficulty was in classification itself, or if difficulty was due to the use of pictures as stimuli.

Groups of middle- and lower-class black and white children were involved in a large scale study. Each child was given the Object Categorization Test (OCT) and the Picture Categorization Test (PCT). The procedure used required the children to label the items in each condition. Then the examiner selected one of the items from the array and asked the child to find as many items from the array that were similar to or belonged to the items selected by the examiner. The child was asked to give a reason for his or her choices. Rarely did children have difficulty labeling the objects or the pictures.

It was found that middle-class children (black or white) tended to classify objects and pictures equivalently and provided reasons for their groupings. Lower-class children, particularly black children, while able to group three dimensional objects, consequently did poorly on the PCT (Sigel, Anderson, and Shapiro, 1966; Sigel and McBane, 1967; Sigel and Olmsted, 1970a).

The consistency of these results was perplexing in view of the studies which report the ease with which children learn to identify pictures of objects (Hochberg and Brooks, 1962; and Reece and Lipsitt, 1970). Results of studies with nonliterate groups report that pictures are not readily identifiable, suggesting that responding to pictorial representation is neither simple nor automatic (Miller, 1973).

What is of particular interest is the fact that all the children in each of the studies could label the pictures correctly. Thus, the discrimination of distinctive cues and employing the correct label was not at issue. The issue was clearly the discrepancy in performance between the picture task and the three-dimensional task.

Perhaps it would help if we examined the task demands. In each set of conditions (OCT, PCT) the child is asked to search for one or more criteria by which to group the items. The child is free to select from among any of the objects as well as to make personal decisions as to the criteria to use, color, form, function, or another. In the OCT tactile test, visual and spatial cues are available allowing direct action on the objects. Piaget argues that "the child acts on the objects, but the knowledge he gains is not derived from these objects; it is derived from the action bearing on the objects, which is not the same at all" (Piaget and Inhelder, 1970, p. 124). This physical action precedes internalized mental actions—an invariant sequence as prelude to logico-mathematical thought. Classification is an instance of this thought. Pictures as representations do not allow for these actions, rather classification of pictures requires internalized action.

The child from a poverty level background may not have internalized the actions, and hence is less able to categorize the pictorial stimuli. Apparently, the meaning and subsequent class membership attributed to an object and its pictorial representation are a function of the way it is represented. Thus, we come full circle to the basic issues stated by Arnheim (1969):

Have we a right to take for granted that a picture shows what

Figure 6.1
Categorization test objects

it represents regardless of what it is like and who is looking? The problem is most easily ignored for photographic material. We feel assured that since the pictures have been taken mechanically, they must be correct; and since they are realistic, they can be trusted to show all the (relevant) facts; and since every human being has practiced from birth how to look at the world, he can have no trouble with life-like pictures. Do the assumptions hold true? (p. 309)

Using evidence from anthropology, art education, and biographical anecdotal material, Arnheim answers his own question by saying "*comprehension* of photographic pictures cannot be taken for granted" (Arnheim, 1969, p. 309, our italics).

If Arnheim is right, to understand that a picture is a representation of an object or an event is the first issue. How, then, do children learn to read pictures?

Secondly, why when the child labels the picture correctly, does the child not react to the picture as an instance of a class? Thus the picture of a horse is not classified in the category "animal" which a three-dimensional representation of the horse might be. This ability to treat objects and pictures as equivalent is referred to as "representational competence" (Sigel and Olmsted, 1970b).

The Conceptual Answer: The Distancing Hypothesis

In a previous paper entitled, "The Distancing Hypothesis: A Causal Hypothesis for the Acquisition of Representational Thought" (Sigel, 1970), the argument was developed that although representational thought is generic to the human, the quality and rate of its development depend upon the individual's life experiences.

The argument to be presented here is that the development of representational thinking is fostered by those life experiences which create temporal, spatial, and psychological distance between the self and object. *Distancing* was proposed as the construct defining those classes of behaviors or events which function to separate the individual from the immediate behavioral environment. For example, asking a child to reconstruct a previous experience poses a challenge to the child to bring an awareness of previous experiences. Thus, the child separates or *distances* himself at that moment from the present in order to reconstruct the past. The child is responding to the *distancing behavior*, to the request to re-present previous experience through separating the self mentally from the here and now.

The concept of distancing is not original with us. It has been used by Egon Brunswick in perceptual studies (Hammond,

1966) and in the discussion of symbol formation by Werner and Kaplan (1963) and casually mentioned by Piaget (1962) in the development of symbolic thought. The fact that three investigators independently arrived at this construct to denote the separation of the individual from the environment, perhaps indicates its importance. Each of these investigators is essentially asking a similar question: How does the organism reconstruct reality and objectify a personal environment in symbolic form?

Distancing is a demand feature of environmental events which serves to stimulate, activate, and energize organismic capabilities to represent experiences. The representation is achieved through reconstructing, anticipating, or integrating experiences in the immediate present.

THE MEANING OF REPRESENTATION. Representation is a frequently used word that has many meanings and many uses. A picture is a representation, as is a sculpture. Paintings are referred to as representational or nonrepresentational depending on whether they depict a shared reality. We also use the word to describe our political system, referring to Representatives in the Congress of the United States. Each of these examples shares a common feature, each has an object, an event, an idea, or a group for which the picture, the event, the idea is the referent. The picture of an apple has as its referent the "real three-dimensional" apple just as the portrait has as its referent a real life individual, and so on. Such representations are external. We also have internal representations. We have mental activity which is representational, such as images or the mental use of words to express ideas. All of these are representations since they too stand for something. In each of these examples, the term representation is used to identify a relationship between an object, event, or idea and its sign or symbol. (See Chapter 5 for a discussion of representation and language.)

Representation can also be the act of *re-presenting*, that is, bringing into awareness or into consciousness ideas, words, songs, or any previous thoughts. Recalling experiences and retelling them is an example of recall as a re-presentation to one's self of previous experience. Retelling the story in words is also re-presenting the experience in a verbal medium. Re-presenting involves the mental activity of bringing forth any experience into awareness.

In our case, "Is looking at a picture a case of re-presentation?" The answer is yes. A picture provides only a limited amount of information about an object. To understand that the item in the picture is a *representation* of another item is one requirement for understanding the picture. Thus, in the Picture Categorizing Test, when the child sees a picture of a pencil, she must realize that it is a representation of a "real" pencil. To demonstrate knowledge about the pencil as a solid object that can be used for writing and that one tip is an eraser used for something else requires a re-presentation of experience with the pencil, either having seen it, used it, been told about it, or all of these. Thus, to know or understand the meaning of an external representation requires a re-presentation of the elaborations of relevant information by which to understand the picture.

SIGNIFICANCE OF REPRESENTATION FOR HUMAN ADAPTATION. Representational thinking plays a critical role in thought since "it is characterized by the fact that it goes beyond the present, extending the field of adaption both in space and time. In other words, it evokes what lies outside the immediate perceptual and active field" (Piaget, 1962, p. 273). Representation becomes the "shorthand" by which the human mind can transcend space and time, reconstruct the past, anticipate and plan for the future because these activities are done through the representational process. Although Piaget also restricts the term mental representation to mental or memory images, other writers such as Werner and Kaplan extend it to include language (Piaget, 1962; Werner and Kaplan, 1963). Irrespective of such differences, the basic meaning is that representation evokes mental activities in some form.

Basically, representational thought is a vital human function. Without it, civilizations could not have developed. Art, science, technology, as well as the demands of everyday life require going beyond what is seen, felt, or heard toward the nonpresent, inobservable, inaudible. The artist painting a scene, the engineer building a bridge, the author writing a novel, all engage in re-presenting experiences and representing them in some form. In everyday living we plan for tomorrow, reconstruct yesterday, respond to external representation, in fact, employ many of the same cognitive processes alluded to above. It is difficult to conceive of human beings in any situation in which some representation does not occur. The central role of representation is well expressed by Cassirer (1957).

Representational activity becomes all knowledge in a sense because knowledge includes and presupposes representation. The representing of an object is quite a different act from the mere handling of it. The latter demands nothing but a definite series of acts of body movements coordinated with each other or followed by each other. It is a matter of habit acquired by constantly repeating, unvarying performance of a certain act. . . . To represent a thing, it is not enough to be able to manipulate it in the right way for practical use; we must have a general conception of the object regarded from different angles in order to find its relation to other objects. We must locate it and determine its position in a general system (Cassirer, 1957, pp. 67–68).

ROLE OF EXPERIENCE IN DEVELOPMENT OF REPRESENTATIONAL THOUGHT. What is at issue is not whether individuals represent or re-present experiences, but the quality of both the re-presentation and representation. The fact that individuals possess the ability to run does not mean we are all track stars. We believe that representational thought, like running, is influenced by experience which includes training.

The problem then is to determine whether the various response levels and quality exist; that is, how do children respond to different representational stimuli? We discovered (see pp. 162–163) that lowerclass black children had more difficulty classifying pictorial representations than their three-dimensional referents, and also had difficulty in dealing with conservation problems in which representational thought is relevant. Yet, there was no doubt that these children had memory, that these children had an awareness of the past as well as an awareness of the future. This evidence indicates that responses to external representations may vary to the degree that children have the necessary prerequisite to respond to different representational forms, in spite of the fact that some fundamental competence for representational thought exists.

Why should this be the case with these children? Fortunately, a set of interviews with the parents of these children was available and reviewed to evaluate the type of interactions that occur between parents and children. It was found that few if any of the parent-child interactions involved strategies which were *distancing*. Techniques of child management, as well as teaching strategies, emphasize the present and the apparent, with little attention for planning or representing anticipated outcomes. The adults are also highly authoritarian, treating the child as a passive respondent rather than an active participant. These characterizations are the opposite of what was found among middle-class parents. In essence, the middle-class parents seemed to be using distancing behaviors while the lower socioeconomic group tended not to do so.

The argument, then, is given that representation is a generic process, opportunities children have to experience various representational demands are variable, depending on the quality and quantity of relevant interactions with significant others. This brings us to the distancing hypothesis which holds that the quantity and quality of distancing behaviors will foster the development of representational competence. To round out the rationale for this hypothesis, aside from our review of different child-rearing practices, it is necessary to spell out how distancing behaviors in fact foster representational competence.

REPRESENTATIONAL COMPETENCE AS ADAPTATION. We have already proposed that representational thought is generic to the human organism and also argued that it is vital for human existence. Now let us entertain the proposition that the condition which activates the organism to respond possesses demand characteristics. Representational behaviors have to meet that demand. Representation is to be construed as an organismic response as breathing is a physiological response to the body's demand for oxygen. So too is representational thought a cognitive response to a psychological demand.

Asking a child to reconstruct an experience, or plan a career, a party, or any activity are examples of the kinds of events which activate representational thought. In order to respond to any distancing demand, the child has to re-present the event. By so doing, the child adapts to the demands presented by the environment.

The child adapts to the demands as expressed in the physical world and in a linguistic environment. Distancing behaviors can be expressed verbally. The language is used and presented by the significant others (such as parents, teachers, older siblings, and others) who structure the child's environment verbally. And simultaneously, the child has experiences with a world of three-dimensional objects. The content of what is represented in these verbal encounters and the form they take are the substance of the child's psychosocial milieu. The principles defining the acquisition and consequent development of representational responses may be similar in any environment, since everyone has to adapt to a social-cultural environment. The content, however, of what is represented and how representations are interpreted will vary among cultures. The child in an African bush culture or the child in middle-class urban America may each be told stories about nonexistent and nonpresent matters. While the story told to the child in the African bush culture may not portray clear-cut distance discriminations in time between the child, the child may believe that the events are happening or have just happened, or will immediately happen. In contrast, the middle-class North American child may hear verbs denoting the past and the parents' response may consistently reinforce the distinction between the present and the past and reality and fantasy. Thus, a particular event may take on considerable differences in meaning by virtue of the style and mode of presentation. The degree to which children can assimilate and use information depends on their particular developmental status. Here we return to Piaget's developmental stages in order to help us conceptualize the kind and quality of information that a child can assimilate. Implicit in the above discussion is the concept that representational thinking is generically a response mechanism and is activated by appropriate external stimulation. The basic assumption is that representational competence will emerge to the degree to which the environment activates it and the degree to which the quality of the activation is acquired through learning. Thus, the specific actions of significant adults through demands made on the child will activate the representational potential capability. These interactions, for a significant class of experience for the child, give rise to representational competence.

Our second question is, "What is the relationship between the broader environment and representational performance?" Representational thought is adaptive, but we need to distinguish what and how the environment can be structured to effect its development.

Contextual Conditions for Distancing Behavior To Be Effective

Distancing behaviors can be pervasive and functionally relevant provided two conditions exist: (1) This class of behaviors engages the child; (2) this class of behaviors is made appropriate and relevant to the varying contexts, such as social or physical.

Distancing behaviors, however, can only be effective, irrespective of frequency or intensity of usage, if the child is attentive and receptive to the message. Receptivity is further dependent on the child's motivational and cognitive states. From the motivational perspective, the child has to be willing and interested in the message. Cognitively the child has to have the capability to process the information. A barrage of exposures can fall on deaf ears or blind eyes unless the child is affectively prepared to "tune" in. The child's relationship to the relevant adult or peer and interest in the action or tasks are very important in determining the impact of distancing behavior. Not only is the motivational aspect relevant but also the capabilities of the child to process and respond to the information.

The child responds to distancing behaviors differentially, since a match is necessary between the particular behavior and the child's capability in *knowing* what is involved. "Any kind of action manifests some knowing" (Furth, 1970, p. 243). This knowing can operate from the sensorimotor level, to operational knowing which is "dissociated from external actions to a certain degree; in this sense it is interiorized knowing, and if language would permit, it would be more accurate to say 'disexternalized' knowing. From now on, human knowing increasingly takes on the characteristics of structures that can be called abstract in that they refer to the 'form' rather than the 'content' of an activity" (Furth, 1970, p. 243). Thus, distancing behaviors function to effect representational response when the child is motivated to receive the message and when the message is comprehensible.

RELATIONSHIP OF DISTANCING BEHAVIORS TO REPRESENTATIONAL COMPETENCE. It will be recalled that representational competence is a broad term referring to the child's ability to deal with external representations, such as pictures, graphic reproductions, and so on, and internal re-presentations, that is, constructions of past or future actions. The link between distancing behaviors and the stimuli can now be made. Thus, *distancing behaviors,* particularly when employing *distal stimuli,* contribute to the development of *representational competence.*

For clarification a distinction should be made between distancing behaviors and distance as expressed in the stimuli. The distinction has been made elsewhere and we quote:

For example, a cutout picture of a chair is closer to the chair or less distal, than is the word chair, simply because the latter contains no overlap of any kind with the actual reality of the chair. A photograph, for example, may be more distal than the cutout, since the cutout contains some notion of dimension or depth in its physical form, whereas the picture (photograph) only represents depth through particular visual cues. The term *distal* will be used to refer to the distance within the domain of the stimuli. Distancing refers to acts or events that may or may not employ distal stimuli to create the separation or differentiation between self and the physical environment. In sum, then, two terms are introduced, distal, referring to the nature of the stimulus, and distancing, referring to those classes of behaviors and events that separate the person from the environment (Sigel, 1970, p. 112).

Through similar engagements the child also learns one other important rule: that objects and events can be represented in different modalities. This rule is crucial to the development of symbolic behaviors. For without knowing this, the child is not able to respond in appropriate and relevant terms. To know that a picture represents a concrete referent means that the child may deal with the picture in ways consonant with the object. Thus, if children realize, for example, that picture and object are members of the same class, that is, equivalent in terms of their meaning, the picture can be substituted for the object. Maps or blueprints are similar—responses in the form of location and direction are representations of geographic or architectural realities.

SOME EVIDENCE FOR THE DISTANCING HYPOTHESIS AND ITS RELATION TO REPRESENTATIONAL COMPETENCE. Is there any evidence providing support for the hypothesis? Inspection of a variety of infant and preschool programs does provide suggestive evidence that is convincing and encouraging.

These programs are good sources of data since they report assessment techniques and intervention strategies. Many of them employ tests that measure those cognitive tasks involving representational skills, such as causality, verbal descriptions of events, number concepts, and others. The teaching strategies use language as a means of reconstructing events, classification skills, and so on (Blank, 1970; Fowler, 1971; Kamii, 1972; Levenstein, 1971; Miller and Dyer, 1975; Sigel, 1969; Weikart, Rogers, Adcock, and McClelland, 1970). The teachers are encouraged to elicit responses that essentially deal with nonpresent phenomena, involve temporal differentiation, and focus on integration of events—the latter requirement forces the child to disengage from the immediacy of perceptual cues, and seek alternative modes of relating events. Each of these programs has reported varying degrees of success in fostering cognitive growth.

None of these programs, however, has conceptualized the significance of their teaching strategies. Rather, they tend to describe their strategies without articulating what may be explanatory constructs.

At issue is determining the explanatory principles that can be used to define the relationship between inputs and outcomes. If explanations are relevant to the behavioral science, then identifying functional relationships is critical. One set of relevant functional relations are distancing behaviors which form the bridge between tasks (materials or requirements) and outcomes. The teaching strategies employed in many of these pre-school programs are, in fact, distancing behaviors. For example, teachers involved in programs teaching classification move from comparison of objects according to class labels, to sorting objects into sets on the basis of these class labels.

Levenstein, in a verbal interaction project, instructs teachers to have the child tell about his experiences (language represen-tation), ask and answer questions about cause-effect relations, respond verbally to pictures, and so on. These teaching tech-niques create distance through verbal modalities (Levenstein, 1971).

Marion Blank describes a program in which teaching strate-gies express the distancing construct proposed here most di-rectly. Working with children in tutorial situations the adult employs teaching strategies whereby the child is "forced" to disengage from the immediate perceptual demands. As she says, "If abstraction is to be achieved, the teaching of concepts must be structured so as to stimulate the child's mental level" (Blank, 1970, p. 8). The procedures employed to accomplish this objective were done by having the desired concept defined not by its presence, but by its relationship to a set of stimuli. For example, the child might be asked to draw something, and she might draw a circle. To encourage the development of exclu-sion, she would then be asked to draw "something other than a circle" (Blank, 1970, p. 8). Blank aims at creating "psycholog-ical distance" between the child and the material. This sep-aration is presumed to facilitate the development of abstract thinking.

These programmatic descriptions are prototypic in that they are intended to provide an environment that stimulates cogni-tive growth. Interestingly, each of these programs reports vari-ous types of "success" where success is defined in terms of in-creased intellectual competence, that is, IQ increases and so on. This is not the place to evaluate the assessment procedures, but rather focus solely on one common element: they all involve some assessment of representational thinking.

The intervention studies involved children from impoverished backgrounds. What is the evidence that distancing behaviors have any relevance for middle-class children? Donovan (1974), working with middle-class mothers, investigated the relationship between representational competence and distancing behaviors. She examined the distancing behaviors of mothers of preschool boys who scored low on tasks requiring representational competence and those who scored high. She found that the distancing behaviors of the mothers of the low performing children used teaching and disciplinary strategies that tended to focus more on the present, and provided children with little opportunity for making choices than mothers of children who were higher in representational competence.

Combining the results of this study with the preschool intervention studies adds to our confidence in the validity of the distancing hypothesis.

Application of Distancing Hypothesis to an Educational Setting

The theoretical exposition provides the background of the concept of distancing, the exposition of its relationships to the development of representational thinking. Further by extrapolating and reinterpreting previous research, there seems to be evidence for the theory. But as is too often the case, there can be a discrepancy between the theory and its application. Thus, the question arises, "How does one apply the theory to the classroom?" (Sigel, Secrist, and Forman, 1973).

The method by which this hypothesis can be put into practice is: (1) to spell out distancing behaviors and (2) define the situations in which they are used. Although we believe that any educational environment could be an appropriate one, we chose the preschool since, from a developmental perspective, systematic exposure to distancing behaviors at an early level should help set the pattern for subsequent thinking.

OBJECTIVES OF AN EDUCATIONAL MODEL. To create an educational model based on the distancing behaviors necessitated two major developments: (1) the articulation of teaching strategies which serve as distancing behaviors and (2) the use of relevant materials which help the child realize that objects and events can be represented in different modes and around which organization of lessons or curriculum units can be created to fulfill the objectives. We have opted at this time to apply these criteria to setting up a preschool program.

Articulation of teaching strategies consistent with the theory.
The teaching strategies are the primary carriers of the model,
since social interactions with adults are critical. These teaching
strategies should activate the child's representational competence and create cognitive conflicts that motivate the child to
take an active role to reduce or resolve the conflict introduced
by adult demand or expectation.

One of the most appropriate teaching strategies for accom-
plishing this objective is *guided inquiry.* Guided inquiry refers
to the use of focused questions which help build a body of
knowledge. These questions are directed toward the task at
hand, providing the child with needed guidance. For example,
imagine a situation in which children are working with "classification blocks"—a set of multi-shaped, multi-colored blocks.
The teacher, using distancing strategies, might pick up a block
and ask the child, "Tell me about what I have in my hand": in
contrast to "Can you tell me the color of the block I have in
my hand." The first question is open-ended, requiring the child
to re-present knowledge about the block with no clues from the
teacher. Further, the teacher can build on the response by further elaborative questioning. If the child says, "You have a
square in your hand," the teacher might say, "What about this
(pointing to square) tells you it is a square?" The child replies
"It has corners." The teacher chooses a triangle and asks, "Does
this have corners?" The child replies, "Yes." Then the teacher
asks, "Can we call this (triangle) then, a square?" The child
responds, "No." This discussion can go on—moving from the
general to the specific building up a knowledge base for the
child and an awareness by the teacher of what the child knows
and how the child is using that knowledge.

The *open-ended inquiry* allows the child greater opportunity
to use language as a medium with which to re-present his ideas.
An open-ended approach has to be carefully developed to avoid
undue ambiguity for the child. The teacher has to judge the
level of appropriateness depending on the child's experience and
developmental level. The point is that inquiry, guided by the
teacher's sensitivity, is a key strategy.

Inquiry describes the form of the statement by the teacher,
not its focus or message. We have identified many strategies
which by their focus or message are distancing behaviors. Strategies which involve *making inference of cause and effect, plan-*

ning for outcomes, classifying, reconstructing previous experience, transforming from one domain to another, are behaviors which contribute to the enhancement of representational behaviors.

Rather than assume that these teaching strategies are *accelerative* in nature, it might be useful to digress for a moment and distinguish between *acceleration* and *elaboration and extension* of children's competence.

Acceleration refers to making demands for which the child does not have the necessary prerequisites. Trying to teach a two-year-old to read or a three-year-old to conserve would be examples.

To elaborate or extend the child's competence necessitates identification of what the child can do through observation or careful inquiry. In this way the teacher can determine the child's knowledge base. Given that information, the teacher works within that framework by providing enriched and elaborated experiences. For example, if a child is asked if he could present some of his ideas through drawing, and he draws scribbles, the teacher would discuss these scribbles as if they are representations with no attempt to suggest or to ask for "better" or more accurate drawings. Thus, the inquiry would be, "Tell me about your picture," rather than, "Show me the person in your picture that really looks like Susie." If alternative representations are described, the child might be asked, "Can you draw it some other way?" having provided support and sincere acceptance of the first production. Basically, the teacher is working from the child's perspective as much as possible. Our argument is that growth will occur as a result of these new experiences in a coherent and integral way rather than as grafted onto an inappropriate experiential base.

To return to our basic argument of teaching strategies, we have emphasized the teacher interacting directly with the child. However, each interaction also provides a good source of environmental demands for representational thinking. Encouraging children to relate and ask questions of each other is useful. For example, two four-year-olds were fighting over the possession of a toy. After some moments of push and pull, the teacher told the children to sit quietly and talk to each other to find a way of sharing the toy. The children sat down and realized that only one of them could have it and came to the conclusion that they

Table 6.1
Distancing Strategies

Observing	"Watch . . . This is how"; examining or asking the child to examine; teacher demonstrating also: "Look at what I'm doing"
Labeling	*Naming* a singular object or event. (To be distinguished from concept labeling.); identifying, for example, "What do you call what she is doing?"
Describing	Provide elaborated information of a single instance; defining. Static; no dynamic relationships among elements, no use, not functional. "Appears like, looks like"; also describing inner states of self such as feeling (an action can be described— "What are you doing?")
interpretation	To attribute or explain meaning, such as "What do you mean?" "What does it mean to be something?"
Demonstrating	Showing primarily through action or gestures that something is to be done: "Show me how . . ."
Sequencing	*Temporal ordering* of events, as in a story or carrying out a task. Steps articulated, next, afterwards, start, begin, last
Reproducing	Construct previous experiences; the dynamic interaction of events; interdependence; functional understanding "How was it done?"
Comparing	
describing similarities	Noting ostensive common characteristics (perceptual analysis), "Are those the same?"
describing differences	Noting ostensive differences among instances (perceptual analysis)
inferring similarities	Noting nonobservational commonalities (conceptual)
inferring differences	Nonobservable differences (conceptual)

Proposing alternatives	Key words: other, another, something different from before
Combining	
symmetrical classifying	Recognition of the commonalities of a class of equivalent instances "How are these alike?"
(counting)	Counting like objects; estimating
asymmetrical classifying (counting)	Organizing instances in some sequences comparative to the previous and the subsequent instances; seriation; relative (big to small). Enumeration of number of things
synthesizing	To reconstruct components into a unified whole; explicit pulling together
Evaluating	
consequence	Assess *quality* of outcome, feasibility, or own competence; right-wrong, good-bad
affect	Assess quality of personal liking, opinion "How do you like the way it looks?"
	Evaluate the quality of a feeling state; "How do you feel about feeling sad?"
Inferring	Nonapparent, unseen properties or relationships
cause-effect	Prediction of causal relationships of instances, "How" "Why"; teacher may state cause and effect as well as infer
feelings	Prediction of how persons will feel; having to do with affect, not descriptive feelings of things
effects	Predictions of what will happen without articulation of causality; effects of a cause
Resolving conflict	Presentation of contradictory or conflicting information and resolution; problem solving
Generalizing	Application of knowledge to other settings or objects
Transforming	Changing the nature, function, appearance of instances

Planning	Arranging conditions to carry out a set of actions in an orderly way; actual carrying out of a task in which the child is involved; acting out a rule of the task (nonverbal)
Concluding	Relating actions, objects or events in a summative way; summarizing

would have to take turns. All this reasoning involved representations—the reconstructions, the anticipations of how they might behave—in effect, they planned. The children reported their conclusion to the teacher.

In sum, then, teaching strategies within the distancing framework involve guided inquiry, discovery, and transformation of those experiences with various media (art, dance, and others). Interrogations are presumed to create the necessary cognitive conflicts that should motivate children to alter or reorganize their customary responses. The task for the teacher is to know *how and when* to inquire, *how* and *when* to seek elaboration or engage in dialogue.

A major effort for the teacher would be to create an atmosphere in which children feel they are participants in decision making. In part, the guided discovery contributes to that feeling.

The use of relevant materials. The materials employed, while of secondary significance, provide support for the teaching strategies. The reason that materials are of secondary significance is because most materials, if properly used, could be employed in the program under discussion.

In order to facilitate a systematic development more easily, thinking through the choice of material is important. Principles that are relevant would be to reduce the preponderance of representational materials and increase the availability of non-representational items. In this way the children would be more challenged to invent and to discover. The argument is that too high a load of representational materials may decrease the child's need to invent new ways of thinking about objects. Boards and blocks, for example, can stimulate more representational constructions, representations re-presented in the child's internal state rather than the dependence on external representation, such as a toy truck.

Other strategies for use of materials to extend representational competence are possible for students at higher grade levels. Alternative perspectives or media that display environments in which students have to re-present ideas in other ways should enhance representational competence. Re-creating historical events in flow charts and anticipating outcomes of a physics or chemical experiment prior to carrying it out, are examples of different media being employed to represent an idea or an event. Instead of using conventional ways of reporting an event, encouraging students to find alternatives extends the task demand of the search for equivalences. In science and in thinking, the search for synthetics necessitates identifying equivalence. Essentially, the idea is that an idea can be expressed in many ways, but to fulfill such an assignment requires the development of the understanding that representations are arbitrary conventions. Alternatives may be available when we understand the cardinal rule. Objects, events, and ideas, while different, at one time can also be the same. This principle of simultaneous similarity and difference is a fundamental cognitive principle. If understood, it should lead to representational competence.

RELEVANCE TO OTHER THAN PRESCHOOL SETTINGS. Although the examples presented are weighted in favor of preschool use, the principles involved are by no means limited to that educational setting. It seems reasonable to asume that creation of a dialogue atmosphere in which students and teachers engage in mutual guided discovery, should also foster representational thinking at every educational level. Essentially the rationale underlying the theoretical position in this discussion is that activating or learning to become an *active participant* in the learning process is critical. Once so engaged it is necessary to think in representational terms.

We do not wish to create the impression that teaching strategies are the sole means of applying the distancing hypothesis to other than preschool environments. Knowledge of a subject matter must be involved. The distancing teaching strategies are teaching methods which necessitate a knowledge base.

Recall that, for Piaget, knowledge was divided into three

areas, social, physical and logico-mathematical. Social knowledge is the knowledge of the society, the cultural conventions; physical knowledge is the knowledge of the physical reality, the physical forces and events, such as space, time, or physical objects; and logico-mathematical knowledge is the reasoning, the use of the mental operations we discussed in Chapters 2, 3, and 4.

Since "no form of knowledge, not even perceptual knowledge, constitutes a simple copy of reality, because it always includes a process of assimilation to previous structures" (Piaget, 1971, p. 4), the student acquires some knowledge by having the information made available by others. Social rules, history, names of objects, places, and events, are types of information that cannot be discovered. However, once such information is available and assimilated, the individual can order it (seriate), classify it (classification), and discover relations among the various knowledges (relations). Thus, at primary, secondary, and college levels, two types of engagement can occur—the assimilation of the knowledge through reading, listening, and actively interacting with relevant experiences; and transforming this knowledge into a symbol system. The processes of transformation come about, in part, through active participation of the student and the teacher. The teacher prepares or provides material with which the student works. The teacher decides what the needed knowledge is, the sequencing of this knowledge, and the format for their presentation.

Further, by using distancing teaching strategies the teacher may help the child re-present the material, reorganize it, and reconstitute it for utilization; in essence, provide the opportunity for developing representational competencies.

Let us apply these ideas to an example in social studies for the elementary grades. It will become readily apparent that the principles guiding this example are applicable to virtually any other area of knowledge. Let us say that the teacher is interested in teaching the concept of "humans need shelter," that is, that humans universally have to solve the problem of protecting themselves from the elements, such as heat, cold, rain, and so on.

Since children may not have articulated the concept "shelter," the first task is to direct attention to the child's own home and to identify its "sheltering" functions. This can be done through inquiry, making articulate that which may be taken for granted, by measuring the child's knowledge of what functions a house serves. After the teacher asks about people in other climates, the child may have to be told that some people live in environments that are extremely cold (Arctic) or extremely hot (equatorial Africa). This information cannot be obtained through direct experience. It requires reading, listening to lectures, watching movies, or some similar mode of transmission. Once the children have been given these data, they come to a position to think about the *shelter* concept. The teacher's inquiry strategy can activate mental operations through appropriate use of distancing behaviors. For example, "Remember we saw some pictures of Eskimos houses; can you describe them?" (strategy of reconstruction of a previous event and transforming it into another symbolic modality). "In what way are their houses like your house?" (comparison of similarities). "If Eskimos made their houses of wood, what might be some of the problems they would have?" (inferring cause-effect). An assignment to build an Eskimo house (transformation from one medium to another) is another distancing strategy that could be used.

This prototypic lesson involves: (1) preparing opportunities for new knoweldge by relating it to previous or current experience; (2) employment of distancing strategies to encourage re-presentation and reorganization of the new information with the old; and (3) encouraging transformation of the knowledge into different representational forms (language and drawing, in this case). In this format, the student is an active participant in the learning guided by the teacher. The sophistication of the materials, the inquiry, and the transformational system will vary with the developmental level of the student.

Space does not permit extensive applications to science, mathematics, literature, or other bodies of knowledge where representational thought is relevant. This application is possible when the key principles are kept in mind, remembering that knowledge is a mental construction of reality and can be represented in a variety of media.

Application of these principles on a broader base than described here is well expressed in a recent book by McKim (1972). In a set of exercises and lessons, he creates opportunities and strategies to facilitate transformation of ideas into various media by altering the modes of re-presenting, altering perspectives, and expanding ways of expression. What McKim advocates is the flexibility to shift from a verbal symbolic mode to ikonic or inactive modes, from words to drawings or sketches, in effect, creating various means of re-presenting the same idea. In sum, materials, thinking strategies, and transformation of ideas into multimedia come to pass in part through use of distancing teaching strategies.

Summary and Conclusions

The hypothesis presented is based on the conviction that use of distancing teaching strategies fosters representational thought. Representational thinking, while generic to the human, will vary in performance level as a consequence of life experiences of the individual. In spite of representational thinking being generic to the human's cognitive competency, there is variation among individuals in their ability to engage in such thinking. The *distancing hypothesis* holds that the reason for variation resides in the degree to which the individual has had distancing experiences. Evidence supporting the relationships between distancing experiences and representational thinking has been presented, limited to preschool settings.

Older children have more sophisticated ways of dealing with representational thinking. They are capable of functioning at the verbal symbolic level to a greater degree than preschoolers. In spite of the developmental level of elementary and high school students, engagement in distancing experiences should prove useful. By so doing, conflicts and constructions inherent in inquiry become resolved. The resolutions lead to new ways of thinking and reasoning.

The applicability of the distancing hypothesis to an elementary school educational level has been demonstrated. This illustration should be construed only as an example, since the principles are applicable to any educational setting. Abstracting the principles and testing their applicability to educational settings involving older children might provide the reader with a useful exercise in representational thinking.

Chapter 7   The Modification of Cognitive Abilities and Implications for Education

A number of recent publications (for example, Inhelder, Sinclair, and Bovet, 1974) have commented upon the widespread interest in the concepts which we discussed as central to the theory developed by Piaget (see Chapter 2). These writers have pointed out that professionals who are interested in the theory and growth of knowledge (epistemologists) such as educators, philosophers, and psychologists, are interested in concepts like conservation because these concepts are "neither preformed in the child nor acquired by simple observation." In Piagetian theory these concepts are the products of equilibration and autoregulation. In Chapter 2, we stated that equilibration is a construct used to describe the organism's constant striving toward a state of balance between the assimilation of new information which is in conflict with existent information and the adjustment to the new information (accommodation). Because infants do not have the same capacities as older children (neural,

muscular, and so on) what each child assimilates and accommo-
dates is limited by the factors related to each stage of development. Those *regulators* of development comprise the notion of
autoregulation—the organism's own system will dictate what is
assimilated and accommodated. The research interest for psychologists and educators into concepts like conservation is that
"their growth is governed by very regular laws of development"
(Inhelder, et al., 1974, p. 32). The concepts are also of interest
to educators and psychologists for their relevance to general
cognitive functioning; retarded children, for example, show limited functioning on tasks to which these concepts (such as conservation) are essential.

The purpose of the present chapter is to look at one of the
two issues which has generated all of this "Piagetian" research.
While we will not look at studies here which investigate the
controversy around the innateness of the concepts, we shall
review the studies which investigate the learning and teaching
issues. Can one teach these concepts? Can children learn about
these processes through observation? Can we tell children about
conservation and will that result in their learning conservation
concepts? The target question asked in this chapter is "Are
cognitive abilities modifiable?"

We have organized our discussion, first around the issue of
modification, examining what we consider to be its essential
parameters: permanence of change, durability of change, and
generalizability of learning. The implications of the modifiability
of concepts are also discussed. The second part of our treatment
of this topic pivots around the training research and the generalizations which might be drawn from these studies. We
analyze the modification studies along two dimensions: inducement of conflict and verbal methods of training. Each of these
dimensions is further divided into its polarities: conflict or no
conflict inducement; verbal training procedures or no verbal
training procedures. In the section, "Piaget and Education," we
discuss the meaning derived from modification studies from two
viewpoints. First, we look at the strategies utilized in the training studies and assert that teachers can learn much from them
as teaching strategies. Second, we point to the implications for
curriculum builders.

The Issue of Modifiability

Ever since Piagetian theory became well known in the United States, a proliferation of research has been directed toward the question of whether or not the course of cognitive development can be modified. As we have indicated from the Piagetian perspective, cognitive growth proceeds in an ordered invariant sequence, correlated with chronological age. Although Piaget uses the child's age as an approximation for appearance of stages of intellectual development, it is, nevertheless, a guide as to what to expect of children at various age levels; for example, children at ages seven or eight are concrete operational, while children at ages four or five are preoperational. Given these age spans and the notion that the sequence is invariant, investigators, mostly in the United States, have vigorous_y investigated the broad questions of modifiability, particularly in relation to conservation problems. Why was conservation selected as the focal problem? For two reasons: (1) It is a central concept to the theory; and (2) *it is amenable to experimental investigation.*

Development of Conservation

Conservation is defined by Flavell (1963, p. 245) as "the cognition that certain properties (quantity, number, length, etc.) remain invariant (are conserved) in the face of certain transformations (displacing objects or object parts in space, sectioning an object into pieces, changing shape, etc.)." This process is considered by Piaget (1952b, p. 3) as "a necessary condition for all rational activity." On the basis of extensive studies, Piaget identifies three stages of development for each type of conservation: stage 1, in which no conservation is found, and the child focuses on irrelevancies; stage 2, a transitional period, in which the child is dominated by perceptual appearances and in which conservation may or may not appear; stage 3, the stage of natural conservation, in which the child readily and logically demonstrates understanding of invariant properties in the face of transformations. The stages are presumed to be fixed and invariant, irrespective of the properties under study. An additional developmental sequence exists across the different quantity subclasses. Conservation of substance, for example, appears at about eight to ten years of age, preceding conservation of weight which is apparent between the ages of ten to twelve. Functional acquisition of volume occurs after the age of twelve. The invariant sequence of the development of substance, weight, and volume conservation has generally been verified, with certain qualifications, in a number of studies.

The question for study is whether conservation can be taught so that a *permanent change* in the child's cognitive structure comes about. If so, how and in which areas? A related problem has to do with the relationship between the child's ability to solve conservation problems and the other aspects of cognitive functioning. For example, if the child is "taught" to conserve number, does this learning influence his ability to solve class inclusion problems? The reason that such relationships would be expected is that Piaget contends that intelligence is an organized structure in which each element is related to the other. In addition to the two criteria of *durability* and *generalizability* (that is, permanence and transfer to other knowledge domains), the research question asks whether the training enables the child, not only to solve problems, but also to explain the basis of the solutions, for example, a child can give the correct answer to a conservation problem but may not be able to give a rational explanation for the answer. The Piagetian criterion of conservation ability requires the child to justify the answer by a *verbal explanation* for what happened, thereby indicating that she knows *why* she answered as she did.

Implications of Modification Studies

The implications of this body of research are widespread. First, this research becomes a test of Piaget's conception of cognitive development. If it is found that children can be taught to conserve in one area, (such as quantity), we can test whether the learning generalizes to other conservation domains; or whether each conservation (such as quantity, weight, volume, or area) has to be taught separately. If the latter is found to be the case, then it is apparent that the child is not truly understanding the principle; rather, the learning has been highly specific. In the other case, if solutions to conservation problems can be taught and generalized, this implies that the theoretical assertion that holds children will achieve their competencies only when they have reached the appropriate stage is questionable; rather, the child's performance level is influenced essentially by experience.

Another implication has evolved in recent years regarding the "teachability" of conservation and this comes from work with poverty children. The implication goes far beyond the applicability of Piagetian theory to special groups; it applies to all pupils equally. The research, however, gained specific support during a time when the educational remedy to the war on poverty was politically popular. The research argument reasons that if there is a normal course of cognitive development, and if it is related to age level, and if conservation is vital, then educators should "train" or "teach" children how to solve cognitive problems. What is required, however, is the discovery of the appropriate technology for achieving this objective.

In the following section we are going to present a few prototypic studies which sought to train children in the concepts which Piaget says emerge in the course of normal development. From these studies we have tried to show where the research emphasis has to be placed in order to understand whether or not conceptual development can be accelerated. We have organized the series of studies on the basis of the essential research parameters which were evident in these training studies. By discussing each of the parameters which appear to aid in the development of Piagetian concepts, we believe that we are giving the reader a basis for deducing principles which are relevant in teaching young children. Modification and training studies provide a body of information which enables us to test some of the basic tenets of Piagetian theory, tells us about the interrelationships among cognitive abilities, and relates developmental theory to certain issues of pedagogy.

Training Research

Let us now consider specific modification studies. These studies are reported in detail for they focus upon a critical element which we shall discuss again in relation to the relevance of

Piaget's theory to education. That critical aspect is the teaching *strategy* employed to induce change. As previously stated, the early training studies point to some general conclusions with regard to the strategies which ought to be employed if change in cognitive abilities is to result. Those conclusions center around the utility of both *conflict-* and *verbal-training* procedures. We should now like to examine these two parameters in detail, and compare and contrast the relative merits of each strategy as a practical technique for the classroom.

Modification Studies of Conservation

Modification studies of conservation can be divided into two broad categories: those studies that deliberately attempt to place the subject in a state of cognitive conflict and those studies that do not. Each of these two categories can be divided further into two types: those that emphasize language as a training device and those that emphasize nonverbal procedures. The studies that use both verbal and nonverbal means to induce conservation are classified, for convenience, under the verbal category when the researchers are deliberately testing the effects of verbal training, and under nonverbal when the major experimental question deals with the effectiveness of the nonverbal aspects of training.

CONFLICT INDUCEMENT–NONVERBAL. Perhaps the clearest studies of this category come from Inhelder, Sinclair, and Bovet (1974). Common to each of their training procedures is an attempt to get the child to make a conserving statement shortly before or shortly after making a nonconserving statement in reference to the same material. By bringing the child to the point of making contradictory statements they discovered that some children soon sense the contradiction and seek to resolve the paradox by engaging in a higher mode of thinking. While language is certainly used by the experimenters to focus the child's attention on various states of the materials, the primary source of conflict comes from seeing the physical result of some transformation which did not agree with the child's prediction. In other studies (Brainerd, 1974), language is used as the primary source of conflict, that is, telling the child directly, "No, you are wrong."

Several examples from Inhelder, Sinclair, and Bovet (1974) should be helpful. In a conservation of continuous quantity (liquid) task, children from five- to seven-years-old were given an arrangement of jars as seen in Figure 7.1. The liquid in the top jars could be drained into the lower jars by opening a stop-cock. Children were given a chance to explore the draining process, how the liquid in *B* increased as the liquid in *A* decreased as the liquid drained, with special attention being drawn to the kinetic properties of the change from vessel to

Figure 7.1
Conservation of continuous quantity apparatus

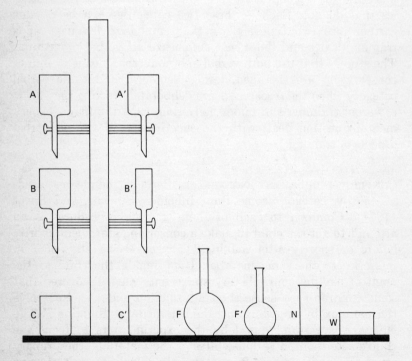

From B. Inhelder, H. Sinclair, and M. Bovet, *Learning and the Development of Cognition.* Cambridge, Mass.: Harvard University Press, 1974.

vessel. Then liquid was poured into F until the level just reached the beginning of the neck. F was poured into A, filled again and poured into A'. At this point the children agreed that jar A and A' contained the same quantity of water. Then A was drained into B and A' drained into B'. Again the children agreed the quantity in B and B' was the same, and they predicted that if B were drained into F the level would come up to the neck; the same holding for draining B' into F. This phase emphasized that liquid could change vessels and still remain a constant quantity, since the change began with F and ended with F. In the second phase a tall, narrow jar (N) or a short, wide jar (W) replaced jar B'. The same procedure was repeated. The child was asked, after A had been drained into B, to fill N from A' with the same amount of water as B. If the child fills N to the same level as B then upon draining both B and N into C and C' respectively the child would see that the levels (and thereby quantities) are not the same. This causes conflict for some children. To accentuate the conflict an opaque shield was placed over the middle jars in a third phase (Figure 7.2). After filling A and A' from the common jar F, the child released both contents into the middle jars, which could not be seen. Then the middle jars were opened so the water could flow into C and C'. Here the child had seen equal levels at A versus A' and equal levels at C versus C'. The second time A and A' were filled with equal quantities the child was asked to predict if the quantity in the two hidden containers were the same. Most children said that they were. When the shield was removed, many children changed their judgments upon seeing the uneven levels. At that point they were asked to predict if the quantity of water released from B to C would be the same as that released from N to C'. Then they were asked to release all of B into C and then release an equal amount of water from N. Here again the children were placed in a conflict situation. If they thought N had more water than B as they began to release only part of N to equal C, they would note that the two levels between C and C' were not the same until they released all of N. By alternating back and forth between situations that elicit a configurational judgment (water levels) and an operational judgment (same quantity), the experimenters effectively generated enough conflict in the children to cause them to think about the compensation be-

Figure 7.2
Conservation of continuous quantity—shielded apparatus

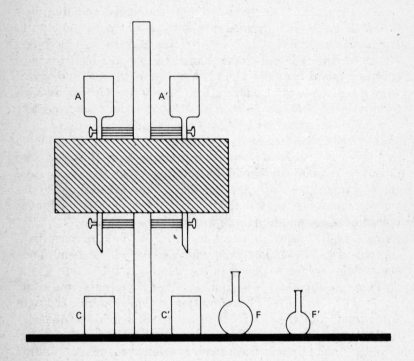

From B. Inhelder, H. Sinclair, and M. Bovet, *Learning and the Development of Cognition.* Cambridge, Mass.: Harvard University Press, 1974.

tween water height and vessel width. The children were not told to ignore the configuration of the liquid, but rather were encouraged to account for the illusion by reasoning that what the liquid gains in height it loses in width, that is, compensation of dimensions. Inhelder, Sinclair, and Bovet (1974) insist that training methods that attempt to shift the child's attention away from perceptual cues are more likely to produce rote learning. However, when static cues, like the water level, are made to conflict with a transformational procedure, that all water came from the common jar F, the meaning of the perceptual variation can be discovered. These training procedures were effective for children who were at least advanced enough to experience the conflict, but not yet advanced to already knowing conservation of liquid quantity. Furthermore, these gains were durable, as indicated on a second posttest, one month after the first posttest.

The conflict that results from a discrepancy between prediction and actual outcome was but one type of conflict used by Inhelder, Sinclair, and Bovet (1974). Similar conflict situations were created with other physical dimensions. In a conservation of length task, equal number was made to conflict with apparent unequal length. In another procedure a one-to-one correspondence was made to conflict with an apparent difference in quantity when small balls in a narrow jar reached a higher level than the same number of small balls in a wide jar. The child has seen balls placed one-at-a-time in each jar simultaneously and repeated eight or ten times. These procedures of generating conflict were effective in causing gains that were durable in conservation concepts one month after training.

CONFLICT INDUCEMENT–VERBAL. The distinguishing feature of these studies is the use of language to direct the child's thought to a contradiction. Instead of physically varying materials until the child discovers a contradiction, the child is told that his judgment is not consistent with his previous statements. Brainerd (1974) conducted one study in which equal length sticks were initially parallel and then one of the sticks was pushed forward as follows:

Red

White

A   B

Children were asked questions about the lengths of the sticks to see if they thought that changes in position affected stick length. Brainerd simply told five-year-olds, who had said that a stick pushed forward was longer than an equal length not moved, "No you are wrong; the red one is still as long as the white." These procedures improved conservation performance that endured at least until a second testing a week later. Brainerd (1973) has also found that verbal correction immediately after the children's responses can be an effective means to engage them to rethink their answers. The conflict which is instigated externally by a teacher evidently arouses enough curiosity within the child so that re-examination of the material leads to internal conflict. Brainerd's results with sticks are similar to Piaget and Inhelder's findings (1971) in which, when children drew the movement of one block across the top surface of another block, they represented both the old location *and* the new position, as in the following illustration.

Position   1   2

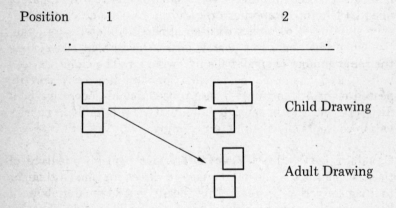

This illustrates the child's failure to compensate for the displacement from position 1 to position 2 when thinking on the basis of static mental images. Here we see a contradiction which emerges when the image of position 1 is juxtaposed with the image of position 2. If centering on the leading edge of two stick lengths as in Brainerd's experiment causes incorrect judgments, the child's search for an alternative basis could lead to the notion of a compensation between leading edge and trailing edge. The internal conflict may come just at the point that the child discovers that the stick seems longer if one looks at the leading edge, but seems shorter if one looks at the trailing edge. The verbal corrective feedback causes the child to decenter from the leading edge only.

There are also studies which have used other children as an external conflict source to increase the probability of an internal conflict. These studies have placed the nonconserving child in a problem-solving situation with more advanced, conserving children. Silverman and Geiringer (1973) and Silverman and Stone (1972) noticed that when nonconservers and conservers disagreed, the nonconservers were more likely to change in the direction of conservation responses than vice versa. Relevant measures indicated that this shift to the higher level of thinking was not due to the greater prestige of age of the conservers. More likely, the disagreement generated a cognitive conflict that could only be resolved by the greater logic of conservation concepts. Murray (1972) discovered that when two conservers and one nonconserver try to reach consensus, all three children show improvements. In sum, many educational studies have found utility in using classmates and somewhat order peers as classroom tutors. The contradictions in child logic are brought to the fore by age-mate tutors and concepts are made more comprehensible. Concepts are apparently clarified on a level understood by the tutored child as well as elaborated in meaning for the tutor. These studies provide support for Piaget's hypothesis that social interaction, through the dialectic of disagreements, is an important source of cognitive development (Piaget, 1967).

One other type of study might, by a stretch of definitions, fit this category. The child's own verbal statements can be made to conflict with the child's perceptions of physical material. Here language does direct the child's thoughts to a contradiction between the way she represents a situation verbally and the way she represents that same situation perceptually. In a training study by Frank (see Bruner, 1964), children were made to state verbally that liquid poured from a wide beaker into a narrow beaker would still have the same quantity. The child could see only the mouth of the narrow beaker, since the remainder of the narrow beaker was shielded from view by a screen. In this situation many children gave conservation replies (such as "They're the same 'cause you only poured the water"). When the screen was removed the children changed their minds upon seeing the high level of liquid in the narrow beaker (such as "There's more in this one 'cause it's higher than this one").

Bruner concludes that the children understand conservation as long as they can represent the transformations in words (symbolic representation) but when they represent the physical features of the task (ikonic representation), the dominance of the visual perceptions of the liquid level inhibits correct responding. The conflict in this case is between a verbal and perceptual mode of thinking.

No CONFLICT–NONVERBAL. A common criticism of most studies of conflict inducement is the failure to provide an independent measure of conflict, that is, a measure independent of the conservation performance itself (Brainerd, 1973). This means that studies have to be differentiated into conflict and no-conflict categories by a plausibility criterion. Was it plausible that the experimental procedure generated conflict? At a minimum, those studies which took deliberate precautions to avoid conflict can be classified *no-conflict*. Training procedures that try to shape correct responses gradually quite plausibly contain little, if any, conflict inducement. Studies that provide critical information, before the child becomes perplexed, are also candidates for this category.

The teacher wishing to train children on conservation might examine the component skills that are required to solve a conservation task. After isolating some of those components, the teacher may proceed to teach one or several of these components in a direct fashion. After successful completion of learning the component skill, the children are tested for conservation itself. This method of training is consistent with the educational tradition of breaking difficult problems down into smaller, thereby less difficult, units.

One component skill of number conservation is the ability to count and equate sets of objects according to number, regardless of the physical arrangement of the sets. That is:

(1) . . . .

(2) . . . .   and

(3) ·   ·   are all equal in number.

In one of Piaget's studies children were asked to choose as many eggs as there were egg cups lined up on the table. At four- or five-years-old, children attack the problem by a one-to-one correspondence strategy—one cup for each egg. Their notions of numerosity are greatly influenced by the physical arrangements of the objects. Piaget uses the term "quotity" to distinguish children's performances on counting tasks from their understanding of actual quantitative concepts. The child may be at a "quotity" level and be able to tell how many objects there are in a collection after counting them, but she may still think that, *even after counting,* one set of the collection has more or less than another set because of their different spatial arrangements. That is, the child does not understand "quantity." The child will say: "There are six there, and six there, the same number of counters when you count them, but it's not the same, there are more counters there" (Inhelder, Sinclair, and Bovet, 1974, p. 37). Quotity is essential, but not sufficient to conserve discontinuous quantity. Often when one of two parallel rows of objects is spread out, the child will agree that the two rows have the same number (a quotity skill) but will still insist that the spread out row has more total quantity. The last object in each row may be given the name "seven," but this does not necessarily imply equal quantity to the nonconserver.

Wallach, Wall, and Anderson (1967) trained children to make a one-to-one correspondence between two equal, parallel rows and between parallel rows of different spans. The training procedure involved transformations, plus reverse transformations; that is, both rearranging rows of items and returning the rearrangement to its original order. This training, in which children counted back and forth across the two rows to check that the numbers were the same, did improve number conservation. Very few children used reversal ("You can make them like they were before") as a justification for number conservation, however. That is, in the testing when the lower row was spread out, few children justified their "same number" judgment with a statement that the transformation could be reversed, thereby reestablishing numerical equality perceptually. Rather, they seemed to learn to ignore the misleading cues of "going beyond." They said that the longer row only looked like it had an extra object (the last bed) but the other row had an "extra" object also, for example, a doll midway between two beds. This training procedure had encouraged the children to look more carefully, but as the investigators admit, it did not train them to understand that number was conserved as a matter of logical necessity. In addition, the training on reversible transformations of number did not transfer to other types of conservation tasks. The study shows that children may become more skilled in their quotity judgments but that their understanding of quantity concepts is not actually altered.

Other studies have shown some success in directly teaching components of conservation. Pufall (1973) found that children learned to conserve the order of three balls in a tube, even when rotated, by watching the rotations and reversals repeatedly. Sheppard (1973) trained children to think about the inverse relation between tall narrow jars and short wide jars. This training, called compensation training, was effective in liquid quantity conservation only when compensation was shown to be relevant to judgments of quantity.

One final type of study fits the *no conflict–nonverbal* category. Studies of this type are particularly relevant for their educational implications. These studies allow children to watch an adult or more advanced peers engage in conservation performance. The observer does not actively interact with the model, therefore the chance of cognitive conflict is reduced, albeit not completely removed.

Rosenthal and Zimmerman (1972) had six- and seven-year-old children watch an adult model answer various conservation questions. In the condition we are calling nonverbal, the model stated her judgments "yes" or "no" without additional justification. After watching the adult, the child's performance on similar conservation tasks improved compared to before observing the model. The investigators conclude that the children induced the principles of conservation through vicarious learning. Their behavior could not have been rote imitation since the child's tasks were sufficiently different from those of the model. Furthermore, the children were able to justify their answers, even though they had not heard the model justify her answers. Another procedure, which we call a *no conflict–verbal* procedure (see p. 201), is to have the model give the rule which justified the conservation answer. Children profited from the model-plus-verbal rule only when the criteria of success on the conservation tasks were increased for them. If the children were only required to say "yes" or "no" to conservation questions, hearing the verbal rule did not make an additional improvement in performance.

No CONFLICT–VERBAL. In this last category, the investigators tried to induce conservation by telling the child either what to watch or a conservation rule. This information was provided, not as a means of reconciling conflict brought about by the presentation of materials, but rather in advance of conflict, as a means of orienting the child's attention and thoughts. This teaching technique is standard in the average classroom.

Beilin (1965) compared several different teaching techniques. Telling the children what dimension to focus on did not significantly improve conservation of number and length, but stating the conservation rule each time a child made an error did improve performance. That is, telling the child to keep track of the number of items in each row on a number conservation task, or telling the child to watch the length of the sticks in a conservation of length task, does not help the child understand these conservation concepts. Verbalizing the rule for the child, on the other hand, does seem to make a difference. The verbal rule was always accompanied by a demonstration of reversing the transformation, so the verbal rule alone may not have caused the improvement. The verbal rule was confused with a physical demonstration. Also, the rule was only given when the child made an error. The child could have felt the same cognitive conflict assumed to occur when nonconservers are placed in the presence of conservers as we discussed in the conflict–verbal section. The verbal feedback at least indicated to the child that he should reconsider this thinking. Beilin (1965) also presented one group of children with corrective feedback only, a buzzer, and reward whenever the correct response was made. The absence of the buzzer and the reward explicitly indicated when an error had been made, but no explanation, no verbal rule was given. Performance did not improve under these conditions. The superiority of the verbal rule condition must have been due to the information contained in the rule itself.

Knowing when an error was made was not as effective as knowing "when" and "why" an error was made.

One study gives data suggesting that children can do more than learn a specific skill when they listen to a verbal rule. Zimmerman and Rosenthal (1974) had either an adult model explain her own conservation judgments or had an adult explain conservation when the child judged incorrectly. Both procedures were effective not only in improving performance on the task used in training, but also in leading the child to apply a derivation of the rule given. In the training phase two sticks were changed from parallel alignment to parallel with one leading forward, as follows:

To the question, "Are the sticks still the same length?" the model answered, "Yes, because they were the same length in the first place." In the transfer test the two sticks were aligned and then transformed to a T-arrangement:

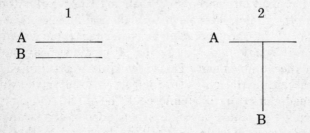

The child was asked, "How would you show a friend that the sticks were still the same length?" The children who had received training could reverse the T-arrangement to the parallel alignment, thereby confirming the sticks' equality. These children (mean age 5.7 years) could apply the reversal of a transformation to explain why two sticks were the same length, even though the reversal rule was not the one given in training. The children without benefit of training could not. The investigators state that the training sessions emphasized only the equality between two lengths. The children deduced the relation between reversibility and equality. A more conservative summary would be, the training sessions emphasized rather explicitly a potential reversal, while the transfer task asked for a direct application of reversibility. These children had learned a specific rule (reverse the transformation), although it was a rule and not a stimulus-specific response.

Summary

We have reviewed the preceding studies so that we might answer some of the questions posed at the beginning of this chapter. Those questions had to do with: (1) the modifiability of cognitive structures; (2) the durability of changes induced during short term training; (3) the generalizability of concepts learned in conservation training; (4) the necessity of altering cognitions; and finally (5) the ease and facility of training cognitive competencies. Our preview of the problem, through early training studies which utilized various techniques (reinforcement, feedback, verbal training, conflict paradigms, and combinations of these procedures) suggested two critical dimensions for organizing modification studies: whether or not verbalization was part of the teaching technique (verbal, nonverbal); and whether or not cognitive conflict was essential to the training procedure (conflict, no-conflict). Let us now consider the relative merits of these procedures and their advantages and limitations for adoption as classroom strategies. A contingency table such as the following might be a helpful organizer for the reader:

	Conflict	No-Conflict
Nonverbal		
Verbal		

Conflict–nonverbal procedures may be regarded as effective teaching strategies as long as the child is advanced enough to recognize and experience the conflict posed in the learning situation. In these studies what the children gained from the strategy was durable (as tested a month after training had ceased) for both continuous quantity (liquid) and discontinuous quantity (small balls in jars) conservation.

Conflict–verbal teaching techniques may be seen by some as a hard-nosed, "reality" approach to teaching. They rely upon telling the person in explicit, absolute terms (1) *that* he or she is wrong; (2) *why* he or she is wrong; and (3) what to do about it. The trainer's verbalizations might be: "No, you're wrong—this is the way it is . . ." when a child commits an error. Such a procedure, we learned from the review, is effective for length conservation training and is durable in so far as the researchers tested permanence of training effects (one week after training). As a result of this technique, the child has to look at what was done and re-think the answer. We might also look at this body of studies and consider the *conflict source* as an important part of educational procedures. Adults were used in the studies from which the foregoing conclusions were drawn. We also learned, however, that peers, both age-mates and tutors who were somewhat older, may be effective in generating verbal conflict and that they, too, produce the changes that studies with adult trainers report. We cannot, however, conclude anything about the *relative* efficacy of adults versus peers in inducing cognitive conflict verbally on the basis of these studies.

The no conflict–nonverbal studies reviewed were of two principal types. The first type involved training children on the subcomponent skills of conservation. While performance often improved on specific skills such as counting (quotity skill), children's thinking was not more advanced conceptually. That is, quantitative concepts involved in number conservation were not altered by this teaching procedure. The second type of study involved observational learning; children observed others performing but not justifying their responses on conservation tasks. Having children observe others is a teaching strategy so effective that even though the performing models did not justify their conservation responses ("You didn't do anything except pour it from one jar into another") the observing child was able to produce such justifications. The researchers concluded that children induce the rules of conservation as a result of being given the opportunity to observe correct performances of others.

The no conflict–verbal teaching strategy consisted of telling the children specifically what to look for as critical dimensions in the learning task; this is probably the most widely used classroom approach. Research data indicate that the task did not aid in the development of conservation concepts. When the technique was combined with telling the child the conservation rule (verbal aspect) and then demonstrating the correct procedure for the child, children grasped the notions embodied in conservation. We cannot confidently conclude that it was solely the verbalization *plus* the no conflict aspect of the teaching approach which accounts for the learning changes, however. This is so because the designs were mixed up by elements such as corrective feedback of child-produced errors and the demonstration techniques of correct problem solution. We can say, however, that knowing when and why errors are made are both critical to learning.

Our next consideration will be determining what constitutes good pedagogy in Piaget's system. We will continue to return to these modification studies and ask for their implication to education. From our statement of the theory in Chapters 3 and 4, one might conclude with Kohnstramm that "the truly pedagogic adult should keep his mouth shut, except for asking the child diagnostic questions" (Kohnstamm, 1970, p. 371). We shall, however, ask whether the training studies tell us anything about how to help a child solve new problems. Kohnstamm (1970) maintains that many strategies which are sound from a pedagogical viewpoint are impossible from the point of view of Piaget's theory. Our focus in the next section, then, will be upon the relevance for the theory to education, and what the educational studies have to say regarding the veridicality of the theory.

Piaget and Education

Interest in the intersection between psychology and education is not new, nor restricted to outcroppings from Piagetian research. From the early days of psychology to the present, dialogues of various kinds have been held between educators and psychologists. However, a fruitful relationship between education and psychology recently has been accentuated by interest in the work of Piaget. Perhaps dissatisfied with the traditional academic work in educational and developmental psychology, Piagetian theory seems to offer much to the educational practitioner, at least at the preschool and elementary school levels.

On the surface Piagetian theory appears to be readily applicable to the educational environment. This point of view is held in spite of the fact that Piaget writes that he is not an educator nor is his system a system of education (Hunt and Sullivan, 1974; Piaget, 1970c; Piaget, 1974). Educators, on the other hand, while struggling to grasp the implications for the theory focus on three main points for which Piagetian theory is suggestive and deemed relevant: (1) the theory provides a developmental perspective for teachers and curriculum builders since it is comprehensive and includes the domains relevant to education; (2) Piaget has offered a mass of substantive data describing the development of particular kinds of knowledge also deemed compatible with most educational objectives; for example, development of knowledge of the physical world, development of logical reasoning abilities at every educational level, and so on; and (3) on the basis of Piaget's description of the conditions of cognitive growth, offering concepts such as autoregulatory mechanisms or the significance of social interaction, educators have extrapolated rationales for teaching strategies. The child uses only partial information in making judgments (height or width, but not both), for example, and Piaget says this illustrates how the child's own cognitive capacities *regulate* his thinking; hence, autoregulation. The question is how this concept might be built upon in a learning curriculum.

Let us turn to a discussion of each of these areas to provide some perspective on the issue of the relationship between Piaget and education.

A Developmental Perspective for Teachers and Curriculum Builders

Prior to Piaget's theory, no educational theory of cognitive development had explained in such detail the stages of cognitive growth. Although contemporaries such as Werner and Dewey have presented developmental perspectives, Piaget has documented the stages of growth in great detail from infancy to adolescence and coordinated these with particular areas of knowledge (e.g., the development of space relations, Euclidean and projective geometry concepts, and so on). (We discuss this in Chapter 8.) Thus armed with knowledge of Piaget, the classroom teacher is presumably sensitized to the child's cognitive level and to the basic notions that development proceeds in an invariant sequence, that children's performances are a reflection of the integrity of their cognitive structures, that movement from one stage to the other is in a sense fixed, and only the rates of appearance of structures will vary across children. Most important in this consideration is the teacher's awareness that the concept of learning and the concept of development for Piaget are distinctly different. This understanding will permeate each of the other two principles to be discussed. On the conceptual level it is a critical distinction. Learning, according to Piaget, is not development, but the application of developing structures to appropriate objects and events. Thus when children classify an object, they are learning about the object and when to apply their classificatory structures. "Functionally, *learning* is the application of an intellectual structure to a wide variety of objects and events. That is, one learns the rules about how to apply the structure, and consequently the structure becomes increasingly elaborated" (Strauss, 1972, p. 331, authors' italics). The curriculum builder using this system has a framework within which to develop materials and to order them. That children fail to grasp meaning from materials when offered to them may be interpreted as a function of an inappropriate match between the materials and the children's developmental levels.

Both the teacher and curriculum builder must be aware that knowledge is not acquired in the sense of bits of information just being added into a system, but that it develops in a given set of sequences. The task for these practitioners is to identify the child's stage and then work accordingly. Two streams of research have emerged as a result of the Piagetian proposition that stages are invariant and that structures evolve as integrated wholes. One set of research attempts to test the sequential nature of the stages. Unfortunately, to do this requires some decisions as to which topics to select. After all, the identification of the stage at which a child is functioning is inferred from performance on the tasks. For the younger children (approximately between the ages of four and nine), many of the studies involved assessment of the child's operational knowledge through *conservation*. The results are generally supportive of Piaget's contention that stages of development are found in the conservation of quantity, area, space, and so on. Thus the vertical décalage, in general terms, has been supported for some selected aspects of knowledge. *Décalage* is a term used to describe the appearance of similar kinds of behaviors at different points in time. The term captures the concept that there are "gaps" in learning and that we see patterns of cognitive development or processes recurring at later times across the developmental span. For example, the child may be able to answer all of the teacher's questions about the quantity of liquid remaining unchanged as it is poured from jar to glass, and so on, but still think that the quantity of coffee has been altered when it goes from coffee bean to ground coffee. This confusion may be expressed as subtly as asking his mother if the pound of coffee is weighed before or after being ground, implying that beans occupy more space and therefore must also weigh more.

Décalage, in Piaget's system, may be of two types: (1) horizontal décalage, referring to repetitions within the same developmental period; and (2) vertical decalage, meaning that the repetition is observed across different levels of cognitive functioning. However, in the relationships among various areas of knowledge (for example, whether the child is at the same stage in conservation of number as in her performance on class inclusion tasks), then the issues that constitute the second research area become more complex and the results more equivocal. Thus the commitment of the educator to the tenet that the details of the developmental perspective are valid has to be held in abeyance pending further research.

But, then, what does the teacher do? Research results support Piaget's perspective of cognitive development (see pp. 32–33) and the teacher, thereby, has some guidelines for how to proceed. But because the data are not definitive, as in the second stream of research, the teacher should not become indolent and do nothing. The teacher should continue to work in ways consistent with the theoretical perspective. That is, *consistency* directed by a rationale, is the best option in the absence of clear-cut feedback from the educational research.

Most developmentalists working within an organismic framework will agree that the general principle of the invariance of stages seems to be valid, but they still hold that further work is necessary to pin down a number of previously untested questions. One manner of research that has tested the question has been the short-term training studies which we discussed (see p. 190). The assumption has been that if the sequence is invariant and fixed, it should not be modifiable, especially in bits and pieces. The issue confronting us at this point, then, is the relationship between the notion of fixed, sequenced stages of intellectual development and the value of education in such development. If one conceives of these stages as immutable, determined by the genetic make-up, then the teacher would be wasting time in trying to accelerate the cognitive development of students. The educator, with this philosophy, merely looks for the match between stage and material appropriate to the stage. Piaget has cited an example of unfettered exploration in the classroom and what it means to children of various ages (Piaget, 1970c, pp. 168–173). The teachers in his example presented a fully equipped laboratory for science exploration (Bunsen burners, test tubes, and so on) and all adult intervention was avoided. Three- to eight-year-old children expressed interest in the materials, as evidenced by their active explorations. Piaget contends that *all* of the children were "learning to observe and reason as they observed." But Piaget's own conclusion of the teaching strategies he witnessed is that they have particular benefits for particular children. Even the most favorable circumstances were "insufficient to erase the various features of the child's mental structure." This means that the children can work only within the limits of their capabilities and that three-year-olds did not learn the same things as eight-year-olds. The value of the adult, which Piaget points out would not have been harmful to the pupils in this example, is that such a person can help provide the necessary rationales for certain activities to the children. Is this, perhaps, what happens in both of the verbal conditions we reviewed? The focus is upon the *systematization* of experiences by the adult. There is corroboration of the sequences of cognitive growth, especially conservation abilities as observed among various cultures (Dasen, 1972). There is some reason, therefore, to believe that the sequences are fixed. The variation in *rate* of growth should not be confused with the sequence issue. In other words, the rates may vary because of social, nutritional, or cultural reasons, but the sequence remains the same. Piaget states that the sequence is invariant, but the rate and the age of appearance may vary (Piaget, 1970a). If the rate is modifiable, then we need to know the factors that aid or impede cognitive growth. If, on the other hand, the rate is not the issue but rather the sequence, then the developmental perspective of Piaget is cast into doubt. To this date, the evidence is in Piaget's favor, but we should not be satisfied until additional research is undertaken. Until then, the skeptics still conclude, "The use of Piaget's stages as indicators of 'learning readiness' seems most premature and needs more careful consideration on both the research and theoretical levels" (Hunt and Sullivan, 1974, p. 156). Piaget himself points out, however, that the major implication for education is first to recognize that "all intellectual raw material is not invariably assimilable at all ages." Interests and needs vary as children grow older. He also emphasizes that the research data point to the decisive role of the environment in mental development: "the thought contents of the stages and the ages at which they occur are not immutably fixed; . . . sound methods can increase the students' efficiency" (Piaget, 1970c, p. 173).

Relationships among Piagetian Research, Specific Knowledge Domains, and Education

Recall that much of Piaget's research has a substantive focus, namely he has been interested in how the child develops the structures for knowledge in general, and how specific knowledge develops. Thus he has studied areas such as the child's developing understanding of morality, natural phenomena (such as dreams or wind); physical phenomena such as flotation, quantity, space, time, geometry, and operational knowledge (such as logical thought). The logical processes were embedded in his study of each domain of knowledge, so that he not only identified the development of logical operations, but also the child's conceptions of time, space, geometry, and so on. For example, Piaget reported that children find it easier to understand topological space, the space dealing with enclosures, than Euclidean space, space defined in terms of angles. He also found that children had difficulty in differentiating between dreams as reality and dreams as distinct from reality. In other words, the body of substantive knowledge that Piaget and his colleagues have presented us with describes developmental sequences. One thing that becomes evident from Piagetian research is that it has focused our attention on knowledge domains that were not part of the educators' framework. Thus, through combining the developmental framework with attention to the child's understanding of particular domains of knowledge, the teacher and the curriculum builders can increase their understanding of the child's knowledge of basic concepts and also foster the expansion of the child's horizons. Our example of a quotity skill versus quantitative concepts is an example. Another is the teacher's use of children's experiences in nature to convey concepts: Wind and cloud movement help the child learn about cause and effect relationships. A by-product of this training quite possibly is that the child's animistic thinking (attributing life qualities to inanimate objects) is also reduced. Curriculum builders are using the naturalistic phenomena for their lessons rather than stolid exercises which have little meaning to the child. Children at very early ages are now learning to think by pondering very basic ideas: Does an ice cube, for example, melt faster in water or out of water? Why? What are the contingencies? For Piaget, education's role is to help children "learn to observe and reason as they observe."

Contribution of Piagetian Theory to Teaching Strategy

Why not try to apply some of the strategies Piaget reports in his work? From the previous sections it is clear that Piagetian theory has some direct relevance to the educational process but the degree of extrapolation is not as great as might be thought at first glance. The developmental perspective provides a rich source of information for the educators to consider and to integrate into their own schemata. However, in relation to teaching strategies we are in a vastly different situation, as seen in the various techniques employed to train conservation (see pp. 191) for the following reasons: (1) Most Piagetian theory comes from either careful observational studies of his own three children (Piaget, 1954) or from interviews and experiments with individual children in one-to-one situations; (2) Piaget's assertions as to how development proceeds, and the experiential conditions deemed essential for growth are hypothetical, or speculative, or inferred from his own observations; therefore the assertion that self-regulatory mechanisms are operative in the development of intelligence needs further study on what initiates these processes; (3) the assertion that actions provide the rudimentary bases for subsequent internalization of knowledge needs much more empirical verification. Yet these kinds of assertions have stimulated educators to extrapolate teaching strategies from Piaget. Thus we must make a distinction here between teaching and instructional strategies based on data presented by Piaget or by Piagetian-stimulated research and extrapolations from the metatheoretical position still awaiting further verification.

One source of verification is in the array of training studies undertaken in the past decade with the intent not of studying teaching strategies, but of evaluating the theory in respect to modifiability of cognitive development. Yet, each of these experiments had to employ an instructional model to induce modification. Some of the training procedures, as we pointed out before, employed highly structured materials and highly structured teaching strategies, focusing the child's attention on various elements in the situation, while others provided information about the objects, or created step-by-step approaches so that each relevant aspect was learned. Still other training studies relied upon conflict strategies in order to induce conservation.

Interestingly, the training study literature did not emphasize the particular strategy employed in the training as much as the model employed. Strauss, for example, refers to a conflict model in which the child is presented with contradictions. Resolution of conflicts, it is asserted, leads to structural changes in development. But the conflict can be induced didactically (through direct teaching) or by inquiry (Why do you suppose that happened? What would have happened if we had done it this way instead? What would we have to do to get it back like it was when we started? and so on). There is also the training model in which children are presented problems known to be one stage advanced of their cognitive stage.

The training *models* all present strategies for achieving their goals, and generally show some shifts in the children's performances. However, the training study *strategies* do not necessarily allow application to the classroom. The findings speak only to the modifiability of the child's cognitive functioning in highly controlled situations; they do not relate to the validity of the teaching strategy in achieving that goal. The research findings do not speak to whether or not the *strategies* can be adopted as general classroom approaches, though the overall *model* may be appropriate. That is, Piaget's model of cognitive development may be a good educational model, allowing for individual differences in rates and stages of development (stage, self-regulation, and the other concepts which we have discussed). At the same time, the Piagetian inquiry strategies, the verbal/nonverbal, conflict/no conflict, or any of the other strategies discussed may not be generally applicable.

What is needed, then, is controlled research to examine in depth the issue of whether the teaching strategies derived from Piagetian theory are, in fact, functional and effective. Further, there is every reason to ask if achievements in cognitive development, in terms described by Piaget, have only one way of emerging. In other words, is a discovery, action-based, method which involves child verbalization the most effective way to accomplish structural transformation? This is a question that has yet to be answered in classrooms, not in laboratories. This leads to another concern, namely, transporting research findings derived from theory or laboratories into a classroom setting.

Relationship between Research and Practice

Clearly there is a missing link between successful laboratory teaching strategies and their application in the classroom. The latter situation is more complex, less controlled, and more variable than laboratory research. More classroom-based research is needed to demonstrate the validity of the laboratory-based strategy when the environmental conditions change. Again we can summarize this position by quoting Hunt and Sullivan:

The ability of Piaget's theory to prescribe a particular type of learning atmosphere is pure extrapolation from his equilibrium model of development. His followers in education who frequently quote him as an authority are the proponents of the "self-discovery" and activity methods. In a sense Piaget is being used to foster the mystique of discovery learning (Hunt and Sullivan, 1974, p. 156).

The use of Piaget to support discovery should be conceptualized as a hypothesis rather than as a finding. And therefore more research is needed.

In closing this discussion we should point out that Piagetian models have been developed as bases for preschool education. The results have not yielded uniform teaching strategies, but rather have produced various approaches, from the highly structured environments and directive teaching (Hooper, 1972) to the type attributed to Piaget (Kamii, 1972). Thus the application of Piaget to education contains many problems, no doubt a function of the complexity and the comprehensiveness of the theory and the differential acquaintance educators have with it. Also, many of the educational issues are not directly broached in the theory. It is difficult to assert, then, that a one-way approach is the most consistent. But what is consistent, is the need for verification, a point of view Piaget would favor, for as a scientist who eschews philosophy, he is a strong advocate of verification and experimentation. The issue confronting educators is the translation of developmental theory into pedagogy. The teacher must engage in classroom activities as if conducting training studies such as those we have presented. "One cannot truly learn child psychology except by collaborating in new research projects and taking part in experiments, and it is useless to limit sources to exercises or practical work directed toward already known results" (Piaget, 1970c, p. 125). Educators must do their best with what is known and orient themselves to carefully watching and examining processes and outcomes consistently. Hopefully, sensitized to the complexity, the teacher can tune in to the classroom and reflect on what is happening there. The teacher's task, in terms of Piagetian theory, is to learn to assess levels of cognitive functioning from child behaviors, and then enter with appropriate mismatches to energize the child toward problem solving. The plea, in a sense, is for the teacher to be reflective in assessing classroom procedures and activities. Finally, the teacher in this case has to be willing to be innovative. This requires administrative support, but only by trying new methods can we come upon the ones which appear to be effective, and in this way define the conditions in which effectiveness occurs.

Summary

In this chapter we have presented once again the ever-present Piagetian concept, conservation, this time as a heuristic. We have organized a series of conservation studies to ask the question: Can one alter the course of development of a naturally emerging phenomenon? We look as these studies, both as a challenge of theoretical tenets and for the teaching strategies which are potentially useful classroom techniques. Presenting children with perceptual conflicts, such as pouring liquids into variously shaped containers, was demonstrated as one technique by which to teach children conservation (conflict–nonverbal). The conflict approach may also be used with verbal procedures, presumably creating cognitive conflict because the new information does not coincide with the children's contemporaneous state and they must re-think their answers to problems (conflict–verbal). Conflict procedures were not the only techniques utilized, however. Children were also trained, nonverbally, on component skills of conservation which aided the specific skill performance but did not alter the quality of conservation response reasoning appreciably (no conflict–nonverbal). Observing correct conservation performances of others, however, appears to promote rule induction. A more direct no conflict–verbal approach of telling the child which critical aspects to concentrate on was not effective unless coupled with the conservation rule itself.

The meaning of these studies for the practitioner was discussed as the intersect between psychology and education. The theory utilizes concepts which are relevant to education in a comprehensive, developmental scheme. Piaget deals with substantive information: knowledge of the physical world is certainly relevant to logical reasoning abilities. Finally, the mechanisms Piaget invokes in describing mental functioning may be useful guides for the teacher. For example, autoregulation, for Piaget, means that the organism assimilates only that information which the system is capable of handling. Teachers must be sensitive to the child's own pacing in classroom lessons. However, the next test of Piagetian theory must be in the classroom, not in the laboratory.

Chapter 8 Modification of Piagetian Theory

We have presented Piagetian theory of cognitive development in the previous chapters. Many would argue that the Piagetian perspective is a self-contained system and adding to or subtracting from it will violate its basic integrity. They suggest that it is illogical to attempt to modify the theory without doing violence to its basic propositions. We do not agree with this assertion, but rather believe that as with all scientific theories, Piaget's is open to modification, elaboration, and extension. This is not the place to show how research in the United States and England, as well as in Geneva, has influenced particular parts of the system or the course of research carried on by Piaget and his colleagues (Inhelder, Sinclair, and Bovet, 1974).

In these last pages, we shall touch on a few issues which we believe will contribute to rounding out the theory. Though we cannot provide an exhaustive list of issues, we shall select those that seem to be most critical and also those about which there is some misunderstanding. These revolve around the issues of *activity, affectivity, acceleration,* and the *role of the environment.*

The Concept of an Active Organism

Piaget makes the case that the living organism is active, reaching out and engaging the environment. Further, the individual engages objects and people directly through motor actions as well as through mental activity. Some argue that Piaget overemphasizes motor action, as in the sensorimotor period. This motor activity is interpreted literally, as though the child has to touch and handle everything in order to learn. This literal translation misrepresents the concept of activity. Activity is a broad concept encompassing motor, perceptual, and mental activity. Reaching out and touching constitute activity for the infant, but visual tracking of a moving object or mentally combining two items to form a chain are also activity-based functions. Activity is both *external* and *internal,* both overt and covert.

Since activity is characteristic of all living organisms, is there reason to expect comparable levels of activity among all individuals? Piaget has little to offer or to say about individual differences. His search is for universal characteristics of the development of human cognition. Yet, it is well known that infants vary in activity level and also in competence; for example, some are better in their visual systems, others are more proficient in their manual dexterity, and so on. Since several variations exist we can ask, how do individual differences in activity influence the course of growth? This is unknown and yet such information would be important for application of Piagetian theory to any educational or clinical setting. Therefore, one area in which more thinking and more research are necessary has to do with the role of individual differences in initial activity levels and in initial or developing competencies among the various perceptual and response systems (such as auditory, visual, or motor).

One way to begin this process is by integrating current knowledge in developmental psychology and education that could elaborate the role of individual differences in activity level.

Examination of the literature on learning disabilities, especially children with perceptual or motor handicaps, is in order. How do blind, deaf, or physically disabled children develop? Describing differences among these children in terms of variations in competence for solving various problems at different stages of growth may shed some light on this question.

The Place of Affectivity

Piaget explicitly states that affect plays a prominent role in the development of intelligence. His apparent lack of developing this idea theoretically or empirically can be interpreted in many ways. The omission, however, seems deliberate in setting priorities in problems of method. Acknowledging the role of affect and some preliminary theorizing has not yet led to a full-scale elaboration of the details.

The body of existent literature in developmental psychology describing social-emotional development has not found its way consistently into Piagetian thinking. The notable exception is the acknowledgement of the contribution of psychoanalytic theory and research to understanding infant development. Piaget argues that the affective system serves as an energizer in its parallel development with cognitive growth. Piaget seems to create a paradox, an integration of the cognitive and the affective, while at the same time acknowledging the two systems co-exist. No doubt there is a need to investigate the particular influence of emotional states in the quality and rate of cognitive growth. Piaget states in an interview that

affectivity does not modify the cognitive structure. Take two school children, for example. One who loves mathematics, who is interested and enthusiastic and anything else you wish, and the other who has feelings of inferiority, dislikes the teacher and so forth. One will go much faster, but for both of them two and two makes four in the end. It does not make three for the one who doesn't like it and five for the one who does. Two and two are still four (Evans, 1973, p. 7).

This quote highlights the issue of the place of affectivity and knowledge acquisition. Note that mathematical knowledge in this case is *objective*. Using the example, however, we might pose a number of questions, such as, do children whose feelings are positive acquire the structures more readily and do they transfer this knowledge more readily? In effect, are there differences in performance as well as in acquisition? These questions are not addressed and so cannot be directly answered within a Piagetian framework.

The problem is to identify affective variables that lend themselves to study. This is especially difficult among very young children whose affective states can only be inferred from observation. Thus, studies have had to focus on infant behaviors, such as restlessness, loss of appetite, weight loss, and fussiness, as indices of distress; and the converse, smiling, gurgling, cooing, reflect more positive states. These states of inferred emotionality in infancy must be examined in greater detail.

To complicate matters, it is necessary to take into account temperamental characteristics of the children. In spite of Piaget's interest in the biological basis of human behavior, he has tended to overlook temperamental factors. Initially, it would appear that temperament should be discussed under the heading of biological factors. The reason we consider the issue in the context of emotions is that temperament seems to contribute to affective states. The quiet baby in comparison to the active one suggests a different emotional state, such as satisfaction as opposed to frustration level. A large body of literature beyond the psychoanalytic studies of Décarie (1965), Escalona (1968), and Spitz (1957) must be incorporated in the framework to round out our knowledge of how cognition develops. The psychoanalytic studies reveal that infants, while going through the various sensorimotor stages, are beginning to define themselves; they relate differently to familiar and unfamiliar individuals, and differentially engage features in the environment. There is still the need to incorporate these results with others in order to demonstrate the effect on developing cognitive structures, rate of growth, and transition from stage to stage within each period, that is, sensorimotor, concrete operations, and formal operations.

Relatively little research or conceptualization has occurred identifying the affective features related to cognitive growth during the preoperational and operational periods. For example, from the preschool period on, children extend their personal-social contacts, gaining experience from such interactions. This assertion, however, does not explain how the necessary conditions for mutual influence occur. For children to socially interact, they have to be outgoing or at least receptive to others. There is some indication, however, that young children begin to show early differential interest in things (objects) compared to persons. How can we ask if this interest difference influences the development of cognitive structures? For example, do children who have had "emotional" difficulties during the first years of life develop similarly intellectually in comparison to those who have benign life experiences? Piagetian theory and these more extensive sets of data on emotional development have not yet been properly integrated.

Another issue that has been raised is that Piagetian theory does not deal with motivation in the context of affect. Motivation in the Piagetian system has its roots, in part, in the biological basis of activity as well as in interests. Although Piaget does not detail the role of interest as an energizer, he does acknowledge that individuals are energized to action by interest. This is another area that needs further amplification. If interest serves as a motivator, the questions arise as to the source of these interests and whether particular interest patterns influence developing cognitive organization. For example, if, for reasons to be identified, children are *thing* oriented, does this facilitate their spatial abilities or their manipulative skills? If motivational factors influence the activities children engage in, then it is possible that cognitive growth is in part directed by motivational factors.

Implied in the above argument is the idea that temperament, activity levels, and interests contribute to individual differences in rate and quality of cognitive development. The Piagetian system addresses universals in human development. Yet, it must be acknowledged that individual differences must be explained for educational application of these ideas.

In general Piaget deals, albeit briefly, with affect in regard to the development of moral judgment, development of value systems, and adult roles. Little if any attention has been paid to the influence of emotional factors in the development of concrete operations and formal operations. The significance resides in the argument that the décalage in development may, in part, be attributed to emotional factors functioning at particular stages in the child's life. Is it not conceivable that the anxiety level might influence the child's learning about characteristics of objects, therefore influencing classificatory skills, since classification depends in part upon substantive knowledge of attributes of a class? Furthermore, the process of classification requires the child to decenter, a process that might be influenced by affect. Integrating the affective component extends Piagetian theory into areas that are intimately involved in cognitive growth. Although Piaget acknowledges the role of affectivity in cognitive development, his descriptions and speculations, however, are not sufficiently detailed to allow for the claim that Piagetian theory truly integrates the role of emotional features with cognitive growth.

The American Question—Acceleration

Piaget has indicated that acceleration—the idea of speeding up the course of development—is an "American" question. For our purposes it might be better to think of acceleration, not as artificial speeding up, but pose the question: What is the effect of enrichment and educational intervention on the rate of growth? Piaget offers only the crudest age-related expectations and these are intended merely as guidelines, not as absolutes. Since there are no norms, just general age graded guidelines, we can ask what is acceleration? What does it mean to speed up the course of growth?

As we have indicated, the rates of cognitive development vary among cultures and among various groups within cultures. If experience does influence rate, then enhancing experiences through educational strategies may alter the expected rate. Thus, preschool or kindergarten age children may be able to solve conservation of quantity problems with ease if exposed to appropriate educational experiences, and at the appropriate stage. Acceleration is a false issue if it refers to the efforts of educating children to engage in groupings (classification, seriation, and so on) at earlier ages than Piaget reports. If the training stays within the stage structure postulated by Piaget, then it would seem that the issue is reduced to one of testing the limits of when children are capable of engaging in and performing certain tasks. For example, solving class inclusion problems may be possible for preschoolers provided the appropriate cognitive structures develop. Undoubtedly, there are practical limits to this since the stages of development cannot be compressed into too short a time. To date, little research has been done on this issue (Wohlwill, 1973).

Related to this issue is the question regarding the invariant order of stages. Again, validity of the invariance has to be demonstrated. In some cases, as in learning subtraction before number correspondence, the order of stages is clear. A child cannot solve subtraction problems before being able to understand number correspondence. Further, it seems doubtful that a child can deal with the logic of problems while in the concrete operational stage. But then, is the order of conservation of quantity fixed? Can one not provide experiences to enable children to solve problems of conservation of volume prior to conservation of weight? As we know, development of the substantive areas (for example, number, space, or area) and the logical processes (causality, classifications) proceed in an orderly sequential way. Some research argues that under certain conditions the defined sequence is open to question: for example, Trabasso claims that children can be taught transitivity problems during the preoperational period (Trabasso, 1975).

In sum, the acceleration issue has to be reviewed, not in the context of speed, but of defining the upper and lower limits within which modification of rate and development of cognitive structures can be determined. Accelerating cognitive growth is superfluous for Piaget. For many American investigators, modification and training studies shed considerable light on the theory itself. Through these studies (see Chapter 7), the necessary or sufficient conditions for cognitive growth can be identified. Thus, the point is not to accelerate development as much as discover the conditions which foster it. Such discoveries can be more readily translated into practical educational or training environments than the concepts directly taken from Piaget's theory.

We could ask what the "danger" is in so-called acceleration. Acceleration assumes a defined rate of growth. If rate is open-ended, then is this a real issue? Knowledge of the directions and stages of growth, and knowledge of the conditions for growth, would then provide the basis for creating an environment that fosters development. If the environment is not oppressive, and if the child evolves in a way that seems affectively positive, then there is, in effect, no acceleration, merely optimal conditions for expression of abilities. Acceleration presupposes a given order and rate of growth. We have a false issue unless development has such a schedule. But we have already stated that Piaget does not base his stage theory upon ages for mental abilities to make their appearances. Since age and stage are not rigorously tied together, acceleration is not an issue.

The Role of Experience

In Chapter 6 we proposed distancing behaviors as one class of experience relevant to the development of representational thinking. We also alluded to the broad role of cultural factors that influence cognitive development. There is ample evidence to show that the rate *and* quality of cognitive development vary according to the type of environment. Children from the African bush, for example, performed less effectively on conservation tasks than city children at a particular age (Dasen, 1972); children from disadvantaged environments in the United States had more difficulty solving conservation and classification tasks than children from more privileged homes (Sigel & Olmsted, 1970). The reasons for these results are not yet clear.

Piagetian theory holds that environmental interactions are necessary for cognitive growth. In environmental interactions, the child has opportunities for spontaneous learning through discovery and invention. Through the presentation of materials and resources (education), cognitive structures evolve. What is needed is greater specification of the particular environmental settings and definition of their specific influences. For example, Murray (1972) found that children were able to solve conservation problems through observing and participating with peers. Research of this type provides the detail that elaborates the role of experience and environments.

The physical and social environments provide the child with the necessary settings for constructing a social and physical reality. The factors that play a role in this context, such as physical resources, types of social interaction, freedom of movement to explore and to discover, are among the factors that must be incorporated into the theory. In this way, the environmental forces become more than mere abstractions.

Epilogue

This final section will be a summary statement of our developmental perspective for providing a coherent theoretical point of view by which many of the developmental concerns previously discussed can be integrated.

Essentially, our point of view can be called *developmental constructivism*, which holds that human organisms actively build their constructs, knowledge base, and views of reality through engagement with the environment. What and how the building varies is a function of the developmental level of each person.

Constructivism is not new or radical in philosophy. In developmental cognitive psychology, however, this point of view is recent, having been inspired to some degree by the work of Piaget. It is important to keep in mind that constructivism as a theoretical perspective is different from the usual use of the term *construct* in psychology. There is no question that all theories in any science are constructed by the scientist. For the scientist organizes his observations and his inferences about events. That all systems made by people are human constructions should not be confused with the idea of constructivism itself as a label for a theoretical perspective. When we think of constructivism as a theoretical perspective, we start with the assumption that the individual, as an active organism, builds or constructs notions of reality, whether physical or social. The principal assumption is that the active organism does not passively assimilate information and construct a knowledge system. Rather, the active organism builds from experience and the process of building results in knowledge. The process may be similar to the scientist building theoretical models, but our interest is in the developmental aspects of such constructions. The metaphor of construction is applicable to each situation, whether the individual is a scientist or not.

The constructivist point of view is antagonistic to the behavioristic perspective. From the constructivist perspective the active organism encounters the environment through actions and this prototype describes the process of knowledge development. Whereas in the behavioristic perspective, the individual emits behaviors, some of which are reinforced and are retained, while others drop out. Of importance is that developmental constructivism be understood as a frame appropriate to the study of mental development.

The process by which Piaget and Skinner come to the conclusions they do about how to view and study human growth is not different in essence from the way each of us comes to define the world we live in, by building a construction of a reality. Because of our active engagement with varieties of objects, persons, events, time frames, and the like, and because we are participants in this endeavor, the inevitable occurs: We create a mental picture of the world about us. We have constructed a reality. The critical issue is that as scientists deliberately set out to define and formalize how each views the world, so too with each of us, although not in a formal way. The homologue is that the scientist builds a world, evolves a world view, but does so in a formal, articulated, systematic way; we, the nonscientists, do the same thing but in an informal, not usually articulated, and not necessarily systematic, way. We are all in a sense scientists, actively engaged in organizing our reality as participants (Kelly, 1955). The world is not fed to us which we then passively ingest; rather, we ingest it through actively reaching out and taking it in. Before elaborating on the processes involved in these developments, it is necessary to clear away some possible misconceptions.

First, does this concept of constructivism mean that each of us builds a *unique* and different world since each of us is different? Are we implying that there is no agreed upon reality? Not at all. The point of our discussion of *constructivism* is that we build a conception of our reality through our experience with it. One constructs a different concept of typewriting just by being told how to type as compared to actively engaging in it. One cannot know about a ball until one has experienced the ball. Participation and engagement in the event are the active bases from which a construction of the particular is developed and from which meaning is extracted, a meaning shared in part with others.

How do we come to experience outer space or other phenomena with which we cannot have direct participation? The answer resides in the conception of humans as symbol-using, symbol-developing organisms who learn to represent mentally many experiences. These representations serve as analogues or approximations of the event. In a sense, it is a vicarious experience. The knowledge of the event is an approximation and may not be in accord with the reality if and when one can experience it. For example, reading travel books and studying about a place at a distance does provide approximations with places, but not identical images. We recreate and re-present those places even though we have never been there. *But* we are familiar with them in a limited sense.

Basically, the human organism constructs a world of experiences using various modes in the process. The modes employed are functions of the person's developmental level. The very young child cannot use language as the older child or adult does; the younger child has more difficulty using writing symbols to express an idea. Irrespective of the mode employed, however, the individual represents personal experiences in some form. This act of representation is a central human capability (see Chapters 5 and 6 on language and the distancing hypothesis, respectively). The ability to represent in any modality provides the individual with an economical means by which to retain considerable information in an efficient form. Stop and think how much information the human mind is capable of retaining in the course of even the short span of childhood. By the age of four the child speaks and understands a language, knows the names of many things, carries on conversations, communicates wants, and the like. How the knowledge is stored is a moot question, but we do know that the young preschool child by age four is able to employ at least three modes, which Bruner has so aptly called enactive, ikonic, and symbolic modes. The enactive is similar to the sensorimotor; the ikonic is comparable to the figural; and the symbolic refers to systems such as written or spoken language, mathematical notation, and so on. The child then uses these modes to assimilate and organize information encountered in everyday activities.

Before we proceed with a somewhat more detailed discussion of developmental constructivism, we should make it clear that this is not the usual philosophical concept of idealism in which the mind is the most important factor in determining the nature of reality. This view emphasizes the uniqueness of experiences, and in this uniqueness there is no shared commonality. Our point of view does not take such an extreme position. There is an OUT THERE. We create representations of trees, buildings, people, of all experiences. We are the only ones that *experience* what we have experienced. But we share these experiences with others through various means of communication.

Let us extend our description of what is constructed. The implication is that what is constructed is a "picture" of the world, a knowledge base. This knowledge consists of two broad domains; operational knowledge, that is, how to do something, and a knowledge about something. We know when a one is a one and not a two; we know a unit from units; singulars from plurals. This is substance. We also know that combining one unit with another unit yields two units. This later is an operation on the knowledge. To achieve the knowledge of the operation and the knowledge of the substance, is a function of growth (physical, neurophysiological) and experience, coming in contact with individuals, objects, and events.

We also experience a relatedness in our knowledge. Things do not exist in isolation, but tend to be organized into units or wholes. These units or wholes are referred to as *schemata*, organizations of experiences which serve as the context by which new knowledge can be assimilated. For example, the individual may have developed a schema of the class *animals*. New instances of animals that are experienced will be assimilated to this one, yielding a more elaborate class *animal*.

The development and organization of knowledge, along with the processes involved in its utilization, come about through the developmental processes of assimilation and accommodation (see Chapters 1-3). Through assimilations and accommodations individuals build their reality; they construct the knowledge they use now and will continue to use.

However, as we have shown, the knowledge base may remain the same, but its meanings will change. The young child in the conservation task recognizes two balls and does not understand that a change in shape does not mean a change in amount; the older individual recognizes the change in shape as does the child, but interprets this differently. The older person sees it as a change in appearance, but not as a change in amount. The stimuli are the same for both parties, but the meanings are different because each constructs the reality differently. This is due to the differences in experience and in maturation. But what experiences make for the differences, and why do they happen? We can only give partial answers to these questions, but they are consistent with our constructivistic developmental perspective.

Let us return to the application of assimilation and accommodation concepts. These are two interdependent processes; one does not exist without the other. Assimilation must lead to some accommodation and the new accommodation creates a new concept or schema which is then assumed until another new experience replaces it. The form of the assimilation-accommodation relationship is a dialectic. Simply, this refers to the process between a given situational state, a thesis, and a new experience which does not fit with what was previously known, the antithesis; both new and old then merge into a new synthesis. The dialectic principle, action-reaction-reorganization, is a constant interactive process which describes how the organism copes with the new experience and leads to engaging in a constant interplay between a given state and an experience.

How does this work? The individual lives in an active relationship with the environment, engaging and participating with the world of objects, people, and events. During this, the individual is in situations which are compatible with his wants, intentions, and expectations. The child reaches for an object and the object is there: confirmation of an expectation. The child cries for the mother and the mother appears: a confirmation of an expectation. The child moves from one activity to another seeking excitement or a change of scenery: A change occurs. All of these are minor, yet prototypes of, engagements where there is consistency, confirmation of the individual's intentions and expectations, and outcomes. But the opportunities for confirmation are not always present. There are times when the child reaches for an object and it moves away or is not within grasp. The child cries for the mother and she does not appear. The child moves from one place to another and the new scene is of no more interest than the old. Confirmations do not appear;

rather there are violations of what is wished for, expected, and intended.

Life is made up of both confirmations and nonconfirmations of expectations. Our contention is that this interplay of confirmation and nonconfirmation, of consistency and inconsistency in one's engagement with the world, provides what Piaget calls the conflict, the disequilibrium. These experiences demonstrate in an experiential way that the world is not always a predictable, consistent set of events. The inconsistency and the consistency, the confirmation and the lack of confirmation, however, are not in the world of events, objects, and people. These phenomena are constructed in the head of the individual. The constructivist point of view would argue that the individual constructs all these consistencies and inconsistencies.

It follows from this line of reasoning that growth occurs as a function of both consistent and inconsistent engagement. Consistent engagement may be interpreted as reinforcement, as a positive reaffirmation of one's own judgment, whereas disconfirmation yielding conflict demands resolution. The reason for this need is that humans cannot tolerate contradictions, and must come to a resolution.

The question then arises as to how the resolutions relate to the outcomes. In general, resolution requires some change in approach to the problem. Change can be expressed by leaving the scene of the encounter and in a sense avoiding it. The child does not obtain the object by reaching for it, so gives up. The adult cannot get a certain job so gives up. Acceptance of the failure is then one approach. The individual may also try to change either the approach or the problem. The child may decide that the means employed to achieve the goal were inappropriate so alters the way of going about it. The adult, not finding the job, surveys the scene and finds that the method employed is not productive, so shifts the strategy. Or the problem itself might be shifted. On the surface this description sounds like we are discussing personality adjustment. That is because in our view engagement and problem solving in the environment are the basic issues and can be expressed in such conceptual systems as personality or cognition. It should be kept in mind, however, that the ways of engagement and coping are fundamental organism-environment developmental cognitive problems. In every case, the individuals develop knowledge of the world and their places in it. Thus if we wish to designate these modes of resolution as cognitive conflict mechanisms of defense, as Freudian psychologists would, or coping mechanisms as other personality theorists might, it does not really matter. Underlying all of these manifestations of differences in theoretical bias is the necessity to indicate how the individual copes with contradictions in the environment. For Piaget, this is the essence of intelligence, since intelligence is solving problems. Problems are present in the eyes of the individual and for their resolution the individual constructs mechanisms of dealing with them.

Knowledge is accumulated during the encounters discussed. The knowledge can only be partial understanding of an event since all events are complex and made of various constituents. Children reaching for the object discover they cannot do it simply by extending their hands, so move their bodies and arrive at the place of the object. They have learned that they can propel themselves and in so doing coordinate this with their eyes and hands and acquire the object. The knowledge so obtained is not the whole story. They have learned nothing about the relationship between voluntary actions and the brain or nervous system; they have learned nothing about the role of friction movement; they have learned nothing about the grasping actions coordinated by the eyes. They have learned some, but not the total, knowledge involved in that set of actions. What they learned is practical. This is true of all assimilations. The children, however, have constructed representations of their experiences. These representations may take the form of motor action (enactive), images or mental pictures (ikonic), or symbols (language). In whatever form the new knowledge is assimilated, it is coordinated with existing knowledge and may result in a new schema.

Another implication of the complexity of the environment is that the particular aspects of items that become salient for the person will depend on individual differences and previous experiences with such stimuli. For example, some individuals may tend to focus on the manifest characteristics of objects, such as color, form, or appearance, while others may be oriented to the functions of objects. The variation in selection of salient cues to be extracted from stimuli is due to the particular style the person develops. Approaches to one's surroundings have been called *cognitive style*, since it is assumed that individuals develop characteristic ways of organizing and defining their environments (Kagan, Moss, and Sigel, 1963).

The selection of particular aspects of the environment as a basis for organizing arrays of stimuli relates to our discussion of formation of concepts. A concept is an organization of an array of independent items. Thus we can argue that concept development is related to the individual's style, to the individual's selection of particular cues by which to organize matters. This concept of cognitive style is of particular significance in our conceptualization of individual differences in development.

To this point we have emphasized general developmental characteristics with little attention paid to the individual differences in such development. We are all aware of the fact that individuals differ in rate of growth and in the quality and quantity of experiences. These background factors are assumed to influence the way people develop concepts.

Not only are there individual differences in direct experiences, there are also differences in the satisfaction individuals have in their engagement with the environment. Piaget speaks of the significance of interest and desire in describing affective concomitants of engagement with objects, events, and people. Although he does not place much emphasis on this aspect of human interaction, its significance is profound. How the individual at any age participates in an activity, overtly or covertly, is tied to affective involvement. There is enough evidence from the clinical research literature to indicate that the role of emotional involvement in encounters with the environment are of considerable significance. The emotional factors contribute to the energizing and persistence with which individuals continue their engagement in activity.

The joy and excitement that individuals have in their encounters with the environment are not the sole sources of motivation to construct reality. It should be kept in mind that the resolution of conflict on the cognitive level is also of import. The discrepancy that is observed or experienced in solving a problem or resolving differences in a situation produces a conflict. There seems to be a basic human need to resolve such discrepancies. To call this emotional would equate emotionality with tension or awareness of difference between two conditions. For this discussion let us keep the two separate. The conflict we are discussing now is cognitive conflict with its own tension system which we conceptualize as different from the affective involvement we have discussed.

Within the context discussed, it becomes clear that the emotional factors provide an additional complication. The source of these factors comes not only from the individual's sense of joy and excitement, but also from the responses of others. Thus, the way significant figures respond to the child's newly found learning and newly developed strategies for dealing with problems should have a profound influence on the child's developing approach to, and engagement in, the world. We can allude to two general sources here. One, the primary familial unit with the significant adults having a particular influence on the very young child, and with increasing age other significant adults such as teacher or similar individuals playing the role of teachers; and the second major influence is the peer group. The balance between the relative influence of one or the other of these classes of individuals influencing the child will vary with the age of the child and the culture. In western societies the adults play the significant role in the early years, with the peer group coming to play an increasing role by the time the child goes to school, usually about age six. From this point on, the teachers and peers enter contributing significant experiences not only to the child's increasingly complex knowledge about the physical world and how to deal with it, but most apparently to the social world. Each component will be influenced differentially. For example, the child's knowledge of how to extract knowledge from the physical world and how to utilize this knowledge are part of the educational experience as well as learning how friends accept this approach. The joy and interest may be influenced by the relationships the children have with their peers. There may be times when the child will surrender a point of view or deny experiences in order to hold on to peer relationships.

The perspectives that are involved in the child's developing knowledge base, however, are intimately tied to the culture. Thus, the child in Africa in a hunting society is different from the child in Europe or America. Each group has experiences and patterns of interrelationships which are culturally defined. That we in the western world do not generally believe in reincarnation leads us to a very different response toward animals than people in India. There are many religious and other belief systems which are highly differentiated among cultures. These differences contribute to differential definitions of reality. However, this should not be construed as implying that the operations performed on these knowledge domains are different from one culture to another. We are talking here essentially of the substance of the knowledge base, not the operations performed on the knowledge.

In sum then, the influence of culture and individual growth experiences, are among the critical features that define the kind of cognitive development the child will exeprience. It is within this context that the child develops conceptions of reality and defines the meanings attributed to various experiences. It is also in this context that the child develops the representational modes used to organize and express this reality. For us then, a constructivist developmental point of view seems to capture the essence of cognitive growth and allows for the inclusion of the factors that contribute to its development. Many gaps exist in our scientific information base, but within the framework proposed here, we see the potential for extending our understanding of cognitive development.

References

Arnheim, R. *Visual thinking*. Berkeley, Calif.: University of California Press, 1969.

Asch, S. E., & Nerlove, H. The development of double function terms in children: An exploratory investigation. In B. Kaplan & S. Wapner (Eds.), *Perspectives in psychological theory: Essays in honor of Heinz Werner*. New York: International Universities Press, 1960.

Ausubel, D. P. *Theory and problems of child development*. New York: Grune & Stratton, 1957.

Bandura, A. Social-learning theory of identificatory processes. In D. A. Gostin (Ed.), *Handbook of socialization theory and research*. Skokie, Ill.: Rand McNally, 1969, 213–262.

Bandura, A. Behavior theory and models of man. *American Psychologist*, 1974, **29**, 859–870.

Beilin, H. Learning and operational convergence in logical thought development. *Journal of Experimental Child Psychology*, 1965, **2**, 317–339.

Beilin, H., & Spontak, G. *Active-passive transformations and operational reversibility*. Paper presented at biennial meeting of the

Society for Research in Child Development, Santa Monica, California, March 1969.

Bellugi, U. Some language comprehension tests. In C. S. Lavatelli (Ed.), *Language training in early childhood education.* Urbana, Ill.: University of Illinois Press, 1971, 157–169.

Bever, T. G., Mehler, J., & Valian, V. V. Linguistic capacity of very young children. Lecture at Graduate School of Education, Harvard University, 1947 (cited in McNeill, 1970b).

Bijou, S. W. Development in the preschool years: A functional analysis. *American Psychologist*, 1975, **30**(8), 829–237.

Blank, M. A methodology for fostering abstract thinking in deprived children. In A. J. Biemiller (Ed.), *Problems in the teaching of young children.* Toronto: Ontario Institute for Studies in Education, 1970.

Bolles, M. M. The basis of pertinence. *Archives of Psychology*, 1937, **212**, 51.

Bower, T. G. R. Stimulus variables determining space perception in infants. *Science*, 1965a, **149**, 88–89.

Bower, T. G. R. The determinants of perceptual units in infancy. *Psychonomic Science*, 1965b, **3**, 323–324.

Bower, T. G. R. Slant perception and shape constancy in infants. *Science*, 1966, **151**, 832–834.

Bower, T. G. R. Phenomenal identity and form perception in an infant. *Perception and Psychophysics*, 1967a, **2**, 74–76.

Bower, T. G. R. The development of object permanence: Some studies of existence constancy. *Perception and Psychophysics*, 1967b, **2**, 411–418.

Bower, T. G. R. *Development in infancy.* San Francisco: W. H. Freeman, 1974.

Bower, T. G. R., Broughton, J. M., & Moore, M. K. Development of the object concept as manifested in change in the tracking behavior of infants between 7 and 20 weeks of age. *Journal of Experimental Child Psychology*, 1971, **11**, 182–193.

Brainerd, C. J. Order of acquisition of transitivity, conservation, and class-inclusion of length and weight. *Developmental Psychology*, 1973, **8**, 105–116.

Brainerd, C. J. Training and transfer of transitivity, conservation, and class-inclusion of length. *Child Development*, 1974, **45**, 324–334.

Brown, R. W. *Words and things.* New York: Free Press, 1958.

Brown, R. W. *Social psychology.* New York: Free Press, 1965, 246–349.

Brown, R. W. *A first language.* Cambridge, Mass.: Harvard University Press, 1973.

Bruner, J. The course of cognitive growth. *American Psychologist*, 1964, **19**, 1–15.

Bruner, J. *Beyond the information given.* J. Anglin (Ed.) New York: Norton, 1973.

Bruner, J. S., & Oliver, R. R. Development of equivalence transformations in children. *Monographs for the Society for Research in Child Development*, 1963, **28**(2), 125–143.

Carlson, P., & Anisfeld, M. Some observations on the linguistic competence of a two-year-old child. *Child Development*, 1969, **40**(2), 569–576.

Cassirer, E. *The philosophy of symbolic forms*. Vol. 3 of *The phenomenology of knowledge*. New Haven, Conn.: Yale University, 1957.

Clark, E. V. What's in a word? On the child's acquisition of semantics in his first language. In T. E. Moore (Ed.), *Cognitive development and the acquisition of language*. New York: Academic Press, 1973, 65–110.

Clark, E. V. Some aspects of the conceptual basis for first language acquisition. In R. Schiefelbusch & L. L. Lloyd (Eds.), *Language perspectives—acquisition, retardation, and intervention*. Baltimore, Md.: University Park Press, 1974, 103–128.

Cocking, R. R. *Cognitive socialization: a social-learning analysis of language acquisition*. Publication of the Mathemagenic Activities Program, January 1972, Athens, Ga.

Cocking, R. R. *Measures of language comprehension: Relations to performance*. Paper presented at Southeastern regional meetings of the Society for Research in Child Development, Williamsburg, Va., April 1972.

Cocking, R., & Potts, M. Social facilitation of language acquisition. *Journal of Genetic Psychology Monographs*, 1976, **94**(2).

Cohen, D. *Deictic reference in children's speech*. Paper presented at Linguistic Society of America meetings, Winter 1973.

Cole, M., & Scribner, S. *Culture and thought: A psychological introduction*. New York: Wiley, 1974.

Dasen, P. Cross-cultural Piagetian research: A summary. *Journal of Cross-Cultural Psychology*, 1972, **3**, 23–40.

Decarie, T. G. *Intelligence and affectivity in early childhood*. New York: International Universities Press, 1965.

Donovan, A. *Parent-child interaction and the development of representational skills in young children*. Unpublished doctoral dissertation. S.U.N.Y. at Buffalo, Buffalo, N.Y., 1974.

Elkind, D. The development of quantitative thinking: A systematic replication of Piaget's studies. *Journal of Genetic Psychology*, 1961, **98**, 37–46.

Elkind, D. Children's discovery of the conservation of mass, weight, and volume: Piaget replication study II. *Journal of Genetic Psychology*, 1961, 98, 219–227.

Elkind, D. *Children and adolescents: Interpretive essays on Jean Piaget*. New York: Oxford University Press, 1970.

Ervin, S. Imitation and structural change in children's language. In E. H. Lenneberg (Ed.), *New directions in the study of language*. Cambridge, Mass.: M.I.T. Press, 1964, 163–189.

Ervin-Tripp, S. Language development. In M. Hoffman & L. Hoffman (Eds.), *Review of child development research, Vol. II.* New York: Russell Sage, 1966, 55–105.

Escalona, S. *Roots of individuality.* Chicago: Aldine, 1968.

Evans, R. L. *Jean Piaget: The man and his ideas.* New York: E. P. Dutton, 1973.

Ezer, M. Effect of religion upon children's responses to questions involving physical causality. In J. Rosenblith & W. Allinsmith (Eds.), *The causes of behavior: Readings in child development and educational psychology.* Boston: Allyn and Bacon, 1962, 481–487.

Fantz, R. L. The origin of form perception. *Scientific American,* 1961a, **204,** 66–72.

Fantz, R. L. A method for studying depth perception in infants under six months of age. *Psychological Record,* 1961b, **11,** 27–32.

Fantz, R. L. Pattern vision in newborn infants. *Science,* 1963, **140,** 296–297.

Fantz, R. L. Visual perception from birth as shown by pattern selectivity. *Annals of the New York Academy of Science,* 1965, **118,** 793–814.

Fantz, R. L., & Nevis, S. Pattern preferences and perceptual cognitive development in early infancy. *Merrill-Palmer Quarterly of Behavior and Development,* 1967, **13,** 77–108.

Fillmore, C. J. *Some problems for case grammar.* Report of the Ohio State University and the Center for Advanced Study in the Behavioral Sciences, 1971.

Fink, R. *The role of imaginative play in cognitive development.* Unpublished doctoral dissertation, S.U.N.Y. at Buffalo, Buffalo, N.Y., 1974.

Flavell, J. *The developmental psychology of Jean Piaget.* Princeton, N.J.: Van Nostrand, 1963.

Flavell, J. State-related properties of cognitive development. *Cognitive Psychology,* 1971, **2,** 421–453.

Fowler, W. Demonstration program in infant care and education. (Final Report), 1971.

Fraser, C., Bellugi, U., & Brown, R. Control of grammar in imitation, comprehension, and production. *Journal of Verbal Learning and Verbal Behavior,* 1963, **2,** 121–135.

Furth, H. G. *Piaget for teachers.* Englewood Cliffs, N.J.: Prentice-Hall, 1970.

Gagné, R. M. *Essentials of learning for instruction.* N.Y.: Holt, Rinehart and Winston, 1974.

Gardner, R. A., & Gardner, B. T. Teaching sign language to a chimpanzee. *Science,* 1969, **165,** 664–672.

Gesell, A., & Amatruda, C. S. *Developmental diagnosis: Normal and abnormal child development.* New York: Hoeber, 1941.

Ginsburg, H., & Opper, S. *Piaget's theory of intellectual development.* Englewood Cliffs, N.J.: Prentice-Hall, 1969.

Gladwin, T. *East is a big bird.* Cambridge, Mass.: Harvard University Press, 1970.

Goldstein, K., & Scheerer, M. Abstract and concrete behavior: An experimental study with special tests. *Psychological Monograph*, 1941, 53(2, Whole No. 239).

Goodenough, F. L., & Tyler, L. E. *Developmental psychology*, 3d ed. New York: Appleton-Century-Crofts, 1959.

Gough, P. B. (Almost a decade of) Experimental psycholinguistics. In W. O. Dingwall (Ed.), *A survey of linguistic science*. College Park, Md.: University of Maryland, Linguistics Program, 1971.

Hammond, K. R. (Ed.). *The psychology of Egon Brunswik*. N.Y.: Holt, Rinehart and Winston, 1966.

Hershenson, M. Development of the perception of form. *Psychological Bulletin*, 1967, 67, 326–336.

Hochberg, J., & Brooks, V. Pictorial recognition as an unlearned ability: A study of one child's performance. *American Journal of Psychology*, 1962, 75, 624–628.

Hoffman, M. Moral development. In P. Mussen (Ed.), *Carmichael's manual of child psychology*, Vol. II. New York: Wiley, 1970.

Hooper, F. An evaluation of logical operations instruction in the preschool. In R. K. Parker (Ed.), *The preschool in action*. Boston: Allyn and Bacon, Inc., 1972.

Hunt, D. E., & Sullivan, E. V. *Between psychology and education*. New York: Holt, Rinehart and Winston, 1974.

Hunt, J. McV. *Intelligence and experience*. New York: Ronald Press, 1961.

Huttenlocher, J., Eisenberg, K., & Strauss, S. Comprehension: Relation between perceived actor and logical subject. *Journal of Verbal Learning and Verbal Behavior*, 1968, 7, 527–530.

Huttenlocher, J., & Strauss, S. Comprehension and a statement's relation to the situation it describes. *Journal of Verbal Learning and Verbal Behavior*, 1968, 7, 300–304.

Inhelder, B. The diagnosis of reasoning in the mentally retarded. New York: John Day, 1968.

Inhelder, B., & Piaget, J. *The growth of logical thinking from childhood to adolescence*. New York: Basic Books, 1958.

Inhelder, B., & Piaget, J. *Early growth of logic*. New York: Harper, 1964.

Inhelder, B., Sinclair, H., & Bovet, M. *Learning and the development of cognition*. Cambridge, Mass.: Harvard University Press, 1974.

Jacobson, R. Concluding statement: Linguistics and poetics. In T. A. Sebok (Ed.), *Style in language*. Cambridge, Mass.: M.I.T. Press, 1960.

Jenkins, J. J. Mediation theory and grammatical behavior. In S. Rosenberg (Ed.), *Directions in psycholinguistics*. New York: Macmillan, 1965.

Johnson, R. C. Linguistic structure as related to concept formation and to concept content. *Psychological Bulletin*, 1962, 59, 468–476.

Kagan, J., Moss, H. A., & Sigel, I. E. Psychological significance of styles of conceptualization. *Monographs of the Society for Research in Child Development*, 1963, **28**(2, Serial Number 86), 73–112.

Kamii, C. An application of Piaget's theory to the conceptualization of a preschool curriculum. In R. K. Parker (Ed.), *The preschool in action*. Boston: Allyn and Bacon, 1972.

Kaplan, E. L. *The role of intonation in the acquisition of language*. Unpublished doctoral dissertation, Cornell University, Ithaca, N.Y., 1969.

Kaplan, E. L., & Kaplan, G. A. Is there any such thing as a prelinguistic child? In J. Eliot (Ed.), *Human development and cognitive processes*. New York: Holt, Rinehart and Winston, 1971.

Katz, E. W., & Brent, S. B. Understanding connectives. *Journal of Verbal Learning and Verbal Behavior*, 1968, **7**, 501–509.

Kelly, G. A. *The psychology of personal constructs*. Vol. I. New York: Norton, 1955.

Kessen, W., Haith, M. M., & Salapatek, P. *The ocular orientation of newborn infants to visual contours*. Paper presented at the meeting of the Psychonomic Society, Chicago, October 1965.

Koffka, K., *The growth of the mind: An introduction to child psychology*, 2d rev. ed. Translated by R. M. Ogden. New York: Harcourt, 1928.

Kohlberg, L. *Stages in children's conceptions of physical and social objects in the years four to eight: A study of developmental theory*. Unpublished manuscript, 1963.

Kohlberg, L. Stage and sequence: The cognitive-developmental approach to socialization. In D. Goslin (Ed.), *Handbook of socialization theory and research*. Skokie, Ill.: Rand McNally, 1969.

Kohnstamm, G. A. Experiments on teaching Piagetian thought operations. In J. Hellmuth (Ed.), *Cognitive studies*, Vol. 1. New York: Brunner/Mazel, 1970.

Kooistra, W. H. *Developmental trends in the attainment of conservation, transitivity, and relativism in the thinking of children: A replication and extension of Piaget's ontogenetic formulations*. Unpublished doctoral dissertation, Wayne State University, Detroit, Mich., 1963.

Laurendeau, M., & Pinard, A. *Causal thinking in the child*. New York: International Universities Press, 1972.

Laurendeau, M., & Pinard A. *The development of the concepts of space in the child*. New York: International Universities Press, 1970.

Lavatelli, C. *Early childhood curriculum: A Piaget program*. Boston: American Service & Engineering, 1970.

Lenneberg, E. H. A biological perspective of language. In E. H. Lenneberg (Ed.), *New directions in the study of language*. Cambridge, Mass.: M.I.T. Press, 1964.

Lenneberg, E. H. On explaining language: The development of

language in children can best be understood in the context of developmental biology. *Science*, 1969, **164**, 635–643.

Lenneberg, E. H. Of language knowledge, apes, and brains. *Journal of Psycholinguistic Research*, 1971, **1**, 1–29.

Lenneberg, E. H., Rebelsky, F., & Nichols, I. The vocalization of infants born to deaf and hearing parents. *Human Development*, 1965, **8**, 23–37.

Levenstein, P. Verbal interaction project, child welfare, research and demonstration project (R-300). Final Report to Children's Bureau, OCD, Washington, D.C., 1971.

Loban, W. D. *Problems in oral English*. Champaign, Ill.: National Council of Teachers of English, 1966.

Luria, S. *Life: The unfinished experiment*. New York: Scribners, 1973.

MacNamara, J. Cognitive basis of language learning in infants. *Psychological Review*, 1972, **79**(1), 1–13.

McKim, R. H. *Experiments in visual thinking*. Belmont, Calif.: Brooks/Cole, 1972.

McNeill, D. *The acquisition of language: The study of developmental psycholinguistics*. New York: Harper & Row, 1970a.

McNeill, D. The development of language. In P. Mussen (Ed.), *Carmichael's manual of child psychology*. Vol. I. New York: Wiley, 1970b.

McNeill, D. *Semiotic extension*. Paper presented at the Loyola Symposium on Cognition, Chicago, April 1974.

Mead, G. H. *Mind, self and society*. Chicago: University of Chicago Press, 1972.

Menyuk, P. Syntactic structures in the language of children. *Child Development*, 1963, **34**, 407–422.

Menyuk, P. *Sentences children use*. Cambridge, Mass.: M.I.T. Press, 1969.

Menyuk, P. *The acquisition and development of language*. Englewood Cliffs, N.J.: Prentice-Hall, 1971.

Miller, R. Cross-cultural research in the perception of pictorial materials. *Psychological Bulletin*, 1973, **80**, 135–150.

Miller, L. B., & Dyer, J. L. Four preschool programs: their dimensions and effects. *Monographs of the Society for Research in Child Development*, 1975, **40**, Serial No. 162.

Mogar, M. Children's causal reasoning about natural phenomena. *Child Development*, 1960, **31**, 59–65.

Moore, M. K., & Clark, D. E. Piaget's State IV error: An identity. Paper presented at the Society for Research in Child Development, Denver, 1975.

Moore, M. K., & Dawson-Myers, G. *The development of object permanence from visual tracking to total hidings: Two new states*. Paper presented at the Society for Research in Child Development, Denver, 1975.

Murray, F. B. Acquisition of conservation through social partici-pation. *Developmental Psychology*, 1972, **6**, 1–6.

Mussen, P. (Ed.). *Carmichael's manual of child psychology*. New York: Wiley, 1970.

Nelson, K. Structure and strategy in learning to talk. *Monographs of the Society for Research in Child Development*, 1973, Serial No. 149.

Nelson, K., & Kessen, W. *What the child brings to language.* Lecture presented at the Jean Piaget Society meetings, Philadelphia, May 1974.

O'Donnell, R. C., Griffin, W. J., & Norris, R. C. *Syntax of kindergarten and elementary school children: A transformational analysis.* Champaign, Ill.: National Council of Teachers of English, 1967.

Palermo, D. S., & Molfese, D. L. Language acquisition from age five onward. *Psychological Bulletin*, 1972, **78**(6), 409–428.

Piaget, J. *Judgment and reasoning in the child*. New York: Harcourt, 1928.

Piaget, J. *The child's conception of physical causality*. New York: Harcourt, 1930.

Piaget, J. *The psychology of intelligence*. London: Routledge and Kegan Paul, 1950 (reprinted 1966).

Piaget, J. *Play, dreams, and imitation in childhood*. New York: Norton, 1951 (reprinted 1962).

Piaget, J. *The origins of intelligence in children*. New York: International Universities Press, 1952a.

Piaget, J. *The child's conception of number*. London: Routledge, 1952b.

Piaget, J. *The construction of reality in the child*. New York: Basic Books, 1954.

Piaget, J. The general problems of the psychobiological development of the child. In J. M. Tanner & B. Inhelder (Eds.), *Discussions of child development*. Volume IV. New York: International Universities Press, 1960.

Piaget, J. The genetic approach to the psychology of thought. *Journal of Educational Psychology*, 1961, **52**, 275–281.

Piaget, J. Introduction to *Causal thinking in the child* by M. Laurendeau & A. Pinard. New York: International Universities Press, 1962.

Piaget, J. *Six psychological studies*. New York: Random House, 1967.

Piaget, J. *Genetic epistemology*. New York: Columbia University Press, 1970a.

Piaget, J. Piaget's theory. In P. Mussen (Ed.), *Carmichael's manual of child psychology,* Volume I. New York: Wiley, 1970b, 703–732.

Piaget, J. *The science of education and the psychology of the child*. New York: Orion Press, 1970c.

Piaget, J. *Biology and knowledge*. Chicago: University of Chicago Press, 1971.

Piaget, J. *Child and reality*. New York: Grossman, 1973.

Piaget, J. *To understand is to invent*. New York: Grossman, 1974.

Piaget, J., & Inhelder, B. *Psychology of the child*. New York: Basic Books, 1969.

Piaget, J., & Inhelder, B. The gaps in empiricism. In A. Koestler, & J. R. Mythies, *Beyond reductionism*. New York: Macmillan, 1970.

Piaget, J., & Inhelder, B. *Mental imagery in the child*. New York: Basic Books, 1971.

Pufall, P. B. Induction of linear-order concepts: A comparison of three training techniques. *Child Development*, 1972, 44, 642.

Reece, H. W., & Lipsitt, L. C. *Experimental child psychology*. New York: Academic Press, 1970.

Ricciuti, H. N. Geometric form and detail as determinants of similarity judgments in young children. In *A Basic Research Program on Reading*. Final Report, Cooperative Research Project No. 639. Washington, D.C.: U.S. Office of Education, 1963, 1–48.

Ricciuti, H. N. Object grouping and selective ordering behavior in infants 12 to 24 months old. *Merrill-Palmer Quarterly*, 1965, 11, 129–148.

Rohwer, W., Ammon, P., & Cramer, P. *Understanding intellectual development*. New York: Holt, Rinehart and Winston, 1974.

Rosenthal, T. L., & Zimmerman, B. Modeling by exemplification and instruction in training conservation. *Developmental Psychology*, 1972, 6, 392–401.

Salapatek, P., & Kessen, W. Visual scanning of triangles by the newborn infant. *Journal of Experimental Child Psychology*, 1966, 3, 155–167.

Selman, R. The relation of role taking to the development of moral judgment in children. *Child Development*, 1971, 42, 79–91.

Shantz, C. U. The development of social cognition. In E. M. Hetherington, J. Hagen, R. Kron, & A. H. Stein (Eds.), *Review of child development research*, Vol. 5. Chicago: University of Chicago Press, 1975.

Sheppard, J. L. Conservation of part and whole in the acquisition of class inclusion. *Child Development*, 1973, 44, 380–383.

Sigel, I. E. Developmental trends in the abstraction ability of children. *Child Development*, 1953, 24, 131–144.

Sigel, I. E. Dominance of meaning. *Journal of Genetic Psychology*, 1954, 85, 201–207.

Sigel, I. E. *Cognitive style and personality dynamics*. Interim progress report for National Institute of Mental Health, M2983, 1961.

Sigel, I. E. Sex and personality correlates of styles of categorization among young children. *American Psychologist*, 1963, 18, 350. (Abstract).

Sigel, I. E. The Piagetian system and the world of education. In D. Elkind, & J. H. Flavell (Eds.), *Studies in cognitive development: Essays in honor of Jean Piaget.* New York: Oxford University Press, 1969.

Sigel, I. E. The distancing hypothesis: A causal hypothesis for the acquisition of representational thought. In M. R. Jones (Ed.), *The effects of early experience.* Miami, Fla.: University of Miami Press, 1970.

Sigel, I. E. Developmental theory and preschool education: Issues, problems, and implications. In J. J. Gordon (Ed.), *Early childhood education.* The 71st Yearbook of The National Society for the Study of Education, Part II: Childhood. Chicago: University of Chicago Press, 1972.

Sigel, I. E., Anderson, L. M., & Shapiro, H. Categorization behavior of lower and middle class Negro preschool children: Differences in dealing with representation of familiar objects. *Journal of Negro Education,* 1966, **35**, 218–229.

Sigel, I. E., & Hooper, F. H. Logical thinking in children. New York: Holt, Rinehart and Winston, 1968.

Sigel, I. E., & McBane, B. Cognitive competence and level of symbolization among five-year-old children. In J. Helmuth (Ed.), *The disadvantaged child,* Vol. 1. New York: Brunner/Mazel, 1967.

Sigel, I. E., & Olmsted, P. Modification of cognitive skills among lower class black children. In J. Helmuth (Ed.), *The disadvantaged child,* Vol. 3. New York: Brunner/Mazel, 1970a.

Sigel, I. E., & Olmsted, P. Modification of classificatory competence and level of representation among lower-class Negro kindergarten. In A. H. Passow (Ed.), *Reaching the disadvantaged learner.* New York: Teachers College, 1970b.

Sigel, I. E., & Olmsted, P. The development of classification and representational competence. In I. Gordon (Ed.), *Readings in research in developmental psychology.* Glenview, Ill.: Scott Foresman, 1971.

Sigel, I. E., Secrist, A., & Forman, G. Psycho-educational intervention beginning at age two: Reflections and outcomes. In J. C. Stanley (Ed.), *Compensatory education for children, ages two to eight: Recent studies of educational intervention.* Baltimore, Md.: Johns Hopkins University Press, 1973.

Silverman, I. W., & Geiringer, E. Dyadic interaction and conservation induction. A test of Piaget's equilibration model. *Child Development,* 1973, **44**, 815–879.

Silverman, I. W., & Stone, J. Modifying cognitive functioning through participation in a problem-solving group. *Journal of Educational Psychology,* 1972, **63**, 603–608.

Sinclair-de-Zwart, H. Developmental psycholinguistics. In D. Elkind & J. Flavell (Eds.), *Studies in cognitive development: Essays in honor of Jean Piaget.* New York: Oxford University Press, 1969, 315–336.

Sinclair, H. Piaget's theory and language acquisition. In M. F. Rasskopf, L. P. Steffe, & S. Taback (Eds.), *Piagetian cognitive development research and mathematical education.* Reston, Va.: National Council of Teachers of Mathematics, 1971.

Slobin, I. Grammatical transformations and sentence comprehension in childhood and adulthood. *Journal of Verbal Learning and Verbal Behavior,* 1966, **5**, 219–227.

Spitz, R. *No and yes: On the beginnings of human communication.* New York: International University Press, 1957.

Strauss, S. Inducing cognitive development and learning: A review of short term training experiments. *I. The organismic-developmental approach to cognition,* 1972, **1**, 329–357.

Sullivan, E. V. Piaget and the school curriculum: A critical appraisal. *Ontario Institute for Studies in Education Bulletin,* No. 2. Toronto: The Institute, 1967.

Sutton-Smith, B. Piaget on play: A critique. *Psychological Review,* 1966, **73**, 111–112.

Tanner, J. M., & Inhelder, B. (Eds.). *Discussions on child development.* New York: International Universities Press, 1960.

Templin, M. C. *Certain language skills in children: Their development and interrelations.* Minneapolis: University of Minnesota, Institute of Child Welfare, 1957. Monograph Series No. 26.

Thompson, J. Ability of children of different grade levels to generalize on sorting tests. *Journal of Psychology,* 1941, **11**, 119–126.

Tough, J. *Focus on meaning.* London: G. Allen, 1973.

Trabasso, T. Representation, meaning and reasoning: How do we make transitive inferences? In A. D. Peck, *Minnesota Symposia on Child Psychology.* Minneapolis: University of Minnesota Press, 1975.

Turner, E. A., & Rommetveit, R. The acquisition of sentence voice and reversibility. *Child Development,* 1967a, **38**, 649–660.

Turner, E. A., & Rommetveit, R. Experimental manipulation of the production of active and passive voice in children. *Language and Speech,* 1967b, **10**, 169–180.

Wallach, L., Wall, A. T., & Anderson, L. Number conservation: The roles of reversibility, addition-subtraction, and misleading perceptual cues. *Child Development,* 1967, **38**, 425–442.

Welch, L. A. A preliminary investigation of some aspects of the hierarchical development of concepts. *Journal of Genetic Psychology,* 1940, **22**, 359–378.

Weikart, D. P. A comparative study of three preschool curricula. In J. E. Frost & G. R. Hawkes (Eds.), *The disadvantaged child.* Boston: Houghton Mifflin, 1970.

Weikart, D. P., Rogers, L., Adcock, C., & McClelland, J. *The cognitively oriented curriculum: A framework for preschool teachers.* Washington, D. C.: National Association for the Education of Young Children, 1970.

Werner, H. *Comparative psychology of mental development*, rev. ed. Chicago: Follett, 1948.

Werner, H., & Kaplan, B. *Symbol formation: An organismic developmental approach to language and the expression of thought.* New York: Wiley, 1963.

Wertheimer, M. Psychomotor coordination of auditory and visual space at birth. *Science*, 1961, **134**, 1962.

White, B. *Human infants: Experience and psychological development.* Englewood Cliffs, N.J.: Prentice-Hall, 1971.

Whorf, B. L. *Language, thought, and reality.* Cambridge, Mass.: Techonology Press, 1956.

Wohlwill, J. F. Absolute versus relational discrimination of the dimension of number. *Journal of Genetic Psychology*, 1960a, **96**, 353–363.

Wohlwill, J. F. A study of the development of the number concept by scalogram analysis. *Journal of Genetic Psychology*, 1960b, **97**, 345–377.

Wohlwill, J. *The study of behavioral development.* New York: Academic Press, 1973.

Wolff, P. H. The natural history of crying and other vocalizations in early infancy. In B. M. Foss (Ed.), *Determinants of infant behavior*, Vol. IV. London: Methuen, 1966.

Woodward, M. Concepts of number of the mentally subnormal studies by Piaget's method. *Journal of Child Psychology and Psychiatry*, 1961, **2**, 249–259.

Zimmerman, B. J., & Rosenthal, T. L. Conserving and retraining equalities and inequalities through observation and correction. *Developmental Psychology*, 1974, **10**, 260.

Index

Abilities, cognitive, modification of, 86, 186–216
  education, Piaget and, 205–216
  modifiability, issues of, 188–190
    conservation, development of, 188–189
    studies of, implications of, 189–190
  Piagetian research, relationship among specific knowledge domains, education and, 210–211
  training research, 190–205
Abstraction, physical, 54
  reflective, 54
Abstract symbols, 111
Acceleration, 178, 218, 222–224
Accommodation, 105, 115
  Piagetian theory concept, 15
Action-pattern basis of language, 115–121
Action of social environment, 18, 20–21
Actions, 24
  reversibility of, 24
Active organism, concept of, 218–219
Activity, 218
  external and internal, 218
Adaptation, representational competence as, 170–172
  systematic, 33–34
Adcock, C., 174
Affective interactions, concrete operational period, 83–88
  games, 83–84
  group action, 84
  language, 84
Affectivity, place of, 219–222
Alternatives, development toward use of, 53–54
Amatruda, C. S., 30
Anderson, L. M., 164, 199
Animism, 31

Anisfeld, M., 119
Arnheim, R., 164, 166
Asch, S. E., 157
Assimilation, 5n., 105
  Piagetian theory concept, 15
Atomism, principle of, 80–81
Ausubel, D. R., 30
Autoregulation, 187

Babbling, 113
Bandura, A., 50
Behavior, 17
  adaptive, 33–34
  distancing, see Distancing behaviors
Beilin, H., 133, 201, 202
Bellugi, U., 134, 135, 142
Bever, T. G., 131
Bijou, S. W., 30
Biological-experimental factors, Piagetian theory, 14–15
Blank, M. A., 174, 175
Bolles, M. M., 73
Bovet, M., 23, 186, 187, 191, 192, 194, 196, 199, 217
Bower, T. G. R., 42
Brainerd, C. J., 31, 32, 191, 195, 196, 198
Brent, S. B., 155
Brooks, V., 164
Brown, R. W., 100, 118, 119, 122, 125, 142, 159
Bruner, J., 163, 197, 198, 227
Brunswik, E., 166

Carlson, P., 119
Cassirer, E., 169
Causality, physical, 80–81
Causal relations, 150
Centration, 72
Chaining, 163
Child psychology, 13–14
Circular reactions, during sensorimotor period, 39–44

Circular reactions (*cont.*)
  language acquisition, 117–118
  secondary, 40–41
  tertiary, 41–42
Clark, E. V., 42
Clark, H., 124, 125, 136
Classification, 65, 70, 71–74, 76
  class-inclusion, 71–73
  materials, nature of, 73–74
Class-inclusion, 71–73
Cocking, R. R., 134, 136, 139, 141,
    142, 148
Cognition, 1–2, 6
Cognitive ability, see Abilities, cog-
    nitive
Cognitive conflict, 22
Cognitive processes, 9
Cohen, D., 137
Cole, M., 4, 27–28
Combinatorial thinking, 61, 75–76
Combining, distancing strategy, 181
Comparison, distancing strategy,
    180
Comprehension, 155, 166
  assessment of, 134–135, 136
  language, 120, 121
Concluding, distancing strategy, 181
Concrete operational period, cogni-
    tive development, 29, 64–88
  cognitive growth from birth to,
    61–62
  description of, schematic, 65–66
  educational implications, 100–104
  genesis of, 66–70
    conservation problem, 66–68
    conservation responses, analy-
      sis of, 68–70
  interactions, social and affective,
    83–84
    games, 83–84
    group action, 84
    language, 84
  interpretations and conclusions,
    98–103
  moral feelings and judgments,
    85–88
    basis of, affective, 85–86
    development of, 86–88

Concrete operational period (*cont.*)
  number and quantity concepts,
    70–79
    classification, 65, 70, 71–74,
      76
    combinatorial thinking, 75–76
    numbers, whole, 77–78
    quantity concept, 78–79
    reversibility, 65–66, 70–71
    seriation, 70, 74–75
  representation of the universe,
    79–82
    causality, physical, 80–81
    sociocentrism, 81–82
Conflict, 45–46, 56
  inducement of, modification stud-
    ies, nonverbal, 191–195
    verbal, 195–198
  resolving, distancing strategy, 181
Congruence, principle of, 136
Consecutive relations, 150
Conservation, 66–70, 117, 208
  of continuous quantity apparatus,
    191
    shielded apparatus, 194
  development of, 188–189
  modification studies of, 191–203
    see also Modification studies
  ontogenesis of, 54–55
  problem of, 66–68
  responses, analysis of, 68–70
Consistency, 208
Construction, 125–127
Construction of Reality in the Child
    (Piaget), 45
Constructivism, 225–226
  Piagetian theory concept, 15–17
Context, meaning and, 137–138
Continuous quantity, 78
Cooing, 112
Coordination, 144
Core concepts, Piagetian theory,
    14–25
Cultural perspective, Piagetian
    theory, 25–29
Culture, influence of, 25–27
Curriculum, organization of, Pia-
    getian theory and, 101–102

Curriculum builders, developmental perspective for, 206–210

Dasen, P., 210, 224
Dawson-Myers, G., 42
Décalage, 79, 208
Décarie, T. G., 220
Decentration, 53–54, 70, 71–72
Deferred imitation, 43, 50–51
Deixis, 137
Demonstration, distancing strategy, 180
Development, cognitive, 6, 8, 29–30, 32
  childhood to adolescence, 64–104
  concrete operational period, see Concrete operational period
  course of, factors influencing, 18–21
  formal operational period, see Formal operational period
  language acquisition in early stages of, 105–160
    action patterns to verbal meaning, from, 122–140
    development in school years, 153–157
    grammarian, child as, 140–153
    preverbal child, 112–122
    representation, symbols, and the semiotic function, 110–112
  order of, 30
  preschool years, during, see Preschool period
  regulators of, 187
  relevance of, to educational process, 9–10
  stages of, 17–18
Developmental constructivism, 225
Discontinuous quantity, 78
Disequilibrium, 22
Displacement, 22
Distal stimuli, 173
Distancing behaviors, 162, 166
  adaptation, representational, competence as, 170–172

Distancing behaviors (*cont.*)
  contextual conditions for, 172–176
    representational competence, relationship of, 173–174
  experience, role of, in development of representational thought, 169–170
  representation, meaning of, 167–168
    significance of, for human adaptation, 168–169
  strategies, 180–181
Distancing hypothesis, 162, 166–172
  application of, to an educational setting, 176–185
  evidence for, and relationship to representational competence, 174–176
"Dominance of Meaning, The" (Sigel), 162
Donovan, A., 176
Drawing, child's, enumerated elements in, 151
  synthesized elements in, 152
Durability, 189
Dyer, J. L., 174

Education, 3–4
  contribution of Piagetian theory to, 211–213
  distancing hypothesis, application of, 176–185
  Piaget and, 205–216
    developmental perspective for teachers and curriculum builders, 206–210
    Piagetian research, relationship among specific knowledge domains and, 210–211
    Piagetian theory, contribution to teaching strategy, 211–213
    research and practice, relationship between, 213–215
  psychology and, 205–206
  relationship among Piagetian research, specific knowledge domains and, 210–211

Education (*cont.*)
  relevance of Piagetian theory to, 100–103
    curriculum organization, 101–102
    intelligence, development of, 100–101
    teaching strategies, 102–103
Egocentrism, 47, 50–53
Eisenberg, K., 133
Elaboration, 178
Elkind, D., 32, 98
Environment, 28, 231–232
  influence of, 4–5
  role of, 218
  social, see Social environment
Epistemology, genetic, 13n.
Equilibration, 18, 21
Ervin-Tripp, S., 113, 142
Escalona, S., 220
Evaluation, distancing strategy, 181
Evans, R. L., 62, 219
Exercise, 19
Expectations, 230
Experience, 18, 19
  role of, 224–225
    in development of representational thought, 169–170
  systematization of, 209
Extension, 178
Ezer, M., 31

Fantasy, 56
Figurative knowledge, 88
Fillmore, C. J., 137
Fink, R., 57–58
Flavell, J., 32, 38, 48, 188
Flotation problem, 91–97
Formal operational period, cognitive development, 29, 88–97
  educational implications, 100–104
  flotation problem, 91–97
  interpretations and conclusions, 98–103
Forman, G., 19, 176
Fowler, W., 174
Frank, J., 197
Fraser, C., 142

Free sorting, 72
Furth, H. G., 172, 173

Gagné, R. M., 9
Games, social interaction, 83–84
Geiringer, E., 197
Generalizability, 189
Generalization, distancing strategy, 181
Generative model, 143–146
  morphological level, 143
  phrase structure level, 143
  transformational level, 143
Genetic psychology, 13–14
Gesell, A., 30
Ginsburg, H., 15, 33
Gladwin, T., 26
Goldstein, K., 30
Gough, P. B., 136
Grammarian, child as, 140–153
  syntax, development of, precursors to, 140–142
    emergence of, 142–143
Grammatical demands, 148
Group action, social interaction, 84
Guided inquiry, 177

Haith, M. M., 116, 117
Hammond, K. R., 166
Heteronomy, 85–86
Hochberg, J., 164
Hoffman, M., 88
Hooper, F., 214
Human adaptation, significance of representation for, 168–169
Hunt, D. E., 210, 213–214
Hunt, J. McV., 30, 31, 66, 90
Huttenlocher, J., 133

Identity, 136
Imitation, 50
  deferred, 43, 50–51
  in preoperational thought, 50–51
Individual-culture intertwining, 28–30
Inference, distancing strategy, 181
Information, accumulation of, 5–6
  exchange of, speech function, 107

Information (*cont.*)
  sensory, infant's abilities to attend to, 126
Inhelder, B., 14, 23, 25, 30, 70, 72, 81, 83, 85, 89, 92, 94, 95, 98, 101, 164, 186, 187, 191, 192, 194, 196, 199, 217
Inquiry, guided, 177
  open-ended, 177–178
Intelligence, 62
  development of, conceptual scheme for, 100–101
  sensorimotor, 44, 110, 117
Interactions, 16
  social and affective, 83–88
    games, 83–84
      group action, 84
      language, 84
Internalization, 50
Interpretation, distancing strategy, 180
Intuitive phase, see Preoperational period
Investigation, experimental, 188

Jenkins, J., 148
Johnson, R. C., 99
Judgements, moral, see Moral feelings and judgements

Kagan, J., 232
Kamii, C., 62, 174, 214
Kaplan, E. L., 112, 166, 168
Kaplan, G. A., 112
Katz, E. W., 155
Kelly, G. A., 226
Kessen, W., 116, 117
Knowing, 1–2, 136, 172
Knowledge, 59, 231
  acquisition of, 2–6, 16
  figurative, 88
  language and, 157–160
Koffka, K., 38
Kohlberg, L., 30, 86
Kohnstamm, G. A., 160, 205
Kooistra, W. H., 32

Labeling, distancing strategy, 180

Labeling (*cont.*)
  function, language acquisition, 158–159
Language, 2–3, 23, 26, 28, 45, 49, 63, 171, 191, 197
  acquisition of, 105–160
    action patterns to verbal meaning, from, 122–140
    development in school years, 153–157
    grammarian, child as, 141–153
    preverbal child, 112–122
    representation, symbols and the semiotic function, 110–112
    semantic development, 122–140
  action-pattern basis of, 115–121
  features of, 147–148
  knowledge and, 157–160
  motor development and, correlation of, 114
  operational thought, influence on, 99–100
  phonological development, 153–154
  representational, 110
  semantic development, 156–157
  semiotic function of, 111
  social interaction, 84
  speech functions, 106–109
  strategies, development of, 133–134
  syntactic development, 154–156
    precursors of, 140–142
  word sequence, meaning and, 128–137
Laurendeau, M., 30, 31, 32, 99
Lavatelli, C., 62
Learning, 6, 9, 207
  process of, 9
Lenneberg, E. H., 112, 113, 114, 117, 158, 159, 160
Levenstein, P., 174, 175
Linguistic algorithms, 133
Lipsitt, L. C., 164
Loban, W. D., 154
Logical necessity, 22

Logical relations, 117
Luria, S., 29

MacNamara, J., 124
McBane, B., 164
McClelland, J., 174
McKim, R. H., 184, 185
McNeill, D., 131, 132, 133
Materials, classification, nature of, 73–74
Maturation, 18
Mead, G. H., 57
Meaning, 156, 123–124
  construction of, 125–127
  context and, 137–138
  word sequence and, 128–137
Mehler, J., 131
Menyuk, P., 130, 142, 143, 144, 145, 146, 153, 154, 155
Method clinique, 68
Miller, L. B., 174
Miller, R., 164
Mimicries, 142
Model, educational, objectives of, 176–182
  generative, 143–146
  training, 213
Modification of cognitive abilities, 186–216
  education, Piaget and, 205–216
    developmental perspective for teachers and curriculum builders, 206–210
    Piagetian research, relationship among specific knowledge domains and, 210–211
    Piagetian theory, contribution to teaching strategy, 211–213
    research and practice, relationship between, 213–215
  issues of, 188–190
    conservation, development of, 188–189
    studies of, implications of, 189–190
  training research, 190–205
    conservation, studies of, 191–203

Modification of Piagetian theory, 217–234
  acceleration, 222–224
  active organism, concept of, 218–219
  affectivity, place of, 219–222
  experience, role of, 224–225
Modification studies, implication of, 189–190
  of conservation, 191–203
    nonverbal conflict induced, 191–195
    nonverbal no conflict, 198–201
    verbal conflict induced, 195–198
    verbal no conflict, 201–203
Mogar, M., 31
Molfese, D. L., 154, 155, 156, 157
Moore, M. K., 42
Moral feelings and judgements, 85–88
  basis of, affective, 85–86
  development of, 86–88
    conventional level, 87–88
    preconventional level, 86
Moss, H. A., 232
Murray, F. B., 197, 224

Negation, 70
Nelson, K., 116, 117, 141
Nerlove, H., 157
Nichols, I., 112
Nomination, 119, 158–159
Nonverbal conflict inducement, modification studies, 191–195
Nonverbal no conflict, modification studies, 198–201
Number and quantity concepts, 65, 70–79
  classification, 65, 70, 71–74, 76
    class-inclusion, 71–73
    materials, nature of, 73–74
  combinatorial thinking, 75–76
  numbers, whole, 77–78
  quantity concept, 78–79
  reversibility, 65–66, 70–71
  seriation, 70, 74–75
    transitivity, 75

Nursery school, 62, 151

Object Categorization Test (OCT), 163–164
Object permanence, 40, 55, 119
Observation, distancing strategy, 180
O'Donnell, R. C., 155
Oliver, R. R., 163
Olmsted, P., 164, 166, 224
Omissions, 144, 145
Open-ended inquiry, 177–178
Operational reversibility, 117
Operational thought, 61
Operations, concept of, 24–25
Opper, S., 15, 33
Overextension, categories of, 125

Palermo, D. S., 154, 155, 156, 157
Phonological development, language acquisition, 153–154
Physical abstraction, 54
Physical causality, 80–81
Piaget, J., 6–8, 10, 11, 14, 15, 17, 20, 21, 23, 24, 25, 30, 32, 33, 36, 37, 38, 39, 42, 44, 45, 46, 47, 48, 49, 50, 54, 56, 59, 63, 66, 69, 72, 79, 81, 83, 85, 88, 91, 92, 94, 95, 98, 101, 102, 103, 111, 117, 118, 120, 125, 137, 138, 140, 150, 157, 161, 164, 167, 168, 183, 186, 188, 196, 197, 199, 206, 207, 208, 210, 211, 212, 214, 215–216, 217, 218, 219, 221, 222, 223, 224, 230
    education and, 205–216
    developmental perspective for teachers and curriculum builders, 206–210
    relevance of, for preschool ages, 62–63
Piagetian theory, 6–8, 11, 12, 186, 190, 206, 217
    contribution of, to teaching strategy, 211–213
    core concepts, 14–25
    accommodation, 15

Piagetian theory (cont.)
    assimilation, 15
    biological-experiential factors, 14–15
    constructivism, 15–17
    course of development, factors influencing, 18–21
    operations, concept of, 24–25
    stages, development by, 17–18
    structure, concept of, 23–24
    transitions from stage to stage, 21–23
    cultural perspective, 25–29
    curriculum organization and, 101–102
    educational implications for concrete and formal operational periods, 100–104
    modification of, 217–234
    acceleration, 222–224
    active organism, concept of, 218–219
    affectivity, place of, 219–222
    experience, role of, 224–225
    overview of, 13–36
    relevance of, for preschool ages, 62–63
    stage theory, critical issues of, 29–33
    teaching strategies and, 102–103
Pictographs, 110
Picture Object Categorization Test (PCT), 163–164
Pinard, A., 30, 31, 32, 99
Planning, distancing strategy, 181
Play, promotion of, speech function, 107–109
    in cognitive growth, significance of, 55–58
Play, Dreams, and Imitation in Childhood (Piaget), 45
Potts, M., 142
Preoperational period, first-level concepts, 47
    intellectual development, 46–49
    intuitive phase, 48–49
    language acquisition in, 106–160
    Piagetian theory, 29

Preoperational period (*cont.*)
  preoperational phase, 46–48
    thought during early phase, characteristics of, 47–48, 49
    transitions to, from sensorimotor period, 44–46
Preoperational thought, meaning of, 59–60
Preschool years, cognitive development during, 37–63
  cognitive growth, from birth to concrete operational period, 61–62
  intellectual development, 38–49
    preoperational period, 46–48
    sensorimotor period, 38–46
  preoperational thought, meaning of, 58–60
  relevance of Piaget for, 62–63
  transitional processes, 49–58
    conservation, ontogenesis of, 54–55
    decentration, 53–54
    frame of reference, child's, 50–52
    imitation in preoperational thought, 50–51
    play in cognitive growth, significance of, 55–58
Preverbal child, language acquisition by, 112–122
Primary circular reaction, 117–118
Production, language, 120
Psychology, child, 13–14
  education and, 205–206
  genetic, 13–14
Pufall, P. B., 200

Quantity concept, see Number and quantity concepts
Quotity, 199

Readiness, 10
Reason and reasoning, 9
Rebelsky, F., 112
Reciprocity, 70
Recognition, 119
Recognitory assimilation, 118

Redundancy, 144
Reece, H. W., 164
Reflective abstraction, 54
Representation, 110–112, 135
  meaning of, 167–168
  significance of, for human adaptation, 168–169
Representational competence, 106
  as adaptation, 170–172
  evidence for distancing hypothesis and its relationship to, 174–176
  relationship of distancing behaviors to, 173–174
Representational thought, development of, 49, 161–185
  distancing behavior, contextual conditions for, 172–176
    strategies, 180–181
  distancing hypothesis, 166–172
    adaptation, representational competence as, 170–172
    application of, to an educational setting, 176–185
    representation, meaning of, 167–168
    significance of representation for human adaptation, 168–169
  experience in, role of, 169–170
  problem, the, 162–185
    background of, 162–166
    conceptual answer, the 166–172
Research, Piagetian, practice and, relationship between, 213–215
  relationship among specific knowledge domains, education and, 210–211
  training, 190–205
    conservation, modification studies of, 191–203
Reversal, 131–132
Reversibility, 65–66, 70–71
  of actions, 24
  semantic, 129
Rogers, L., 174
Rommetveit, R., 155

Rosenthal, T. L., 200
Rules, social interaction, 84

Salapatek, P., 116, 117
Scheerer, M., 30
Schema (schemata), 15
Scribner, S., 4, 27–28
Secondary circular reactions, 118
  sensorimotor period, 40–41
Secrist, A., 19, 176
Selman, R., 86
Semantic development, language
  acquisition, 156–157
Semantic force, 124
Semantic reversibility, 129
Semiotic function, 42, 49
Sensorimotor intelligence, 44, 110,
  117
Sensorimotor period, intellectual
  development, 29, 38–46
  circular reactions, 38–44
    secondary, 40–41
    tertiary, 41–42
  language acquisition in, 110, 113–
    115
  transitions from, to preopera-
    tional period, 44–46
Sentence, complete, 134
  comprehension, 135
  elements of, 159
Sequencing, distancing strategy,
  180
Seriation, 70, 74–75
  transitivity, 75
Shantz, C. U., 52
Shapiro, H., 164
Shelter concept, 184
Sheltering functions, 183
Sheppard, J. L., 200
Sigel, I. E., 19, 62, 73, 74, 162, 164,
  166, 173, 174, 176, 224, 232
Signs, 111
Silverman, I. W., 197
Similarities, structural, 73
Sinclair, H., 23, 153, 186, 187, 191,
  192, 194, 196, 199, 217
Situational demands, 148
Skinner, B. F., 226

Slobin, I., 155
Social environment, 62–63
  action of, 18, 20–21
Social interactions, 83–88
  games, 83–84
  group action, 84
  language, 84
Sociocentrism, 81–82
Spitz, R., 220
Spontak, G., 133
Stage-dependent theory, 30–31
Stage theory, 17–18
  critical issues of, 29–33
  transitions from stage to stage,
    21–23, 31, 32
Stimuli, distal, 173
Stone, J., 197
Strauss, S., 32, 133, 207
Structural similarities, 73
Structures, cognitive, concept of,
  23–24
Substitution, 144, 145
Sullivan, E. V., 102, 210, 213–214
Sutton-Smith, B., 56, 57
Symbols, 110–112
  abstract, 111
Syncretic conceptualizations, 48
Syntax, 159
  development of, language acqui-
    sition, 154–156
    precursors to, 140–141
  emergence of, 142–143

Tanner, J. M., 30
Teachers, developmental perspective for, 206–210
Teaching strategies, articulation of,
  consistent with distancing
  theory, 176–179
  contribution of Piagetian theory
    to, 211–213
  Piagetian theory and, 102–103
Templin, M. C., 154
Thinking, combinatorial, 61, 75–
  76
  representational, 49
  transductive, 48
Thompson, J., 73

Thought, operational, 61
  preoperational, characteristics of, 47–48, 49
    imitation in, 50–51
    meaning of, 58–60
  representational, see Representational thought
Tough, J., 109
Trabasso, T., 223
Training, research, 190–205
  conservation, modification studies of, 191–203
Transductive thinking, 48
Transformation, distancing strategy, 181
Transitional processes, preschool years, 49–58
  conservation, ontogenesis of, 54–55
  decentration, 53–54
  frame of reference, children's, 51–53
  imitation in preoperational thought, 50–51
  play in cognitive growth, significance of, 55–58

Transitivity, 75
Turner, E. A., 155

Understanding, 20, 61
Universe, causality, physical, 80–81
  sociocentrism, 81–82
  representation of, 79–82

Valian, V. V., 131
Verbalizations, 157, 159

Wall, A. T., 199
Wallach, L., 199
Weikart, D. P., 62, 174
Welch, L. A., 44
Werner, H., 30, 32, 38, 47, 167, 168
White, B., 44
Whorf, B. L., 100
Wohlwill, J. F., 32, 224
Woodward, M., 30
Word order, 123
Word sequence, meaning and, 128–137

Zimmerman, B., 200, 202